BRIDGING A GULF

Toda Institute Book Series on Global Peace and Policy

Series Editor: Majid Tehranian

Published and forthcoming:

1. *Worlds Apart: Human Security and Global Governance*, edited by Majid Tehranian. London & New York: I.B.Tauris, 1999.
2. *Asian Peace: Security and Governance in the Asia-Pacific Region*, edited by Majid Tehranian. London & New York: I.B.Tauris, 1999.
3. *Not By Bread Alone: Food Security and Governance in Africa*, edited by Adelane Ogunrinade, Ruth Oniang'o, and Julian May. Johannesburg: University of Witwatersrand Press, 1999.
4. *Nuclear Disarmament: Obstacles to Banishing the Bomb*, edited by Jozef Goldblat. London & New York: I.B.Tauris, 2000.
5. *Reimagining the Future: Towards Democratic Governance*, by Joseph A. Camilleri, Kamal Malhotra, Majid Tehranian *et al.* Bundoora, Australia: The Department of Politics, La Trobe University, 2000.
6. *Managing the Global: Globalization, Employment, and Quality of Life*, edited by Don Lamberton. London & New York: I.B.Tauris, 2002.
7. *Dialogue of Civilizations: A New Peace Agenda for a New Millennium*, edited by Majid Tehranian and David W. Chappell. London & New York: I.B.Tauris, 2002.
8. *Democratizing Global Governance*, edited by Joseph A. Camilleri & Esref Aksu. New York: Palgrave Macmillan, 2002.
9. *Bridging a Gulf: Peacebuilding in West Asia*, edited by Majid Tehranian. London & New York: I.B.Tauris, forthcoming.
10. *Worlds on the Move: Globalization, Migration, and Cultural Security*, edited by Jonathan Friedman and Shalini Randeria. London & New York: I.B.Tauris, forthcoming.

BRIDGING A GULF

Peacebuilding in West Asia

Edited by

Majid Tehranian

I.B.Tauris *Publishers*
LONDON • NEW YORK

in association with
The Toda Institute for Global Peace and Policy Research

Published in 2003 by I.B.Tauris & Co Ltd
6 Salem Road, London W2 4BU
175 Fifth Avenue, New York NY 10010
www.ibtauris.com
in association with the Toda Institute for Global Peace and Policy Research

In the United States and Canada distributed by Palgrave Macmillan, a division of
St. Martin's Press
175 Fifth Avenue, New York NY 10010

ISBN 1 86064 884 3

A full CIP record for this book is available from the British Library

Typeset in Baskerville 11/12 pt by Q3 Bookwork
Printed and bound in Great Britain by MPG Books Ltd, Bodmin

Contents

Part Three: Future Visions

In Loving Memory of

Saif A. Abdulla Dehrab

Who Bridged the Gulf by His Life and Scholarship
in Peacebuilding

Contributors

Amir A. Alanbari is currently Iraq Ambassador to the Vatican. He was Ambassador Extraordinary and Plenipotentiary, Permanent Delegate of the Republic of Iraq to UNESCO, Paris from 1992–1998, and Ambassador Extraordinary and Plenipotentiary, Permanent Representative of the Republic of Iraq to the United Nations from 1989–1992. He was leader of the Iraqi delegation to the negotiations with the UN Secretariat for the conclusions of the Memorandum of Understanding May 20, 1996 for the implementation of Resolution 986 (1995). He was also Ambassador Extraordinary and Plenipotentiary to the United States of America from 1987–1989 (non-residential), to the state of Ireland from 1985–1987, to the Court of St. James, United Kingdom from 1985 to 1987. He was Director General of the Department of International Organizations, Ministry of Foreign Affairs from January to August 1985. Recently Dr. Alanbari was Member of the High Council of International Education Center, Geneva and Vice-President of NESCO Ministerial Conference and Member of the Executive Board of UNESCO.

Saleh Alkhatlan is Associate Professor of Political Science at the Department of Political Science, King Saud University, Riyadh, Saudi Arabia. He received his Ph.D. in Political Science from the University of Kansas in 1993. His interest areas include Arab national security, Arab relations with the CIS countries, Islam, and democratization in Central Asia. He has participated in a number of conferences in the Arab world, Central Asia and Caucasus.

Shahram Chubin is currently the Executive Director of Research, at the Geneva Centre for Security Policy. Formerly he has held a number of positions in the academic and policy analysis field. He was Director of Regional Studies at the International Institute of International Studies, London, a Visiting Fellow at the Wilson Center in Washington, DC, and has taught or lectured at numerous universities, including the Graduate Institute of International Studies (Geneva), Columbia, Harvard, Oxford, and the Fletcher School of Law and Diplomacy. He has written extensively on the security problems of non-Western states, especially those of the Middle East region.

Saif A. Abdulla Dehrab is Chairman of the Political Science Department at Kuwait University. Formerly he was a Visiting Professor at the University of Texas.

Peter Jones is a Senior Analyst in the Privy Council Office, Ottawa, Canada. From 1995 to 1999 he was the project leader for Stockholm International Peace Research Institute's Middle East Security and Arms Control Project.

Bjørn Møller holds an MA in History and a Ph.D. in International Relations, both from the University of Copenhagen. Since 1985, he has been (senior) research fellow, subsequently program director and board member at the Copenhagen Peace Research Institute (COPRI, formerly Centre for Peace and Conflict Research). Furthermore he is a lecturer at the Institute of Political Studies, University of Copenhagen and was Secretary General of the International Peace Research Association (IPRA) 1997–2000. He is the author of numerous articles and three books: *Resolving the Security Dilemma in Europe: The German Debate on Non-Offensive Defence* (1991); *Common Security and Nonoffensive Defense: A Neorealist Perspective* (1992); and *Dictionary of Alternative Defense* (1995). He is further the editor or co-editor of six anthologies, most recently *Oil and Water: Towards Cooperative Security in the Persian Gulf* (London: I.B.Tauris, forthcoming 2001).

Pirouz Mojtahed-Zadeh is Professor of Geopolitics at Tarbiat Modarres University, Tehran. He is Chairman of the Urosovic Research Foundation, London, and Senior Research Associate of GRC/SOAS, University of London. In the late 1970s he spent three years at Oxford University working for a M. Phil. Born in 1946, Dr. Mojtahed-Zadeh has published extensively in both Persian and English, some of which have been translated into Arabic and French. His English publications include *The Islands of Tunb and Abu Musa* (CNMES/SOAS, University of London Publication, 1994); and *The Amirs of the Borderlands and Eastern Iranian Borders* (Urosovic Foundation Publication, 1995). Dr. Mojtahed-Zadeh has lectured extensively in North America, Western Europe, the Middle East, and the Far East, and contributes regularly to international media. His latest book, *Security and Territoriality in the*

Persian Gulf (a maritime political geography) was published in 1999 by Curzon Press of London.

Richard Murphy has been Senior Fellow for the Middle East at the Council on Foreign Relations, New York since 1989. He was Assistant Secretary for the Near East and South Asia between 1983 and 1989, Ambassador to Saudi Arabia, the Philippines, Syria, and Mauritania from 1971 to 1983 and Chairman for the Middle East Institute, Washington. He has been a Trustee for the American University of Beirut since 1995.

Vitaly Naumkin has been President of the Russian Center for Strategic Research and International Studies since 1991. He was also Deputy Director for the Institute of Political Studies, Russian Academy from 1989 to 1994, Head of the Middle East Department, 1984–1989, and Professor at the Moscow University, 1980–84. He worked at the Moscow University as Senior Researcher between 1972 and 1980, and in diplomatic mission from 1972 to 1977. He did post-graduate work between 1970 and 1972 and lectured at the Military University from 1968 to 1970.

Leanne Piggott is a Lecturer in the Department of Government and International Relations at the University of Sydney. She is a member of the Center for Peace and Conflict Studies at the University and teaches in their graduate program in Peace Studies and Conflict Resolution. In addition to her university work, Leanne is the Director of Scholars Ink, an education consultancy. She is presently working on an assessment and revision of school curricula in the areas of religious studies and personal development.

Amin Saikal is Director of the Center for Arab and Islamic Studies and Professor of Political Science at the Australian National University, where he teaches and writes about the politics, history, political economy, and international relations of the Middle East and Central Asia. He has been a visiting fellow at Princeton University, Cambridge University, and the Institute of Development Studies (University of Sussex) as well as a Rockefeller Foundation Fellow in International Relations (1983–88). He is the author of numerous works on the Middle East, Central Asia, and Russia. His recent works include "Iran's Foreign Policy 1921–1979." *Cambridge History of Iran*, Vol. 7 (1991); (co-author) *Regime Change in Afghanistan: Foreign Intervention and the Politics of Legitimacy* (1991); (co-editor) *Russia in Search* *of Its Future* (1995); (co-editor) *The Middle East: Prospects for Settlement and Stability?* (1995); (editor) *Turkey: A Bridge between East and West* (1996); (co-author) *Security and Security Building in the Indian Ocean Region* (Canberra Papers on Strategy and Defense No. 116, Canberra: Strategic and Defense Studies Center, ANU); (co-editor) *Lebanon and Beyond 2000* (1997); and *Emerging Powers: The Case of China, India, Iran, Iraq and Israel* (1997) Emirates Occasional Paper No. 12 (Abu Dhabi: The Emirates Center for Strategic Studies and Research).

Mohammad El-Sayed Selim is Professor of Political Science and Director of the Centre for Asian Studies, Cairo University. He received his Ph.D. from Carleton University, Canada in 1979. His book publications include *Foreign Policy Analysis* (1998); *Asia and the Global Transformations* (1999); and *Relations Among Muslim States* (1999).

Behzad Shahandeh is Associate Professor of Politics at the Department of Law and Political Science, Tehran University. He is a graduate of Utah State University, Southhampton University (US), Cambridge University (UK), Beijing University, and Tehran University. He has a Ph.D. in Sinology and is a specialist in East Asian politics and economy. He is fluent in Persian, English, French, and Chinese (Mandarin). He is the director of the Asia-Pacific Group at the International Center for the Dialogue of Civilizations, Tehran.

Majid Tehranian is professor of international communication at the University of Hawaii and director of the Toda Institute for Global Peace and Policy Research. A graduate of Dartmouth and Harvard, Tehranian's publications include 20 books and more than 100 articles in over a dozen languages. He also edits *Peace & Policy* as well as the Toda Institute Book Series. Email: majid@hawaii.edu Website: www2.hawaii.edu/~majid

Nur Yalman received his B.A., M.A., and Ph.D. (1958) from Cambridge University, and was a fellow of the Peterhouse, Cambridge. He was Professor of Social Anthropology at the Chicago University from 1964 to 1972 and Director of the Center for Middle Eastern Studies at Harvard University from 1973 to 1976. He also did his fieldwork in Sri Lanka, India, Iran, and Turkey. He has produced publications on social anthropology, Islam, Buddhism, democracy and politics of culture.

Stephen Zunes is Associate Professor of Politics and Chair of the Peace and Justice Studies Program at the University of San Francisco. He is the author of *Nonviolent Social Movements: A Geographical Perspective* (Blackwell, 1999) as well as numerous articles and three forthcoming books on conflict resolution in North Africa and the Middle East and United States policy towards the region. He received his doctorate in Government from Cornell University, has served as a research fellow at the Institute for Policy Studies and the Institute for Global Studies and served as Founding Director of the Institute for a New Middle East Policy.

Preface

The September 11 terrorist attacks on the United States have dramatically changed the world situation. This volume has called for a strategy of cooperative rather than competitive security in West Asia. Zero-sum security games in the Israeli-Palestinian conflict have led to a new cycle of violence characterized by Palestinian suicide bombings and Israeli reoccupation of the West Bank and Gaza Strip. The situation has effectively terrorized both the Israelis and Palestinians. Meanwhile, the US threats to invade Iraq have polarized world public opinion and created new anti-American sentiments in the Islamic world.

Since September 11, the Bush Administration has moved from a neo-isolationist to an interventionist foreign policy. Before that, the new Republican Administration had refused to engage in 'nation building'. Following September 11, the Bush Administration chose to pursue a largely unilateral and competitive security policy. It has toppled the Taliban regime in Afghanistan while attempting to build a nation out of a tribal society. By declaring its right to attack an "Axis of Evil" consisting of Iran, Iraq, and North Korea, it has also turned a police action into a global war on terrorism. By adopting a policy of pre-emptive attacks against such nuclear powers as Russia and China, the United States has asserted its unilateral superpower prerogatives. By following a unilateralist policy toward international cooperation in a variety of fields, the Bush Administration has thus created doubts about US leadership among its own allies.

The Bush Doctrine has brought about significant domestic and international consequences. To build defenses against terrorism, the new policies have led to the creation of a new Department of Home Security and extension of the government's rights of surveillance. On the international front, Bush policies have led to a dissension among Western allies, particularly noticeable with respect to Iran, Iraq, and Palestine. In the case of Iran, the European and Japanese governments have opted for continued engagement while Bush has reversed Clinton's policies of cautious rapprochement. Bush plans to attack Iraq in order to topple Saddam Hussein have similarly found little support among US allies.

What is the alternative to the current competitive security polices? To bring about greater benefits to all the stakeholders, we have recommended the establishment of a regional collective security. See particularly the chapters by Møller, Jones, and the late Dehrab to whose fond memory the book is dedicated. Saudi Arabian Crown Prince Abdullah's peace proposal of March 2002 has provided a useful framework. It has been endorsed by the Arab League, supported by the international community, and remained unopposed by the United States and Israel. The proposal calls for a normalization of relations between Israel and the Arab states if and when Israel withdraws to its 1967 borders. That is, in essence, a restatement of UN Resolution 242, which guided the Oslo peace process restated, in October 2001, as US policy. The sweetener is the notion of 'normalization' that goes beyond the 242's requirements for a simple recognition of Israel by the Arab states. The proposal may open the rich Arab markets to Israeli consumer goods, technological know-how, and investment.

Wars are failures of human imagination. However, peace building is not easy. The easiest road for governments to take is to fall back on competitive zero-sum strategic thinking. That is what the US and West Asian governments have largely done so far. Meanwhile, government follies have produced enormous suffering for Americans, Arabs, Iranians, Afghans, and Israelis alike. Can an informed peace movement sponsored by concerned global citizens reverse the course? We hope it can.

CHAPTER 1

Introduction: Triple Track Diplomacy in West Asia[1]

Majid Tehranian

The role of multiple-track diplomacy in peace negotiations has received increasing attention in the post-Cold War era (Väyrynen 1991; Carroll 1992; Folger & Jones 1994; Mayer 1995; Kriesberg 1998; Fisher 1998; Lepgold & Weiss 1998). It is generally recognized that the role of civil society in international relations is on the rise. Market forces from the top and civil society forces from the bottom have undermined the authority of the territorial states in a post-Westphalian world order. Global communications and markets are increasingly undermining the physical borders. The boundaries between domestic and foreign policy are also increasingly blurred. While global market forces are imposing serious constraints on the power of the smaller and medium sized states, an international civil society is pressuring the states to observe the global norms in human rights and environmental protection. The role of non-governmental organizations (NGOs) in peacemaking and peacebuilding is of critical importance. Given the enormous sensitivity of the states to "foreign" interference, this role would be more effective if mediated by independent agencies that enjoy the confidence of the contending governments. Dual track diplomacy typically provides an NGO channel parallel to official diplomatic negotiations. By contrast, triple track diplomacy attempts to build a bridge between civil societies and governments by creating a commission composed of distinguished scholars and diplomats in their own personal capacities. This case study of a triple track diplomatic initiative presents the problems and prospects of such an approach.

In collaboration with several other non-governmental organizations (NGOs), in 1998, the Toda Institute for Global Peace and Policy Research initiated a project on Persian Gulf security. As part of its Human Security and Global Governance (HUGG) research program, the project is named HUGG West Asia. In its first phase, the project focused on confidence building among the Gulf states by establishing the International Commission for Security and Cooperation in West Asia (SACWA). The Commission consists of distinguished diplomats and scholars from the eight littoral states plus the five permanent member-states of the United Nations Security Council and a UN representative. The project has acted as a third track diplomatic bridge between the regional governments and civil societies by opening up channels of communication, massaging all submitted peace proposals to prepare them for the consideration of the relevant governments, and promoting a regional security regime for durable peace. The project thus aims at mobilizing a social movement for regional peace in the Persian Gulf area. The Commission met in Istanbul on March 6–7, 1999, for the first time and unanimously recommended the establishment of a center for the promotion of regional cooperation and confidence building in security, political, economic, social, and cultural arenas. The Commission met for the second time in Limassol, Cyprus, on May 27–29, 2000, to focus on arms control, border disputes, as well as social, economic, and cultural cooperation.

At the invitation of the government of Qatar, the third meeting of the Commission took place in Doha on January 5–7, 2001. This meeting represented a major breakthrough in that it was taking place in one of the Persian Gulf littoral states. The meeting thus received significant media attention from the local press and such Pan-Arab media as *The Al-Hayat* newspaper in London and the *Al-Jazirah* television station, situated in Doha but broadcast via satellite to all of the Arab world. At the Doha meeting, the Commission reached the following conclusions:

- In the light of its past wars, current tensions, and the continuing humanitarian tragedy in Iraq, the region is desperately in need of a Regional Center for Dialogue and Cooperation (RCDC) to promote peace, security, and development in the area.
- To be an effective channel for communication among the peoples and governments of the region, the center should be an independent, non-profit, non-partisan, and non-governmental organization that is recognized as such by the governments of the littoral states.
- To ensure its independence, the center should have its own board of trustees drawn from distinguished academic, governmental, business, and civil society leaders willing and able to

bring moral and material support from both private and public sources.

- To plan for the establishment of such a center, the Commission charged a steering committee with preparing for a larger conference to be held in Cyprus or Beirut in collaboration with any number of non-governmental organizations willing to assist.
- In the meantime, expert advisors from the co-sponsoring organizations are urged to give support for the Commission. Toda Institute for Global Peace and Policy Research, Copenhagen Peace Research Institute, Norwegian Institute of International Affairs, Center for Islamic and Arab Studies of Australian National University, Center for World Dialogue, and Institute for Political and International Studies are the present co-sponsors of the project.
- To disseminate past conference papers, a book should be published as soon as possible.

This essay reviews the evolving security regimes in the Gulf region, provides a background to the HUGG West Asia project, reports on the substance of the discussions at the three conferences held so far, and concludes with the prospects for the establishment of an indigenous security regime in the Gulf region.

The Evolving Gulf Security Regimes

During the 20th century, the Persian Gulf seems to have gone through at least three distinctly different security regimes, including Pax Britannica, Pax Saudi-Iranica, and Pax Americana.[2]

Pax Britannica lasted from 1918, the conclusion of World War I, to 1971, which marked the withdrawal of British forces from the East of the Suez. The destruction of the Ottoman Empire and the transfer of Iraq, Trans-Jordan, and Palestine to Britain as League of Nations mandates inaugurated this period. The Iranian Parliament (*Majlis*) turned down the proposed Anglo-Iranian Treaty of 1919. The treaty would have reduced Iran to the status of a protectorate like Egypt. Nevertheless, Britain exercised considerable influence in the political affairs of Iran. The *coup d'état* of 1921 by Colonel Reza Khan, masterminded by the British, brought Iran for the next 20 years under a dictatorship. Although much less independent, the Gulf Arab Emirates (Kuwait, Bahrain, Oman, and what now constitutes the United Arab Emirates (UAE)) were at the same time carved out of the nominally Ottoman territories by the British. Like Iraq and Trans-Jordan, the borders of the Emirates were drawn up to pay political debts while ensuring a system of divide and rule. Many of the current border disputes in the region stem from such colonial schemes (e.g. disputes between Iraq and Kuwait, Qatar and Bahrain, and Iran and the UAE).

The era of Pax Britannica came to an end with the postwar dismemberment of the British Empire and the rise of nationalist regimes in Iran, Iraq, Syria, Palestine/Israel, and Egypt. A new era emerged in 1971 when the British forces were withdrawn from the East of the Suez. Under the circumstances, Pax Americana could have effectively replaced Pax Britannica. However, the United States withdrawal from Vietnam had led to the emergence of the Nixon Doctrine calling for the establishment of proxy powers in various regions of the world to act on behalf of the United States interests. In the Persian Gulf, the monarchist regimes of Saudi Arabia and Iran presented themselves as candidates for this role. The two regimes were thus bolstered by extensive US political and military aid. The emergence of a Pax Saudi-Iranica had anticipated and unanticipated consequences. It led to Saudi-Iranian rapprochement on the Shi'i-Sunni conflicts, the Organization of the Islamic Conference (OIC), and to a new unity in the Organization of Petroleum Exporting Countries (OPEC) that quadrupled the price of oil in 1973. Some boundary disputes were resolved, including the Iranian abandonment of sovereignty claims over Bahrain, an understanding between Iran and Sharjah on Abu Musa Island, and continental shelf agreements among the littoral states. In 1975, Iran and Iraq also reached an agreement in Algiers regarding their boundary dispute over Shatt-ul-Arab and the withdrawal of Iranian support for the Kurdish rebellion in Iraq. As part of the new security regime, Iran also assisted the government of Oman to successfully defeat a Marxist rebellion in the Dhofar Province.

The Islamic revolution of 1979 in Iran brought Pax Saudi-Iranica to an end. With the tacit support of Saudi Arabia, Kuwait, as well as Western powers, Iraq invaded Iran in 1980. A historical pattern was repeating itself. As in the case of modern revolutions in France, Russia, China, and Cuba, the new revolutionary regime in Iran presented a threat to its neighboring conservative governments. Although the rhetoric far outweighed the power of a newly established and disorganized government, it was considered opportune by Iraq and its Arab and Western allies to nip the revolution in the bud. However, as in other historical instances, the Iraqi invasion had a counter-intuitive effect. It unified a divided revolutionary regime against the enemy in a patriotic war that "imperialists and their lackeys had imposed on the country" (*jang-e tahmili*). The consequence was an eight-year tug-of-war in which both sides suffered incalculable material and human costs. Initially, Iraq had the upper hand, but as the Iranians better organized themselves, the tide turned against Iraq in roughly 1987. During a tanker war that threatened oil exports from the Gulf, Kuwait also requested the United States to protect its ships. These dual circumstances brought the United States with full force into the region.

A third period thus began under the aegis of Pax Americana. The approaching end of the Cold War had made it possible for the US and Soviet Union to jointly pressure Iran and Iraq to accept a ceasefire in 1988 (Hume 1994). Under the threat of great power intervention, Ayatollah Khomeini had no choice but to drink the "poisonous cup" of peace with his enemy Saddam Hussein. Later, the invasion of Kuwait by Iraq on August 2, 1990 ensured direct US intervention in Gulf conflicts.

Thanks to his Arab and Western allies, by 1990 Saddam Hussein had acquired a new powerful war machine and tested armed forces (Tehranian 1999). He therefore turned his attention to Iraq's old territorial ambition of incorporating Kuwait, which was now demanding repayments for its wartime loans. Iraq invaded and occupied Kuwait in August 1990 by a *blitzkrieg*. The United States response was a rapid deployment of forces to oppose the Iraqi invasion. It is not entirely certain if this turn of events was premeditated. On the one hand, the massive destruction of Saddam's war machine may be considered a calculated strategy by the United States to undo the Frankenstein monster that was created during the Iraqi war against Iran. This interpretation is supported by US Ambassador April Glaspie's assurances of neutrality between Iraq and Kuwait. That assurance must have encouraged Saddam to gamble on an invasion of Kuwait. The interpretation is further supported by the subsequent US refusal to allow Saddam a face-saving exit out of Kuwait. On the other hand, the US responses to the events could be considered to have been spontaneous and without premeditation.

At any rate, the events were unanticipated by Saddam. Coming at the heel of the end of the Cold War and the disappearance of the Soviet Union as a superpower, Saddam was gambling on an easy victory. During the Iran-Iraq War, he had assumed a new stature as a *Pan-Arab nationalist*, following the footsteps of President Nasser of Egypt. He was hoping to cash in on his prestige by championing the cause of a united Arab world against all enemies. But he had miscalculated for a second time. From the *globalist* perspective of the United States and its allies, the emergence of a hostile regional superpower in the Persian Gulf would have proved disastrous for Western oil and strategic interests. From a domestic perspective also, the Republican Party in power in Washington wished to exorcise the "Vietnam syndrome" in the United States that had deterred it from playing a more active global, military role. The invasion of Kuwait assumed a symbolic significance in the post-Cold War era. Should a potentate be allowed to seize regional power by virtue of a Western default? President Bush quickly responded to that question by deploying the largest post-war military force into Saudi Arabia. Following fruitless peace negotiations in which the United States was unwilling to allow Saddam a face-saving withdrawal, the United Nations forces with the tacit approval of all five Great Powers, and led by the United States, re-conquered Kuwait and restored its monarchy to power. Iraq itself came under UN economic sanctions, and no-fly zones in the north and the south were established in order to protect the dissident Kurds and Shi'ites. Following Egyptian President Nasser's challenges of the 1950s and 60s, the colliding moral spaces of Western globalism and Pan-Arabism led in 1991 to a decisive defeat for the latter.

Although Pax Americana has been a fact of life in the Gulf during the 1990s, it has proved to be an unstable regional security regime. The failure of the US policy of dual containment of Iran and Iraq called for a new design. Since 1996 under the leadership of President Khatami, Iran has regained the respect of the international community for its restrained foreign policies. Although Saddam Hussein is still in power and defiant in Iraq, France, Russia, and China have diverged from the United States and Britain in their recommendation for ending the isolation of the country. The time is thus ripe for inaugurating a new indigenous security regime under which Iran, Iraq, and the Gulf Cooperation Council (GCC) can settle their border disputes, guarantee non-interference in each other's internal affairs, and cooperate for a durable peace. The new regime, however, would be impossible without guarantees from the Great Powers.

Why HUGG West Asia?

The two Gulf Wars (1980–88 and 1990–91) and the risks of an impending third one have created grave threats to international peace and security. As the source of some 60 percent of the world oil reserves and exports, the region has invited unprecedented numbers of foreign interventions and spiraling arms races that lead nowhere except to greater insecurity for the regional states and further threats to world peace. The human costs during the two decades of warfare (1980–99) in the region have been staggering. Hundreds of thousands of people were killed and maimed in the Iran-Iraq War of 1980–88. The invasion of Kuwait by Iraq on August 2, 1990 and the subsequent high technology war against Iraq by the UN forces involved fewer casualties, but it nonetheless entailed disastrous results. The breakdown of the Iraqi physical and social infrastructure as well as the continuing economic sanctions against Iraq have resulted in the premature death of about half a million Iraqi children each year due to malnutrition and infectious diseases. Under present circumstances, normalization of relations among several of the contending states in this affair appears dim. Iran, Iraq, and the United States have severed their diplomatic relations. Similarly, Kuwait, Saudi Arabia, and Iraq continue to act as belligerents.

In the absence of diplomatic relations among the main parties to the regional disputes, prospects for peace are slim, unless international civil society assumes its responsibility by providing alternative channels of communication and negotiation. The role of NGOs in multiple-track diplomacy is thus indispensable. Although governments are often protective of their "rights" to conduct foreign relations without interference from "meddlers", they would welcome the additional information and facilitation that may result from NGO involvement. For instance, the US Department of State has often treated the role of such figures as Jimmy Carter and Jesse Jackson in supervising elections and releasing hostages with disdain. However, it has also had to acknowledge the positive contributions they have made in the process. These include the release of hostages, supervision of elections, and a general opening of channels of communication.

The design for the Toda Institute's initiative took place largely in 1998. In this process, three major obstacles had to be overcome. First, the conflict over the name of the project was resolved by changing it from HUGG Gulf to HUGG West Asia. The Arab participants would not have taken part in the project if the region were to be called by its historic name, the Persian Gulf. The Iranians would have refused participation if the project were to be called "the Arab Gulf". A compromise was reached by calling the project HUGG West Asia, a label that more accurately fits the region than its colonial label of "the Middle East". The latter is a strategic label devoid of any historical or cultural content. Captain Alfred Mahan, Theodore Roosevelt's close friend and colleague in the US Navy, coined the term "the Middle East" in the late-19th century (Mahan 1894). He argued that in order to have world domination, a state must have naval superiority through control of landmasses lying between the Near East and Far East, i.e. the Middle East. The control of this piece of real estate was therefore critical to Captain Mahan, who probably had no notion of the region's cultural and historical complexity.

A second obstacle to overcome was the traditional suspicions and conspiracy theories that characterize the colonial past of the region. Two bloody wars in the last two decades and a creeping third one have taken their toll on trust. We faced a triple-T problem: Tehranian, Toda, and Tudeh. Initially some Arab colleagues suspected that the project was an Iranian government conspiracy because the director of the Toda Institute is Iranian-born. Once they were dissuaded from this thought, an imaginative colleague in the region suggested that Toda resembled Tudeh, the name of the Iranian communist party. The project therefore must be a communist conspiracy! The Institute obviously had to explain that it had been named after Mr. Toda, the second President of Soka Gakkai, to honor his work for peace and global citizenship. Finally, someone suggested that since the conference is being held in Istanbul, it must be a Turkish-American-Israeli conspiracy against the rest of West Asia. Reasons for the choice of Istanbul, however, were convincing enough to dispel that suspicion: to avoid partiality, the first conference could not be held at any of the littoral states. Thus, Istanbul was the nearest convenient major city to the region that could be found.

A third obstacle presented itself as the conference time approached. The capture of Ocalan, the Kurdish nationalist leader, and his dispatch to Turkey to stand trial created some security fears. In the light of worldwide Kurdish demonstrations against Ocalan's capture, we considered a postponement of the conference. But assurances by the Turkish government of the security of the participants and the determination to press on kept us on target.

Despite these difficulties, there were many good omens as well. Because the project was an independent initiative supported by several peace and policy research institutes from outside the region, fears of partiality and manipulation were allayed. The co-sponsoring organizations included the Toda Institute, Copenhagen Peace Research Institute, Norwegian Institute of International Affairs, and the Center for Middle Eastern and Central Asian Studies of

Australian National University. The distinguished diplomats and scholars who accepted our invitation to join the International Commission also helped to diminish the anxiety about "conspiracies".

To further allay any fears or suspicions, a letter of request was sent to all of the foreign ministers of the eight littoral states and the five permanent state-members of the UN Security Council. It listed the purpose of the project, and requested them to nominate someone from their own country for Commission membership. The letter emphasized that the Commission members should have the confidence of their own governments and civil societies without necessarily representing them. The objective was clearly to have a non-governmental commission whose members were participating in the security dialogue in their personal capacity rather than as officials of their governments. One foreign minister, that of Britain, responded negatively to our request. Russia, Iran and Oman nominated representatives, while the remaining foreign ministers left our request unanswered. Informal contacts with non-responding government officials, however, indicated a bemused interest in the project. Selection of other representatives thus had to employ the project's informal academic and governmental channels to identify those who might qualify as eminent citizens of their own countries, enjoying equal respect from their governments and civil societies.

The first meeting of SACWA took place successfully on March 6–7, 1999, in Istanbul, Turkey. The fact that representatives of countries with broken diplomatic relations could meet in an atmosphere of friendship helped build confidence among them as a prelude to serious discussions. This was some proof of Woody Allen's assertion that "ninety percent of life is just being there!" Professor Saleh Alkhatlan, the Commission member from Saudi Arabia, has best expressed the positive feelings and the results that came out of the Istanbul conference:

> I send you my deepest thanks for two days of fruitful and informative discussion. I really enjoyed our meetings and strongly believe that the conference was a big success. As it was discussed in the meetings, misperception is a major obstacle to security and cooperation in the region, so please see if Toda's experience in enhancing communications and global understanding may help in overcoming such cognitive problems. You will be happy to know that today I am sending an e-mail to our colleagues from the Iranian Institute of Political and International Studies (IPIS) to say hello and thank them for frank and sincere discussions. To my knowledge this is the first e-mail contact between Riyadh and Tehran and it would have not been, if it were not for Toda (not Tudeh). May Allah help us in

achieving our objectives and see the Gulf stable and its peoples happy and prosperous. Thanks again and keep up the good work.

On a sad note, however, *Tehran Times* of March 6, 1999 (Internet version), reported on the conference under the headline: "Institute close to CIA hosts conference on Persian Gulf security in Turkey." The report stated "the conference has been organized by Toda Institute for Global Peace and Policy Research, which is headed by an Iranian Majid Tehranian, who has close links with the CIA … This is the first time Iran is involved in negotiations with the US focusing on the Persian Gulf security."[3] *Kayhan*, another newspaper controlled by the conservatives, also falsely accused me of CIA ties in order to discredit my peacebuilding efforts.

I wrote to the editors to deplore their irresponsible and false reports while denying the allegations of any CIA connection and emphasizing the NGO nature of the project. However, the incident showed once again that the lot of peacemakers is not easy. The project was being abused as a pawn in the power struggles between the conservatives and liberals in Tehran. As the mouthpiece of the conservatives, *Tehran Times* was thus trying to discredit the peacemaking initiatives of President Mohammad Khatami's government towards the Arab states and the West.

Regardless of the hurdles, what are the objectives and methods of the project? As a triple-track diplomatic initiative, the project consists of an International Commission acting as a second track while a third track of peace scholars feed it with proposals to promote a regional non-aggression pact, an arms control agreement, and a regional cooperation organization. Mr. Yasushi Akashi, former UN undersecretary-general and director of the Hiroshima Peace Institute, initially accepted to chair the Commission until a permanent chair was elected. However, due to his decision to run for the governor of Tokyo at about the time of the Istanbul conference, he had to withdraw. Mr. Vladimir Petrovsky, director-general and undersecretary-general of the United Nations office in Geneva, also had to decline participation while assuring us of his continued support for the project.

The Istanbul, Limassol, and Doha Conferences

Invitees to the Istanbul conference consisted of representatives from the eight littoral states, the five permanent members of the UN Security Council, the UN Secretary-General's office, and a number of observers (see Appendix I). Despite considerable efforts, no representatives from Kuwait and Bahrain attended the conference. Due to circumstances beyond their control, the UAE representatives also excused themselves with assurances of continued support of the project and promises to attend future meetings.

The conference agenda called for a preliminary discussion on various models of regional security and cooperation to be followed by explorations of the possibilities for a regional non-aggression pact, an arms control treaty, and a regional organization for security and cooperation. At the conclusion of the conference, we reached a unanimous agreement on the future of the Commission with a press release that called for the establishment of a regional research center for security and cooperation in the Gulf (see Appendix III).

Here are the main themes that were discussed at the conference:

1. Procedural Matters. Conference participants agreed first and foremost that the Chatham House confidentiality rules must apply to discussions, i.e. conference reports must refrain from any direct attribution of comments. This rule provided a secure atmosphere for open and frank discussions. The participants agreed that Yemen should be added to the Commission. Yemen is expected to join the GCC and its participation is vital to a viable security regime in the region. Participants also expressed a preference for soft rather than hard agenda items, as well as concrete rather than vague measures. They added that the language and framing of problems must be free of stereotypes and threats. The Commission should work first on confidence building measures and common grounds.

2. Models of Regional Cooperation. There are currently two good models for regional security regimes established by the Organization for Security and Cooperation in Europe (OSCE) and the Association of South East Asian Nations (ASEAN) in which arms control, transparency, and preventive diplomacy have been combined to provide enduring regional peace. Past security organizations in West Asia have been often prompted from the outside, e.g. the Baghdad Pact followed by the Central Treaty Organization. The Commission could learn from such examples. To succeed, however, the new regional organization must be initiated from within the region itself. Furthermore, participants felt the support and guarantees of the five permanent members of the UN Security Council were vital to regional security in the Gulf.

The experiences of other regional groupings are not, however, directly transferable to the Gulf. Despite this warning, there are three basic requirements for any successful regional formation: *consensus, inclusiveness,* and *functionalism.* Consensus building means regular visits by government officials to develop a common view on regional problems and possible solutions. Inclusiveness means to include all states of a given region regardless of their ideological or political orientations. Functionalism suggests that it is easier to achieve agreement on functional cooperation such as regional transportation and telecommunication, than sensitive political and economic issues.

It takes a long time before the potential member-states of a regional organization can gain sufficient confidence and trust in each other to commit to long-term, cooperative relations. In the case of the Gulf states, the following confidence building measures will help:

- Agreement on frontiers by peaceful negotiation for any needed adjustments
- Prior notification of military exercises
- Reciprocal observation of military exercises
- Reciprocal inspection of military facilities
- Transparency in arms production and imports
- Replacement of US with UN forces in the Gulf
- Great power guarantees of regional security through United Nations Security Council
- Preventive diplomacy through regular exchange of views on outstanding problems
- Regional games in popular sports such as soccer
- Regional exchange of performing artists
- Regional research and training center for security and cooperation
- Regional educational exchange programs
- Studies of security perceptions of the Gulf states
- Studies of mutual misperceptions and stereotypes in order to remove them
- Delinkage of Gulf issues from the Arab-Israeli disputes
- Focus on process rather than outcome
- Cultural exchange among non-governmental organizations
- Regional exchange among journalists and other critical professionals
- Encouragement of European Union to get more involved in the Gulf security issues
- Starting perhaps with a single step such as the formation of a regional center for security studies

3. Major Security Concerns. It is important to recognize the legitimate security concerns of the Gulf states before responding to them in a new regional security regime. While the Gulf region as a whole shares some common security concerns, each state in the region also has its own unique preoccupations. However, stability in the flows and price of oil, non-interference in their internal affairs, and long-term economic development, are the common concerns of all of the Gulf petroleum exporting states. A review of the main security concerns of each state might be useful here.

At the crossroads of East and West, Iran is bordering 12 different sovereign states, all of which are characterized by internal and external insecurity. Iran's security anxieties are thus real. Witness the Iraqi invasion of 1980 and the skirmishes with Afghanistan in 1998. As the largest of the Gulf states in population, Iran views its role as the balancer of power. Although successive Iranian governments have consistently denied any hegemonic intentions, they are often accused of such designs. To assume domination, however, Iran faces competition with the outside powers. Under Pax Saudi-Iranica, for a short period, Iran assumed a proxy role for the United States. After the Iranian Revolution, however, the United States has tried to isolate Iran. The two Gulf Wars and increasing political maturity have led the Iranian regime to make greater efforts toward confidence building with the Gulf states. Ever since the Iran-Iraq War, relations between the two countries have been tense. Each regime provides a base of operation for opposition groups to the other regime. War reparations, return of Iraqi jets that are claimed by Iran as part of war reparations, exchange of war prisoners, and ideological differences are the main issues at stake. However, both states wish for the United States to leave the Persian Gulf. Both desire higher prices for oil. And both consider themselves vanguards of the revolutionary movements in the region. Iraq claims leadership of the secular nationalists and republicans while Iran champions the cause of an Islamic revolution.

Iraq's internal divisions (60 percent Shi'i, 20 percent Sunni, and 20 percent Kurdish) have shaped its security perceptions. With its historical memories of grandeur as the center of the Abbasid Dynasty during the 9th–13th centuries, Iraq has in modern times competed with Egypt and Syria for leadership in the Arab world. Following 1968, under the Ba'athist regime, this competition reached its peak during the Iraqi invasions of Iran and Kuwait. During the first Gulf War, Iraq enjoyed the support of Arab countries except Libya and Syria. In the second Gulf War, however, it was isolated except for

Jordanian and Palestinian support. Having been subjected to over a decade of economic sanctions, the Iraqi regime suffers from intense insecurity. It views itself as the victim of Western imperialism, conservative Arab perfidy, and Iranian hostility. Dominated by Sunni Arab leadership, the Ba'athist regime's suspicion of its own Shi'i and Kurdish population adds to this sense of insecurity.

The GCC consists of six countries that vary in size and attitudes. Saudi Arabia has successfully served as the GCC leader shaping its policies in the Gulf. As a group, the GCC considers itself a balancing power *vis-à-vis* the two Gulf big boys, namely Iran and Iraq. As relatively rich but less populated countries, the GCC governments also look for protection from the United States against possible threats from Iran and Iraq. However, feelings about the presence of the US forces are mixed. Too close an identification with the US opens the GCC regimes to accusations of complicity with un-Islamic and imperialist powers. Although the recent rapprochement with Iran is not universal among the GCC members, Saudi Arabia has led the way. The United Arab Emirates continues to have a serious conflict with Iran on the issue of sovereignty over the three Gulf islands (Abu Musa, Greater and Smaller Tunbs). Bahrain has accused the Iranian regime of subversive activities within its borders. Bahrain and Qatar have had some territorial disputes that were finally settled in 2001 by the World Court. Oman and Qatar seem to enjoy the best relations with Iran. Expanding commercial relations between Iran and the southern Gulf states, however, are paving the way for greater common and enduring interests. Saudi Arabia and the UAE are currently at odds over the GCC opening to Iran. Symbolic issues such as the name of "the Gulf" and practical issues such as the control of the three Gulf islands (Abu Musa, Greater and Smaller Tunbs) continue to divide the two sides of the Gulf.

The Cyprus and Qatar meetings in 2000 and 2001 carried the work of the Commission forward and gained the support of new sponsoring organizations and governments, notably the Center for World Dialogue in Cyprus and the government of Qatar. The Doha meeting was particularly significant in that it was taking place in the region. The project thus received significant attention in such media as *Al-Hayat*, *Al-Jazirah* Satellite Television, *Al-Sharq*, *The Gulf Times*, and *The Peninsula Times*. *Al-Hayat*, published in London, and *Al-Jazirah*, broadcast from Doha, are particularly important media because they reach the entire Arab world and enjoy top audience ratings and credibility. Moreover, the Doha meeting reached significant decisions on the future of the project and conflict resolution between Iran and the UAE.

Conclusion

This brief account of an effort at peacebuilding in a war-torn region of the world has reviewed the historical evolution of security regimes in the Persian Gulf. It has argued that the current situation is both untenable and conducive to a new, indigenous security regime for long-term regional security and cooperation. The essay has provided the background to the HUGG West Asia Project, an NGO initiative aiming at the establishment of such a regime. It has reported on the deliberations of the three meetings of the International Commission for Security and Cooperation in West Asia, held in Istanbul. Limassol, and Doha. The essay also has outlined the main obstacles to establishing regional cooperation for security as well as the opportunities that present circumstances offer.

What lies ahead? (Sick & Potter 1997). As soon as the Gulf states adopt the Commission's recommendation for the establishment of a regional center for security and cooperation, the task of the HUGG West Asia Project may be considered completed. However, until such time, much needs to be done. Regular meetings of the Commission are planned for the next few years. In preparation for these meetings, research projects are under way exploring the security perceptions of Iran, Iraq, and the GCC and how a common ground can be developed among them. Other topics for research and policy development may include arms control, border disputes, trade and development problems, oil production controls and prices, scientific, technological, and cultural cooperation, the role of great powers, the European Union, and the United Nations.

Each of the three meetings came to the same conclusion, i.e. that in the current regional atmosphere, a soft rather than hard approach to security and cooperation is preferable. For this reason, the Doha meeting recommended the establishment of a West Asian Regional Institute for Dialogue (WARID) to be taken up at a larger conference to be held outside of the region either in Beirut or Cyprus. WARID's central objective will be to mobilize the governments and civil societies of the region toward a movement for peace and security through dialogue and cooperation.

APPENDIX I.
INTERNATIONAL COMMISSION FOR SECURITY AND COOPERATION IN WEST ASIA
LIST OF PARTICIPANTS

First Meeting, Istanbul, Turkey, March 6–7, 1999
Second Meeting, Limassol, Cyprus, May 27–29, 2000
Third Meeting, Doha, Qatar, January 5–7, 2001
Fourth Meeting, Limassol, Cyprus, March 29–31, 2002

Commission Members

Bahrain:	Unrepresented
Iraq:	Ambassador Amir Alanbari, Ambassador to the Vatican
Iran:	Dr. Seyyed Kazem Sajjadpour, Director of the Institute for Political and International Studies (IPIS), Tehran
Kuwait:	Professor Saif A. Al-Dehrab, University of Kuwait
Oman:	Ambassador Mohammad Nasser Al-Wahabi
	Ambassador Nasser bin Khalfan Al-Kharoosi
Qatar:	Ambassador Nasser al-Khalifa, Ministry of Foreign Affairs
Saudi Arabia:	Professor Saleh Alkhatlan, King Saud University, Riyadh
UAE:	Dr. Jamal S. Al-Suwaidi, Director, Emirate Center for Strategic Studies & Research
	Dr. Abdalla M. Al-Shaiba, Emirate Center for Strategic Studies & Research
China:	Dr. Jingo-lie Wang, Secretary-General, Gulf Research Center, Beijing
France:	Ambassador Eric Rouleau, *Le Monde Diplomatique*
Russia:	Professor Vitally V. Naumkin, President of International Strategic Research Center
UK:	Lord Judd, House of Lords
US:	Ambassador Richard Murphy, Council on Foreign Relations
UN:	Mr. Vladimir Petrovsky, Director General and Under-Secretary General, United Nations Office, Geneva

Expert Advisors

Australia:	Professor Leanne Piggott, Center for Peace and Conflict Studies, Sydney University
	Professor Amin Saikal, Director, Center for Arab and Islamic Studies, ANU
Denmark:	Professor Bjoern Moeller, Copenhagen Peace Research Institute, Copenhagen
Egypt:	Professor Mohammad El-Sayed Selim, Director for West Asian Studies, University of Cairo
Iran:	Dr. Seyyed Abbas Araghchi, Institute of Political and International Studies (IPIS), Tehran
	Ambassador Ali Asghar Mehrabi, Research Associate, IPIS
	Mr. Ali Akbar Rezaei, Research Associate, IPIS

	Dr. Jalil Roshandel, IPIS
	Professor Behzad Shahandeh, Tehran University
New Zealand:	Dr. Kevin Clements, Director, Alert, London
Norway:	Sverre Lodgaard, Norwegian Institute of International Affairs
Qatar:	Abdullah bin Saleh Al-Khulaifi, President, University of Qatar
	Abdul Rahman Alattiyah, Under-Secretary, Ministry of Foreign Affairs
	Mohammad Al-Malki, Minister Plen., Ministry of Foreign Affairs
	Ambassador Fahed Alkawari, Ministry of Foreign Affairs
	Professor Mohammad S. Al-Musafir, Qatar University
Switzerland:	M. Jean F. Freymond, Director, Center for Applied International Negotiations
Turkey:	Oguz Celikkol, Director General Of Ministry Of Foreign Affairs, Turkey
United States:	Mr. Jack Maresca, Vice-President, Unocal, Geneva
	Ambassador Roscoe S. Suddarth, President, The Middle East Institute, Washington, DC
	Professor Stephen Zunes, University of San Francisco
	Professor Nur Yalman, Harvard University

Toda Institute Staff

Professor Majid Tehranian, Director, Toda Institute, University of Hawaii at Manoa

Mr. Tomosaburo Hirano, Deputy Director, Toda Institute, Honolulu Center

Dr. Satoko Takahashi, Program Manager, Toda Institute, Honolulu Center

Appendix II. Proposal for a West Asian Regional Institute for Dialogue (WARID)

The Doha Conference (January 5–7, 2001) resolved to organize a conference in either Cyprus or Beirut in the near future to consider the establishment of a West Asian Regional Institute for Dialogue.

Purpose: As a non-governmental organization, WARID aims at promoting peace and security among the states of West Asia by opening channels of dialogue, exchange, mutual understanding, and confidence building among the peoples of the region.

Governance: WARID shall be governed by a Board of Trustees composed of 15 members, including one representative from each of the following countries or organizations serving in their own personal capacities: Bahrain, Iraq, Iran, Kuwait, Oman, Qatar, Saudi Arabia, United Arab Emirates, Yemen, United States, Russia, China, Japan, European Union, and the United Nations. The Board shall appoint a Secretary-General for a renewable term of three years.

Budget: WARID shall be financed by a consortium of peace and security research centers, academic institutions, and charitable foundations able and willing to support its programs. WARID would also welcome contributions from non-partisan organizations and philanthropists as a source of income.

Program: WARID shall undertake a series of three-year plans focused on peacebuilding among the states and people of West Asia, including, but not limited to, dialogue and cooperation among professional groups (doctors, teachers, nurses, lawyers, politicians, journalists, etc.) focusing on regional collaboration in their own areas of expertise.

Headquarters: Offers shall be accepted from all of the regional states to house the Institute.

Organizing Conference: An organizing conference shall be called by either Center for World Dialogue in Cyprus OR the American University of Beirut inviting about 5 representatives from each regional state. In collaboration with the host organization, Ambassador Nasser Al-Khalifa and Professors Amin Saikal and Majid Tehranian shall prepare the conference program focusing both on substantive and organizational issues.

Notes

1. Despite the controversy over the name of the Gulf, this essay employs the historical name sanctioned by the United Nations. While this article is in line with the peacebuilding objectives of the project it describes, the voice is my own. I am deeply grateful to the HUGG West Asia project participants but absolve them of all responsibility for the errors of fact or interpretation herein.
2. This part borrows from Pirouz Mojtahed-Zadeh (1998a) without necessarily implicating him in my terminology and analysis.
3. On a lighter note, I am tempted to use "the authority" of *Tehran Times* and *Kayhan* to demand my back pay from CIA!

Part One: THE PAST AS PROLOGUE

CHAPTER 2

West Asia from Mansur to Saddam

Nur Yalman

It was Mansur, the second Abbasid caliph (754–775) who built the city of Baghdad on the banks of Tigris near the ruins of the old Sasanid capital of Ctesiphon. The geographer Ya'qubi describes the idea:

> This island between the Tigris in the East and the Euphrates in the West is a market place for the world. All the ships that come up the Tigris from Wasit, Basra, Ubulla, Ahwaz, Fars, Uman, Yamama, Bahrain and beyond will go up and anchor here; wares brought on ships down the Tigris from Mosul, Diyar-Rabi'a, Adharbaijan and Armenia, and along the Euphrates from Diyar-Mudar, Syria and the border marshes, Egypt and North Africa will be brought and unloaded here. It will be the highway for the people of the Jabal, Isfahan and the districts of Khurasan ... It will surely be the most flourishing city in the world. (Lewis 1958, 82)

The civilization of the early Islamic Empire fulfilled those hopes. Historians report that "Muslim merchants [leaving the Gulf ports] traveled to India, Ceylon, the East Indies and China, bringing silks, spices, aromatics, woods, tin, and other commodities ... Alternative routes to India and China ran overland through Central Asia. The goods brought from China included, silk, crockery, paper, ink, peacocks, horses, saddles, felt, cinnamon, pure Greek rhubarb; from the Byzantine Empire ... gold and silver utensils, gold coins, drugs, brocades, slave girls, trinkets, locks, hydraulic engineers, agronomes, marble workers, and eunuchs; from India ... tigers, panthers, elephants, panther skins, rubies, white sandalwood, ebony, and coconuts." Muslim navigators were quite at home in eastern seas, where Arab traders were established in China as early as the 8th century.

There was also extensive trade between the Islamic Empire and the Baltic via the Caspian, the Black Sea, and Russia. "With Africa too, the Arabs carried on an extensive overland trade." The Jews served as a link with Europe. The early-19th century geographer, Ibn Khurradadhbeh, tells of Jewish merchants from the south of France "... who speak Arabic, Persian, Greek, Frankish, Spanish, and Slavonic. They travel from west to east and from east to west, by land and sea. From the west they bring eunuchs, salve-girls, boys, brocade, castor-skins, marten and other furs, and swords ... they sail on the eastern (Red) Sea from Qulzum to Al-Jar and Jedda, and onward to Sind, India and China. From China they bring back musk, aloes, camphor, cinnamon, and other products ... Some sail with their goods to Constantinople, and sell them to the Greeks, and some take them to the king of Franks and sell them there."

In other words, a "common market" without boundaries and with considerable mobility was evidently a characteristic of the brilliant period of the early Islamic Empire. The historian again, "We hear of banks with a head office in Baghdad and branches in the other cities of the Empire and of an elaborate system of cheques, letters of credit, etc. so developed that it was possible to draw a cheque in Baghdad and cash it in Morocco" (Lewis 1958).

This open market continues well into the 19th century, when Sir Adolphus Slade, a British naval officer, who spent a great deal of time in the service of the Ottoman navy, wrote of the sense of equality among Muslims of the last great Islamic Empire:

> Hitherto the Osmanley has enjoyed by custom some of the dearest privileges of freemen, for which Christian nations have so long struggled. He paid nothing to the government beyond a moderate land-tax ... He paid no tithes, the vacouf sufficing for the maintenance of the ministers of Islamism. He traveled where he pleased without passports; no customhouse officer intruded his eyes and dirty fingers among his baggage; no police watched his motions, or listened to his words. His house was sacred ... His views of ambition were not restricted by barriers of birth and wealth: from the lowest origin he might aspire without presumptions to the rank of pasha; if he could read, to that of grand vesir; and this consciousness, instilled and supported by numberless precedents, ennobled his mind, and enables him to enter on the duties of his office without embarrassment.

And significantly, Slade goes on to remark, "Is not this the advantage so prized by free nations? Did not the exclusion of the people from posts of honor tend to the French revolution?" (Lewis 1968, 125).

The reason it is worth mentioning these matters is twofold: first, the idea of a "common market" among Muslim countries at least, is as old as Islam, and second, equality and freedom of movement was the norm until very recent times. Many commentators from the West remark in astonishment on the cultural uniformity of the peoples from Morocco to Central Asia. Ernst Gellner, one of the most learned observers, finds this homogeneity difficult to explain, when in fact, it is the result of centuries of common education and administration over the central lands of Islam. After all, it was not at all surprising for the intrepid and indefatigable traveler Ibn Batuta to go from Fez to Meknes in Morocco all the way to Cairo, Anatolia, Crimea, Baghdad, Delhi and the Maldives and to be received as a learned 'Alim in the royal courts of all those places. He even found the time and energy to make a trip to West Africa after his return to Fez.

It was this unity of the Islamic lands that the Ottomans had tried to preserve against the predatory attacks from the West. It is also astonishing that they were relatively successful in doing so until 1918, the end of World War I. It is true that the French had penetrated into Algeria in the middle of the 19th century, and that the British established themselves in Egypt by the end of the century. We can hardly overlook the fact that one European power or another had in fact colonized most of the so-called newly discovered world. Only faraway Japan, perhaps Thailand, Persia just barely, and the Ottoman Empire had been able to escape from direct European domination. As Richard Crampton, The Oxford historian, notes in a brilliant review on the Balkans, "despite the lurid pictures of Muslim persecution painted by many 19th-century European Christian observers or commentators, there was a great deal of intermixing in the Ottoman Empire. Muslim, Orthodox Christians, Jews, and others became members of the same guilds, and would even ... join the same labor organizations or gentlemen's clubs ... There was ... usually more hostility between Orthodox Christians and Roman Catholics than there was between Orthodox and Muslim: 'better the Sultan than the Pope' was a sentiment entertained by many of the Orthodox throughout the southern and eastern Balkans after the Crusaders sacked Constantinople" (Crampton 2001).

An example of the cosmopolitan complexity of the Ottoman world is provided by the following description of a visitor to the great city. In 1896 Edmondo de Amicis walked down the Galata Bridge across the Golden Horn where he saw "all the Constantinople pass in an hour." He described it:

> A mussulman woman on foot, a veiled female slave, a Greek with her long flowing hair surmounted by a little red cap, a Maltese hidden in her black faletta,

> a Jewess in the ancient costume of her nation, a negress wrapped in a many tinted Cairo shawl, an Armenia woman from Trebizond, all veiled in black ... The Syrians, clad in a long Byzantine dolman, with a gold-striped handkerchief wrapped around his head; the Bulgarian, in somber-coloured tunic and fur-edged cap; the Georgian, with his casque of dressed leather and tunic gathered into a metal belt; The Greek from the Archipelago, covered with lace, silver tassels, and shining buttons ... the crows ... in great overpowering waves of colour crested with white turbans like foam, in whose midst may occasionally be seen a high hat or umbrella of some European lady ... Every tint of skin can be found, from the milk-white Albanian to the jet-black slave from central Africa or the blue-black native of Dafur ... While you are trying to make out the designs tattooed on an arm, your guide is calling your attention to a Serb, a Montenegrin, a Wallach, a Ukrainian Cossack of the Don, or Egyptian, a native of Tunis, a prince of Imerzi ... An expert eye can distinguish ... the distinctive features and costumes of Caramania and Anatolia, of Cypress and Candia, of Damascus and Jerusalem—Druses, Kurds, Maronites, Telemans, Pumacs, and Kroats ... No two persons are dressed alike. Some heads are enveloped in shawls, others crowned with rags, others decked out like savages ... belts bristling with weapons, some of them reaching from the waist to the arm-pits; mameluke trousers, knee-breeches, tunics, togas, long cloaks which sweep the ground, capes trimmed with ermine, waistcoats encrusted with gold, short sleeves and balloon-shaped ones, monastic garbs and theatre costumes; men dressed like women, women who seem to be men and peasants with the air of princes. (Goodwin 1998, 320–21)

The Jews of the Muslim lands had much to be grateful for: the Ottomans invited the Jewish communities who had been expelled from Spain in 1492 to come and settle in their cities so that they could enrich these communities with their enterprise. Bernard Lewis quotes the famous Edirne letter "written in the first half of the 15th century":

> I have heard of the afflictions, more bitter than death, that have befallen our brethren in Germany—of the tyrannical laws, the compulsory baptisms and the banishments, which are of daily occurrence ... on all sides I learn of anguish of soul and torment of body ... brothers and teachers, friends and acquaintances! I, Isaac Zarfati, though I spring from a French stock, yet I was born in Germany, and sat at the feet of my esteemed teachers. I proclaim to you that Turkey is a land wherein nothing is lacking, and where, if you will, all shall be met with you. The way of the Holy Land lies open to you through Turkey ... Here every man may dwell at peace under his own vine and fig tree. Here you are allowed to wear the most precious garments. In Christendom, on the contrary, you dare not even venture to clothe your children in red or blue, according to your taste, without exposing them to the insult of being beaten black and blue, or kicked green and red, and therefore are ye condemned to go about meanly clad in sad colored

> raiment … and now, seeing all these things, O Israel, wherefore sleepiest thou? Arise! And leave this accursed land forever.

Lewis goes on to quote from a Portuguese Jew a century later, Samuel Usque:

> Most signal (among human consolations) is great Turkey, a broad and spacious sea which God opened with the rod of His mercy as He opened the Red Sea at the time of the exodus … here the gates of liberty are always open for the observance of Judaism.

And Lewis adds, "this must come as a considerable surprise to a traveler from 16th-century Portugal" (Lewis 1984).

How is it that we have arrived at the catastrophic state of affairs that have characterized much of Western Asia in the 20th century? Surely the blame must be placed squarely where it belongs—the shortsighted, self-serving, predatory, and malign policy of many of the foreign powers that have meddled in the affairs of the region. To this must be added the poor leadership and the lack of foresight shown by the political elites in much of Western Asia, including Turkey and Egypt. The sad story begins with the defeat of the Ottoman Empire and continues with the games played between France and Britain up to and including the Suez Canal War. The disaster that befell the Jews in Europe was certainly not the fault of the Palestinians. The horrors of the 1930s were the end product of a long history of anti-Semitism far beyond Germany. It has been highly convenient for the European countries to have the Arabs pay for the sins of European racism, and to pretend, without a trace of cynicism, that Europe is now the repository of universal human rights.

Thus the cultural unity of the Islamic lands was shattered by the experiences of World War I. One by one the different countries began to experiment with ideas of "nationalism". By adopting a European designation for the "new nation" that emerged after the end of the empire, Turkey was the first to move. The Italian "Turchia" became "Turkiye". The population was encouraged to call itself "Turks" to the great astonishment of ordinary Muslims. Sevket Syreya Aydemir describes the amazed reaction of villagers in Thrace when he, as a schoolteacher, informs them that henceforth they are "Turks". "Estaghfurullah", they say, "we are Muslims". In time, Iran, with Reza Shah, and Egypt, especially under Nasser, became preoccupied with the search for the "essence" of the Persian or Arab "nation". Just as Johann Gottfried von Herder has hoped to discover the "Geist" of the German "nation" among ordinary people speaking "their" language, writers and thinkers in the "new" countries in West Asia began the frustrating search for ancient "roots" in the repositories of archaeological museums, and in ethological explorations. It was not by accident that the prime mover of nationalism, Mustafa Kemal Ataturk, was interred in the Ethnological Museum in Ankara after his death in 1939. It was only much later that his remains were transferred to the magnificent mausoleum that has become the symbol of Turkish national identity.

The problem today is that "nationalism" is unlikely to serve as an effective framework for the world that is emerging before us. The peoples of West Asia are once again likely to be left behind in the search for more effective societies. The US has shown that a vast economic empire can be built on the basis of a commitment to a brilliantly conceived "Constitution". The American Constitution allows people of the most diverse backgrounds to come together and to work effectively under the rule of law. At this time nearly 10 percent of the American population is foreign born. In its essence, this was what had been achieved under the Muslim empires and the rule of the Shari'a. The example of the US, its effectiveness as an economic and political regime, has not been lost on European and Asian thinkers. So, now we have two important developments on the Atlantic and Pacific Rim of the Eurasian space. The European Union is an exciting prospect for all those liberal thinkers since the French Revolution who have dreamed of a more inclusive realm, which could contain the ethnic hostilities that had plagued the ancient continent for so long. It will be recalled that Hegel and Goethe as well as Beethoven and Mozart had lent their considerable talents to supporting Napoleon's vision for an "enlightened" Europe. The Eroica symphony and the Magic Flute are witnesses to the attractions of the European idea.

It is difficult to predict how this experiment will work out. In a world of much increased communications, it is inevitable that we shall be faced with much greater needs for international collaboration and administration. In that sense, a larger entity beyond the narrow confines of the "nation-state" has already found many supporters. There is also the hope that supra-national entities may be appealed to for the perceived redress of injustices in the "national" sphere. Hence the appeal of the European Court of Justice.

Similar processes are at work in the Pacific region even though they are far less advanced. Here Japan and the US are playing a key role to encourage regional cooperation, which may have very positive results. ASEAN has already been very helpful in establishing more forthright communications among states, which had largely been closed to each other. The efforts of persons such as Lee Kwan Yew in Singapore and Surin Pitsuwan, the brilliant foreign minister of Thailand, are clearly in this direction.

When we consider the situation in West Asia in the context of such international developments, it becomes clear that conditions are much more promising for the building of institutions beyond the boundaries of the nation-states in the region. In sociological, cultural, and linguistic terms, Europe is more diverse than West Asia. Three great languages, Arabic, Persian, and Turkish are likely to provide communications in a region from Morocco to China. That is the great benefit of the historical legacy of the Ottoman, Persian, and Mogul Empires. Many customs, much of the way of life, from food to dress to gesture is similar in large sections of the region. The profound unifying and purifying experience of the Hajj in Mecca is indeed an effective metaphor for the cultural unity of the peoples of West Asia. In this respect, the unity of the region is in stark contrast to the diversity of Europe. A Turk traveling in Egypt or Iran is immediately at home. Iranians and Arabs are assimilated into Turkish society with hardly any notice taken of their origins. Many persons of Turkish origin are in high places in Saudi Arabia. All this is part of an ancient process that has been going on since the time of the Tulunids in the 10th century in Baghdad and Egypt. This is hardly the case with a Spaniard in Scandinavia or an Italian in England. The ethnic sensitivities of Europe have been much more pronounced than those in the West Asian region.

In Europe two processes have been going on at the same time. There is the desire for higher integration into the larger supranational entity. There is, at the same time, the emphasis on regional cultural autonomy. The process is much in evidence in Spain, with the Catalans and the Basques, in Italy, between North and South, in France with Basques, Bretons, Corsicans and others. There are similar problems in Low Countries. So far the matter has been handled fairly effectively at the level of the European Parliament. There is a long way to go. Still, Europe has given an excellent example of how to handle these matters concerning the evolution and devolution of political power through negotiations. It is greatly to be hoped that a liberal and open society will emerge which recognizes the cultural and political needs of smaller sections of the population in the larger European context.

The need for institutions that bring about better and more effective communications between the peoples of the West Asian region is now more pronounced than ever. With all the cultural similarities, it is also true that the writers, painters, academics, journalists, and thinkers know very little about each other in the major cultural spheres in our region. Institutions, which may remedy this lack of cultural literacy, are likely to be of great benefit to all concerned. And it is here that institutions such as the ones envisaged in this peace building project may play a crucial role.

There is one other reason to think ahead. It is no secret that large young populations in West Asia are extremely frustrated. This deep sense of malaise is expressed in different ways in almost all countries of the region. This is not simply a matter of economic difficulties though they certainly play a part. More importantly there is the need to provide a better model for the future. We need to think ahead to be able to provide the next generations with a vision of more humane, more effective, more free, more decent, more promising societies. This can only come about with free discussions, open disagreements, but also with a view of creating a larger world, with better linkages that provides hope, challenges, and encouragement for the next generations.

CHAPTER 3

Trans-Mediterranean-Gulf Geostrategic Security Linkages

Mohammad El-Sayed Selim

The 20th-century revolution of communications technology has unleashed *inter alia* the linkages between various geographical regions. Such linkages were always present, albeit on a limited scale. The revolution created new forms of linkages, and intensified the existing ones. It also generated various geopolitical theories, conceptualizing inter-regional linkages and their strategic implications. Among the most important of these theories in the field of geopolitics is the Heartland Theory put forth by Sir Halford Mackinder and the Rimland Theory advocated by Nicholas Spykman. Whereas the first theory postulated linkages between the Heartland, the World Island, and the World, the second emphasized that the Rimlands of Europe, the Middle East, Africa, South, and East Asia are keys to the security of the United States (Plano & Olton 1982, 95–6). In the field of International Relations, James Rosenau presented the concept of "linkage politics," by which he meant "any recurrent sequence of behavior that originates in one system and is reacted to in another". He also introduced the concepts of "the Contiguous Environment". This concept refers to the linkages between a national system and the adjacent regions (Rosenau 1969). He also advocated a new form of across-system theorizing which attempts to explore such linkages and assess their implications (Rosenau 1973). The end result of these theoretical advances was the emergence of the concept of the "geostrategic space", of regions. This concept refers to the set of transregional linkages, which influence the dynamics of that region. It is based on the assumption of the complex interplay between variables emanating from the region and adjacent regions. In conceptualizing the dynamics of a region, one must not be limited by what happens within the immediate geographical boundary of the region. One must also take into account the wider strategic space with which it is inter-linked. This new conceptualization has been reflected in recent writings defining geo-strategic regions. For example, Julius Caesar Parrenas, a Filipino scholar, has recently argued that the geo-strategic space of the Gulf is linked to the Southeast Asian space in strategic and developmental terms (Parrenas 1998). This was also reflected in recent writings on the Mediterranean. It is argued that in thinking about the Mediterranean region, one must also be alert to the risks and opportunities inherent in adjacent systems such as Eastern Europe, West Asia, and Central Asia. In their review of the various dimensions of Mediterranean security, Larrabee *et al.* acknowledged the relevance of "transregional" variables to Mediterranean security (Larrabee *et al.* 1998, 13–14).

The objective of this chapter is to review the linkages between the Mediterranean and the Gulf regions, and to assess the risks and opportunities emanating from them, and their implications for Gulf security. The concept of the Gulf region will be broadly defined as referring to the water and land mass, which extends from the Red Sea to the Gulf. This area includes the Red Sea, the Arabian Peninsula, and the Gulf. This is a huge area, which comprise at its core seven countries, Yemen and the Gulf Cooperation Council (GCC) countries, namely Saudi Arabia, Oman, the United Arab Emirates, Qatar, Bahrain, and Kuwait. At the periphery of this core, there are eleven countries, four of which are members in the Euro-Mediterranean Partnership (EMP), Egypt, Israel, Jordan, and Syria, in addition to Sudan, Eritrea, Ethiopia, Djioubti, Somalia on the African side of the Red Sea.

The linkages between the Gulf and the Mediterranean have been widely acknowledged by academicians and policy makers in both regions. For example, in our review of the Arab literature on the Red Sea's transregional linkages, we found that such literature has grasped the linkages between the Red Sea and the Gulf or the Indian Ocean (Selim 1998, 12). One could also identify an emerging acknowledgement of the Mediterranean-Gulf links, among southern Mediterranean and European analysts and policy makers. In conceptualizing the institutions of the Mediterranean Forum, Egypt argued that the Arab countries in the Orient should be brought into the Forum by virtue of their Mediterranean linkages, thereby implying a link between Mediterranean and Arab security (Selim 1995, 22). In 1985, Aliboni conceptualized the Mediterranean, the Red Sea, and the Gulf as a single strategic space. He asserted that the Red Sea is an "area in the midst, working like a pivot for those who want to have access to the

Persian Gulf, Africa, and the Mediterranean or to control them. To a certain extent, this strategic unity of the different regions lying southeast of Western Europe marks the return to a 'classical' situation" (Aliboni 1985, 113–14). In 1996, Abdel-Halim, an Egyptian strategic analyst, argued that "the security of the Red Sea is closely inter-linked with the security of the Mediterranean to the north, and the security of the Indian Ocean and the Gulf to the south. All of them are a part of a larger geo-strategic area which is under the control of a certain superpower" (Abdel-Halim 1996, 16). Further, El-Misfer, a Qatarai analyst, contended that the Mediterranean region should be defined so as to include all Arab countries. No Arab country should be excluded from the EMP. He went on to argue that the EMP and the Euro-GCC partnerships should be inter-linked (El-Misfer 1998, 171). The 1997 agreement signed between Yemen and the EU reiterated the awareness of the EU which states that "Yemen is a part of the Arab states in the Middle East and the Mediterranean." During his visit to Brussels in February 2000, the Yemeni president Abdulla Saleh also expressed an interest in joining the Euro-Mediterranean Partnership (EMP) as an observer. Chris Patten, the European Commissioner for Foreign Affairs, also asserted that the European Commission would link its relations with Yemen with its relations with the Mediterranean states (Al-Saggaf 2000). Underlying these articulations is an awareness of the strong strategic linkages between the Mediterranean and Arabian regions.

Conceptual Issues

In assessing the linkages between the Mediterranean and Gulf regions the methodology of assessment needs to be addressed. The first question relates to the direction of assessment. This analysis is based on the assumption that risks and opportunities located in the Gulf region should be assessed in the light of their counterparts in the Mediterranean region. This is essentially because we are dealing with relational variables (linkages). The dynamics of such variables can only be grasped if we comprehend the distance between the actors as far as these variables are concerned. For example, one cannot understand the risks emanating from the presence of weapons of mass destruction and missile technology in the Gulf region without taking into consideration the availability of the same weapons and technology in the Mediterranean region. Most analysts tend to view developments in one region as posing risks *par excellence* to other regions without taking into account that developments in the latter may neutralize such risks. This also means that one should also assess the risks and opportunities, which the Mediterranean poses to the countries of the Gulf region. The second issue deals with the categories of assessment. Four major categories of assessment have been identified, namely, geopolitical, historical, balance of power, and interdependence linkages (Said 1987, 20–32).

The first category focuses on defining the natural and human geography affecting interactions between the two regions, such as the extent of geographic contiguity, the availability of land and sea routes, and human migration. Although the influence of these factors has been reduced as a result of new communications technologies, they still exercise a significant role in defining perceptions of security in both regions. The second category deals with the development of relationships among the Mediterranean and Gulf peoples and states, the engagement of foreign powers in both regions, and the lessons that could be drawn from the historical record of interactions. The historical approach could reveal the patterns of interactions between the two regions, and their applicability to new conditions in the 21st century. It is also important to define the security threats and regional conflicts, which could influence Mediterranean security including the pattern of power correlation between the two regions. The identification of such pattern will help us assess the direction of the flow of security threats. Finally, the interdependence category focuses on the issues raised as a result of the pursuit of economic interests by various actors. It deals mainly with areas of complementarity without being oblivious to the areas of friction and threat perceptions, which they may raise. In the following sections we will review each category with a view of assessing its impact on the definition of the Mediterranean space.

Mediterranean-Gulf Geopolitical Linkages

From a geopolitical perspective, the Mediterranean is directly linked with the Gulf region through two major channels, geographical co-membership and contiguity and the Suez Canal. Egypt and Jordan, member states in the EMP and the Mediterranean Forum, are Arab states, member states in the Arab regional system, and direct neighbors of the Gulf region. This means that the Gulf region is not a mere neighbor of the Mediterranean region. The two regions overlap through co-membership in both regions of two states. As a result, Egyptian and Jordanian views of Mediterranean security are heavily influenced by their Arab commitments, and their views of the security of the Arab regional system are shaped by their Mediterranean commitments. Further, Mediterranean security structures cannot be established without taking into account Egyptian and Jordanian views of the relationship between Mediterranean and Arab regional security. According to Egypt and Jordan, their membership in Mediterranean security structures does not necessarily exclude their active involvement in Arab security arrangements. This means that the Arab dimension should be considered in future proposals to establish Mediterranean security institutions.

The Suez Canal directly connects the Gulf of Suez with the Red Sea and the Gulf. The canal is a sea level waterway with an overall length of 190 km of which 78 km are doubled parts. It considerably shortens the shipping distance between the Red Sea—Gulf ports, and European ports. For example, ships carrying oil from Ras Tannoura in Saudi Arabia to Rotterdam in Holland though the Suez Canal save 42 percent of the length of the trip if the Cape route is used. Consequently, most European trade with the Gulf region, southern and eastern Asia goes through the Suez Canal. Seven out of the top ten countries using the Suez Canal for southbound destinations in 1999 were European-Mediterranean countries. Their cargo tons in the canal represented 59 percent of the total cargo tons transiting the canal in that year. About 38 percent of the southbound trade transiting the canal in 1999 originated from the Mediterranean region. Furthermore 85 percent of the northbound oil (almost 15 million cargo tons) transiting the canal went to Mediterranean countries and EU states (Suez Canal Authority 2000).

Equally important are the Bab Al-Mandab Straits to the south of the Red Sea and the Hormuz Strait connecting the Gulf and the Arabian Sea. The straits represent the gateway to the Gulf, the Arabian Sea, the Indian Ocean, and beyond. Located in the middle of the Straits are the Hanish and Zuqar archipelagoes. During the October 1973 war, Egypt and Yemen collaborated to close the straits to international shipping destined for Israel. In fact, closure of the straits could render the Suez Canal almost useless except for the littoral states of the Red Sea. In December 1995 troops from Eritrea seized control of Al-Hanish Al-Kabir (Greater Hanish Island) in the southern sector of the archipelago, which was under Yemeni control. Because of this, Eritrea and Yemen were on the brink of war and international navigation in the Straits was seriously threatened. The Hormuz Strait is a narrow and curved shaped channel, connecting the Gulf to the Indian Ocean. It is approximately 100 nautical miles long. The narrowest part of the strait—21 nautical miles—lies between the Iranian island of Larak and the Omani islet of Greater Quoin. Iran and Oman have agreed to define a median line as their demarcation line in the strait (Mojtahed-Zadeh 1990). During the Iraq-Iran War (1980–88), oil shipping in the strait was seriously threatened. Iran had closed off Iraq's access to the Gulf in the initial stages of the war. Iraq replied by launching the "Tanker War", through which the Iraqi air force attacked tankers carrying Iranian oil hoping to attract international attention to end the war. Iran, in turn, retaliated against ships dealing with Saudi Arabia and Kuwait on the grounds that they were supporting Iraq. In response, the US dispatched a naval task force to the Indian Ocean. It also assisted in providing air cover for tankers carrying Saudi and Kuwaiti oil to international markets, and provided Saudi Arabia with stinger missiles and their launchers. Further, the US reflagged tankers carrying Kuwaiti oil, and the Soviet Union chartered three vessels (Gamlen 1993).

Most of the oil produced in the Gulf en route to the Mediterranean countries pass through the Strait of Hormuz, Bab al-Mandab Straits, and the Suez Canal. Part of this oil is also transported through the SUMED pipeline across Egypt to its destination on the Mediterranean. The implication of all of this is that safe and secure passage in the Suez Canal, Bab Al-Mandab Straits, and the Strait of Hormuz, and the security of the oil pipelines should be connected with enterprises to build Mediterranean security. The economies of most Mediterranean powers are bound to be negatively influenced if these international waterways and pipelines are controlled by a hostile power, or if safe passage and transportation is jeopardized by other means.

The Gulf region is also connected with the South Asian and Indian Ocean regions. The South Asian region is heavily dependent upon oil and natural gas imported from the GCC states. India and Pakistan purchase almost 90 percent of their imported oil and natural gas from the Gulf region states. Pakistan alone imports 80 percent of its oil from Kuwait. These countries compete for the oil of the Gulf region with the Mediterranean states; India and Pakistan have entered into a number of joint ventures with the GCC states to secure the flow of oil and natural gas to them. They also have around 4 million expatriates working in the GCC states. Further, the escalating tension between India and Pakistan will be reflected in the Gulf region in the form of pressures for increased economic ties. The emerging Indo-Pakistani naval arms race occurs at the gates of the Gulf states and its impact will be felt by these states in the eventuality of a war in South Asia. In fact the scenario of the outbreak of a fourth Indo-Pakistani war should not be ruled out given the present ominous signs in that region. One can also detect a tendency among the Gulf states to "Go East". This tendency can be established if one examines the number of joint ventures, and institutional arrangements which these countries have been increasingly building with South and East Asia over the last decade. Recently, four of the Gulf region states (Iran, Oman, United Arab Emirates, and Yemen) have joined the newly established Indian Ocean Rim Community-Association for Regional Cooperation (IORC-ARC). Egypt has also joined as a dialogue partner (Saeed 1995–96). The IORC-ARC presents the GCC states with an alternative to its stagnating dialogue with the EU, and a number of business groups in the region are arguing that the GCC states should opt for an eastward policy rather than a Euro-Mediterranean option. The IORC-ARC has also established a number of non-governmental (business and academic) forms of cooperation and it is likely that other GCC states will join in the near future. These emerging trends call for an enhanced involvement of the Gulf region states in developing concepts of Mediterranean security.

Historical Interactions between the Mediterranean and Gulf Regions

The linkages between the Mediterranean and Gulf regions have always existed since the advent of the Ptolemaic dynasty to Egypt around 300 B.C. The Ptolemaics were a northern Mediterranean power, but they managed to control Egypt on the southern shores of the Mediterranean. From their new power base they strove to control the Red Sea, which put them in collision with the Yemeni Arabs. The Ptolemaics undertook the task of shipping the spices and incense, which the Arabs brought, from India to Europe. To this end they re-opened the canal connecting the Red Sea with the Nile during the rule of Ptolemy II (285–246 B.C.) (Fahmy 1966, 41–2). The Romans, the successors of the Ptolemaics in Egypt, continued the tradition of controlling trade between Europe and India through Arabia. Emperor Augustus sent an expedition in 24 B.C. from Egypt to control southern Arabian trade routes. Such control led to the economic demise of the Arabian Peninsula. Such demise was reversed after the advent and spread of Islam in the Arabian peninsula, the Arab Orient, and North Africa in the second half of the 7th century. This area was turned into a single geo-strategic space controlled by the Arabs. For the first time, the Gulf region extended its influence to the Mediterranean region, and the two regions (with the exception of the northern part of the Mediterranean) became a part of a larger geo-strategic space. This process lasted only for two centuries (650–850 A.M.). By the beginning of the second Abbaside, Arab advances into the Mediterranean region were halted and the Arab-Muslim state began to disintegrate. In this process, Egypt, a Mediterranean power under the Arab-Muslim, rule began to enjoy a semi-independent position and the dynasty that ruled Egypt also controlled the Western shores of the Arabian Peninsula and the Red Sea trade routes. It seems that Mediterranean powers are re-assuming the role, which the Ptolemaics initiated eleven centuries ago. The Ottoman rule of the Arab orient, Egypt, and the Arabian Peninsula, which began in 1516, reinforced this trend. The Ottoman Empire was a Euro-Mediterranean power, which managed to control the Red Sea until Aden, which it controlled in 1538. By the beginning of the 17th century, the British began to appear in the southern shores of the Red Sea and the Indian Ocean and eventually they exercised control over both in addition to their dominant role in the Mediterranean. Further, under Mohammad Ali and his successors, Egypt reached the southern shores of the Red Sea, and emerged as a link between the Mediterranean and the Red Sea (Al-Sultan 1985).

By the beginning of the 19th century, European powers began to encroach upon the Arabian region. This was exemplified in the European consortium against Mohammad Ali in 1839–40 and the control of Aden in 1839. They also managed to mobilize capital and resources necessary for the digging of the Suez Canal, which was opened for international shipping in 1869. For the first time, a direct link between the Mediterranean Sea and the Red Sea was established. By the end of the century, Egypt, Sudan, and the Gulf sheikdoms were under British control. An Anglo-French rivalry over the control of the Red Sea flared up and by the beginning of the 20th century, such rivalry was almost settled as a part of the new European new alignments. Further, during World War I, the Gulf region became one of the main theatres of the war against the Ottomans. The Arabs led by Sherif Hussein of Mecca aligned themselves with Britain and France against the Ottomans hoping to establish an Arab state in the Arabian Peninsula and the Arab Orient. However, the post-war response of the two European powers was to divide the Orient.

In addition to the impact of the opening of the Suez Canal on the Gulf-Mediterranean linkages, the discovery of oil in the Gulf region, and the outbreak of the Cold War in Europe reinforced these linkages. Because of the poor endowment in hydrocarbons of northern Mediterranean powers, the Gulf region became increasingly crucial for the security of these countries in energy supplies. The continuous and secure flow of oil from the Gulf region became one of the major interests and concerns of the northern Mediterranean powers. From now on, the question of oil became a major item in the security agenda of the Gulf and Mediterranean states. Further, for the first time since the era of Arab advances in the southern and eastern Mediterranean, the Arab states in the Gulf began to exercise some influence on the security of northern Mediterranean states. This was exemplified in the Arab oil embargo against some European powers during the October 1973 war. The Cold War in the European theatre was also fought in the Gulf region. Western and Soviet fleets were stationed in that region in order to protect Western oil interests by keeping the Soviets away from the region. Western powers managed to exclude the Soviets from the Gulf region properly with the exception of the short-lived Soviet linkages with Southern Yemen and Ethiopia.

The main conclusions to be drawn from the historical review of Mediterranean-Gulf interactions are that such interactions are twenty-two centuries old. These interactions began with the encroachments of Mediterranean powers on the region, rather than vice versa. Such a pattern has continued to characterize Gulf-Mediterranean interactions for almost two thousand years with some exceptions.

Mediterranean—Gulf Security Issues

The Gulf region states are among the highest military spenders in the world. Military expenditures account for almost 9 percent of their total GNP. This is almost double the global average. Between 1993 and 1997, the seven core Arab Gulf countries and Iran imported conventional weapons totaling US$21 billion. This represented 19 percent of global purchases of conventional weapons (SIPRI 1999, 300). Some of these countries, namely Saudi Arabia and Iran have long range missile capabilities. Iran's nuclear capabilities are still in their infancy and it will be a number of years before Iran can realize its nuclear aspirations.

The military capabilities of Gulf region states are perceived as posing a security threat to Europe and the Mediterranean. For example, Larrabee *et al.* argue that "Europe's greater Mediterranean periphery, from Algeria to Pakistan, displays a striking concentration of proliferation risks. The spread of WMD-nuclear, biological, and chemical—coupled with the proliferation of ballistic missile systems of steady increasing range—is transforming the strategic environment around the Mediterranean. Southern Europe and Turkey will be the first within NATO to feel the existential effects of this exposure ... Not long after the year 2000, it is likely that every European capital will be within range of such systems" (Larabee *et al.* 1998, 15). It is our argument that the military capabilities of the Gulf countries do not pose a threat to Mediterranean security given three major factors: (i) Mediterranean countries possess military capabilities far superior to those of the Gulf countries. France is a nuclear power under the Nuclear Non-proliferation Treaty (NPT), most of northern Mediterranean countries are NATO members, and as such protected by the alliance nuclear umbrella, and there is a strong Western naval presence in the Mediterranean; (ii) The pattern of military armament, procurement, and training of Gulf countries is heavily influenced by the West and its military doctrine; and (iii) There is a strong American presence in virtually all the Gulf states.

Iran's strategic posture is mainly oriented toward the Gulf and Central Asia. Its interest in the Mediterranean is restricted to the Arab-Israeli conflict. It is known that Iran supports Hizbullah in southern Lebanon, which has been labeled by European powers as a terrorist organization. One should remember that because of the actions of Hizbullah, supported by Iran, Israel implemented Security Council resolution 425, calling upon her to withdraw from southern Lebanon. Iran is also a strong ally to Syria. All of this calls for involving Iran in the ongoing thinking about Mediterranean security. Such involvement is increasingly needed if we are to achieve a durable settlement to the Arab-Israeli conflict. It is also needed given Israel's concern about the Iranian nuclear program and its request to discuss the question of arms control in the Middle East and establishing a Middle Eastern area free from weapons of mass destruction in a framework in which Iran is involved. The political changes in Iran after the election of Khatami provide opportunities to engage Iran in the ongoing debate on the architecture of Mediterranean security. Iran, in cooperation with Egypt, represent the Organization of the Islamic Conference, in the Dialogue among Civilizations with European countries. This serves already as a viable cultural link between Iran and the Mediterranean space.

Closely related to these security threats are those threats related to the rise of anti-status quo forces in the region. Most of these forces are connected with the Mujahedeen movements in Afghanistan. They are concentrated in the eastern shores of the Gulf and Yemen. They fight for the establishment of "true" Muslim states in the region, and are against foreign military presence in the Gulf region. They have launched a number of successful attacks against American troops in the Gulf region; the most recent of which was the attack on the American destroyer in the port of Aden in October 2000. These forces pose a threat not only to Mediterranean security, but also to the security of their countries. This question could be one of the items on the agenda of a newly defined Mediterranean-Gulf framework for dialogue.

However one must not minimize the security threats resulting from the modest social and economic performance of most Gulf region countries. The GCC states have achieved, thanks to the petro-dollars, welfare states. But there are cross pressures for increased political participation and deeper Islamism. In other states, such as Iran, Iraq, and Egypt, one can identify problems of high unemployment, and limited economic performance (Richards 1995). These problems may not be confined to the respective states for too long. They call for a balanced approach to help these countries to overcome such difficulties in a larger geo-strategic space.

Mediterranean—Gulf Interdependence

In economic terms, there are various linkages between the Mediterranean and Gulf regions. These linkages are highly asymmetrical, as the Gulf states largely depend on the European states. Such asymmetry is reflected in the pattern of trade, and investment between the two regions. Exports of the northern Mediterranean and European countries to the GCC countries are almost double their imports from them. EU states are the largest trade partner to the GCC states. However, the opposite is not true. EU states trade with the GCC states represents around 3 percent of European foreign trade, and 35 percent of the GCC foreign trade. In fact, the major market in which the EU states achieve a trade surplus is the GCC market. Whereas almost 70 percent of the GCC exports states are raw materials (oil), almost 90 percent of European exports to the GCC are manufactured goods. Further, the GCC states invest in

Europe almost 35 percent of their foreign investments (US$122 billion). However, Europe invests 0.3 percent of its foreign investments in the GCC states (almost US$365 million). European countries are not as dependent on oil imported from the Gulf states as commonly thought. Oil exports from the GCC states to European countries represent almost 23 percent of the total European oil imports. If one adds Iran, the percentage increases to almost 30 percent. European northern Mediterranean states largely depend on oil imports from southern Mediterranean states (Khedr 1997; Abu Dahab 1999; Nash'at 2000; Soliman 1999).

In order to expand areas of cooperation, on 15 June 1988 European countries signed a comprehensive agreement with the GCC countries. The agreement dealt with cooperation in the area of industry, agriculture, trade, energy, technology, and investment. According to the agreement, a ministerial joint council was established to explore modalities of the implementation of the agreement. In its first meeting in March 1990, the council discussed the establishment of a free trade area between the European and Gulf states. However, progress on this proposal has been slow as the Europeans requested that the GCC countries should establish a customs union before the projected Euro-Gulf free trade area is operationalized. They also raised certain claims concerning the questions of democracy and human rights in the GCC states, as was articulated in the July 1992 resolution of the European Parliament (El-Misfer 1998).

Further, there are serious problems constraining Euro-Gulf relations: (i) The EU countries levy 14 percent tariffs on their petrochemical imports from the GCC states; (ii) EU countries have targeted the aluminium imports from the GCC countries with a 6 percent tax that is not imposed on imports on a number of other countries; (iii) EU countries impose a carbon tax on their GCC oil imports; and (iv) The EU has not endorsed the application of some GCC states (Saudi Arabia and Oman) to join the World Trade Organization arguing that they have not done enough to liberalize their economies. The taxes imposed by the EU on imports from the GCC have limited the competitiveness of Gulf exports to European countries. They also account for the dependent pattern of trade between the EU and the GCC. As the EU countries insisted on these restrictive measures, the ninth joint council meeting between the GCC and the EU held in Dubai in November 1999 ended with almost no prospect of a future agreement on any of these issues.

Although the GCC states have been expressing grievances about the European restrictive policies and pursuing a diversification of partners strategy in Asia and the Indian Ocean, they are keen to maintain and develop their trade and investment interests with the Euro-Mediterranean countries. Euro-Gulf debates during the 1999 Euro-Gulf ministerial meetings showed that the two sides are cognizant of their interdependent interests and that that the pursuit of these interests cannot be insulated from the wider Euro-Mediterranean concerns. For example, establishing a Euro-Gulf free trade will be influenced by ongoing projects to build Euro-Mediterranean and Arab free trade areas. Given these areas of interdependence and the awareness of both parties of their vitality to their security, it may be advisable to think of mechanisms to bring the wider Arabian states into the Euro-Mediterranean projects.

Finally, the EU has already triggered a projected Euro-Mediterranean Partnership (EMD) of which 12 are Arab countries. Four Arab countries (Tunisia, Morocco, Jordan, and the Palestinian Authority) have already signed partnership (association) agreements with the EU. The objective is to create economic (free trade area) security, and cultural-social cooperation in the Euro-Mediterranean world. The EMP is bound to have detrimental influences on the Gulf states at least as far as their trade interests in the participating Mediterranean states is concerned.

Conclusion

Any comprehensive vision of Gulf security would necessarily bring developments into the picture in the Mediterranean region. Gulf countries have trade and oil interests with this region. These interests are highly influenced by what happens in the international waterway in the region, such as the Suez Canal, the Red Sea, and the Mediterranean. These linkages call for an expansion of the concept of Gulf space to comprise the Mediterranean. This is particularly desirable not only to avoid possible threats to Gulf security, but also to deal with Arab concerns that the EMP and EU-GCC dialogue are two separate tracks. When the EU initiated the EMP in the 1994 proposal, it was criticized as dividing the Arabs into Mediterraneanists and non-Mediterraneanists, thereby preventing Arab regional integration. By bringing the Gulf region states into the Mediterranean and Euro-Mediterranean projects, such concerns will be partially allayed.

One can envisage various modalities for bringing the Gulf region states into the Mediterranean space. One of these modalities is to establish a new category of membership in the EMP for "dialogue partners". This category was first introduced by the Association for Southeast Asian Nations (ASEAN), and later adopted by the IORC-ARC. The dialogue partners of ASEAN are friendly outside actors important to ASEAN for trade and investments and political support. They attend meetings, benefit from economic measures taken within ASEAN, and participate in the ASEAN Regional Forum (ARF) which is a forum to discuss security issues in Southeast Asia.

Another modality is to turn the Euro-Med, and the Euro-Gulf dialogues into Euro-Arab dialogues or partnerships. Three of the Mediterranean states (Turkey, Cyprus, and Malta) participating in the EMP will eventually join the EU as member-states. The only remaining non-Arab state will be Israel. Under these conditions, it is highly undesirable that the EU maintains two separate tracks with the Arab states as the EU will be viewed as exercising a divisive impact on the Arab World.

In thinking of expanding the Mediterranean space into the Gulf region one must take into account three major factors, American, European, and Pan-Arab. Arrangements for expanding the Mediterranean space into the Gulf region must safeguard against a possible impingement upon American strategic concerns in the region. The US linkages with the Gulf states are stronger than those with the Mediterranean actors. It is the major arms exporter to the GCC states and has a strong military presence in almost all of them (Kechichian 1993). Further, the re-definition of the Mediterranean space to include the Gulf region will only achieve significant results if the EU changed its restrictive approach to Euro-Arab cooperation. Arab Mediterranean and Gulf countries have serious reservations over the EU approach to expand cooperation with them. Elsewhere we have reviewed these reservations and concluded that a change in the EU approach is a prerequisite for a sustainable Mediterranean, Euro-Mediterranean and Euro-Gulf cooperation (Selim 2000). Further, in expanding the concept of the Gulf space, it is advisable to bring the League of Arab States into the process. The league could serve to reduce the number of activities needed into order to reach a consensus on Mediterranean security by harmonizing Arab policies and articulating them. The experience of the Asia – Europe Meeting (ASEM), the EU dialogue with the MERCUSOR countries, and the Euro-African Summit could provide useful clues on how to proceed in this respect.

Part Two: PRESENT CHALLENGES AND OPPORTUNITIES

CHAPTER 4

Security, Cooperation, and the US Role in the Gulf

Amin Saikal

The geopolitical situation in the Gulf is going through some important changes. On the one hand, Iran's process of Islamic democratization is consolidating; the Arab perception of an Iranian threat has substantially diminished; Saddam Hussein, while still an irritant, remains incapable of seriously threatening any of Iraq's neighbors; and all the littoral states have once again rediscovered their common oil interests to cooperate to boost their revenues. All this can be conducive to wider regional cooperation in all areas, including security. On the other hand, these are also the very developments that have the potential to heighten tensions in the region, imperilling the chances of wider cooperation. How the United States will manage the changes and determine its own role in the region will prove to be critical to the outcome in the coming years.

The Iranian reform process of President Mohammad Khatami, who was elected in a landslide victory in mid-1997 has gradually changed the face of Iranian politics. Khatami's *ijtihadi* (creatively interpretive) push to create an Islamic civil society and an Islamic democracy and to establish the rule of law, with the principles of dialogue and cooperation rather than a claim of ideological supremacy underlining the conduct of Iran's foreign relations, has now found a place in Iranian politics. By overwhelmingly winning the municipal elections of early-1999 and the parliamentary (Majlis) elections a year later, President Khatami and his supporters have clearly demonstrated that their factional Islamic conservative opponents have no popular legitimacy to discredit the reform agenda any longer.

The conservative forces, which have enjoyed sympathy from the supreme religious-political leader, Ayatollah Ali Khamanei, an essentially appointed office holder but with enormous constitutional powers, still control some of the instrumentalities of state power. They dominate the judiciary, the security and armed forces, the state-run media, and a set of complex decision-making councils and committees. This has enabled them to become increasingly vocal in their opposition to the reform process, especially since their massive losses in the parliamentary elections. They have unleashed a more vigorous campaign of intimidation and obstruction than ever before. Targeting the freedom of the press, which goes to the heart of the reform program, they have closed down a number of pro-reform newspapers and jailed some of their editors for "anti-Islamic" activities. One of their alleged victims has been Saeed Hajjarian, a close associate of Khatami, whom an assailant critically wounded in April 2000.

Even so, the reform process has progressed to the point that the conservatives will not be able to tear the heart out of it. The intensification of their anti-reform campaign may be more to vent their frustration resulting from their electoral defeat than to demonstrate a capacity to sustain their obstructionist behavior in the long run. As long as the reform process has the support of the great majority of the Iranians, its opponents may find it increasingly difficult to maintain their rage against it indefinitely. In the end, many of them may find it convenient to adopt the process quietly, although perhaps somewhat selectively, and thus to bow to the weight of popular will. This is something that has already begun with a number of conservative figures either defecting to the side of reform or adopting its language and culture.

Khatami's reform agenda has emphasized the importance of dialogue of civilizations and international cooperation, based on the common bond of humanity rather than political and ideological differences. Khatami has sought a reformation of Iran not only with reference to the country's own deeply ingrained Shi'ite Islamic cultural identity and historical riches, but also in a cooperative discourse and journey of discovery with other peoples and civilizations. He has considered the diversity of identity and culture among states or clusters of states as a foundation for, rather than a hindrance to, meaningful cultural and inter-civilizational dialogues. Within this framework, early in his presidency, Khatami even called for a dialogue with Iran's arch enemy, the United States, although he stressed that the process in the first instance should begin with a people-to-people, rather than government-to-government, interface, given the political complexity underpinning Iran-US relations. He regarded the people-to-people dialogue through educational and cultural exchanges as the best means of opening the way for eventual direct official contacts. He has quietly taken a number of steps in giving practical expression to such contacts, although in a manner that would not galvanize his opponents.

Khatami's whole approach has indeed put his reform agenda on a par with many Western democratic and universal human rights practices. It has already led to a major improvement in the outside world's perception of Iran's Islamic regime and in the country's foreign relations. The Iranian regime is no longer regarded as a main source of support and inspiration for Islamic militancy in the region and beyond. The regime stands in total contrast to the ultra-orthodox Islamic Taliban militia, which rules most of neighboring Afghanistan but is widely condemned for its medievalism, support of international terrorism and protection of America's most wanted man, the Saudi dissident, Osama bin Laden. The US has indicted bin Laden for allegedly masterminding the bombing of American embassies in Nairobi and Dar es Salaam in August 1998, in which scores of people were killed and hundreds injured. The only radical Islamic group with which Iran still maintains serious contact is the Lebanese Shi'ite Hezbullah (Party of God), and that is for two main reasons. First, Hezbullah has grown to become a popular Arab national liberationist group, given its successful military campaign against Israel's occupation of southern Lebanon. Second, support for Hezbullah is firmly tied to the Iranian conservatives' deep links to the militia and to their opposition to the Middle East peace process, and therefore to the current Iranian power struggle. This is a factor that cautions Iranian reformists against any immediate de-linking with Hezbullah lest they risk providing more ammunition to their domestic opponents.

The regional Arab states and Turkey, which once reviled the Iranian regime, and with the help of the United States aided the Iraqi dictator Saddam Hussein to wage a bloody eight-year long war against Iran in the 1980s, today have little to complain about from Tehran. Even Saudi Arabia—a traditional Sunni regional rival of Shi'ite Iran—has found it imperative to respond warmly to Khatami's overtures, as has Turkey in the last year. Iranian-Saudi relations have improved to the extent that the two sides have now signed a security agreement. The only state of the Gulf Cooperation Council (GCC)—comprising Saudi Arabia, Oman, the United Arab Emirates, Kuwait, Bahrain and Qatar—with which Iran's relations still remain tense is the United Arab Emirates. The issue however is not one of serious ideological-political differences between them, but rather a territorial dispute over the islands of Abu Musa, and the two Tunbs, which Iran took over in the wake of the British withdrawal from the Gulf in 1971 and the UAE wants back. This is a dispute that has echoed well beyond the Gulf. Iran's refusal to enter a serious discussion on the issue has prompted the UAE to support the Taliban in Afghanistan and the militia's patron, Pakistan, as an anti-Iranian leverage, and to deny Iran the degree of commercial and economic benefit that it could reap from improved relations with the UAE. Although at present there is little bilateral contact between the two sides on the issue, a peaceful resolution of it can prove to be very beneficial to both sides. The Iranian reformists are aware of the benefits, but appear to be unable to do anything substantial in resolving the dispute until such time as they have achieved political ascendancy over their domestic conservative opponents.

Iran's problems with Iraq are by no means insurmountable either. From Iran's perspective, as is also the case with other regional states, the Iraqi regime of President Saddam Hussein may still be an irritant, but it is certainly not a real threat to any state in the area. Despite Saddam Hussein's repeated claim of victory, the regime is substantially weakened, with no military or economic capacity to wage and sustain an aggressive foreign policy adventure. It is capable only of maintaining Saddam Hussein's dictatorship inside Iraq, whose territorial integrity is under enormous strain and where a majority of the people's standard of living has degraded to abject poverty, partly because of UN sanctions, and partly due to Saddam Hussein's methods of governance. Even Iraq's middle class is virtually destroyed—a fact which will make Iraq's long-term recovery more difficult than one can anticipate at this point. Whatever the complaints of Iraq's neighbors (including Kuwait) from time to time, they are more for national and regional consumption than anything else.

Indeed, Iran, or for that matter, any other regional state, cannot ignore Iraq, and must work to enhance the conditions for its long-term stability as a responsible actor in the region, and to settle their problems with it peacefully. Yet there is little reason either to be fearful of Iraq or to hold back measures that could strengthen the case for regional cooperation. It is also time for the UN to end sanctions against Iraq, which have done little to damage Saddam Hussein's capacity to maintain his rule, but have caused immeasurable suffering for the Iraqi people. If the UN objective is to steer Iraq in the direction of becoming a more responsible actor then it is necessary to promote such conditions that could lock the country into wider regional responsibilities from a position of weakness rather than strength.

In the climate generated since the advent of Khatami's reforms and concomitant changes in Iran's geo-political outlook, and since the erosion of Saddam Hussein's aggressive capacity, conditions have never been as conducive for cooperation and peaceful settlement of problems in the Gulf as they are today. Had it not been for this development, it is highly doubtful that the oil-rich constituent states of the region would have been able to cooperate once again within OPEC to increase oil prices and almost double their oil revenues since the beginning of 1999. This has been despite the American pressure on two of its allies and key producers within OPEC, Saudi Arabia and Kuwait, to moderate OPEC's price increases in order to restore some stability to the world oil market.

The other side of the coin of course is that these developments also generate their own challenges. Iran is surrounded by states that are mostly ruled either by ultra-orthodox theocratic groups or by authoritarian or concealed authoritarian regimes. To the east, in Afghanistan, the Pakistan-backed Taliban's adoption of a highly repressive, discriminatory form of Islam, which is also preached and implemented in many parts of Pakistan, has become a source of much international trepidation. The Iranian reforms can only reveal the Taliban and Pakistani Islam in the worst light possible and increase domestic and international pressure for their reformation. The danger is that, by the same token, a tacit alliance could develop between the Iranian Islamic conservatives and some Taliban and Pakistani extremists in a regional opposition to Khatami's brand of Islam.

It may be partly because of such a possibility that, despite the massacre by the Taliban of eleven Iranian diplomats and thousands of Iranian-supported Afghan Shi'ites in the wake of the militia's push into northern Afghanistan in mid-1998, which prompted an Iranian troop mobilization along the border with Afghanistan, the Khatami government has precipitously adopted a policy of ambivalence towards the Taliban. Since late 1999, it has even opened dialogue and trade with the militia in an effort to moderate their extremism and delink them from Pakistan. In 2000, it also used Iran's presidency of the Organization of the Islamic Conference (OIC) to initiate a new round of indirect talks between the Taliban and their Islamic moderate northern alliance opposition, led by Commander Ahmed Shah Massoud, for a peaceful resolution of the Afghan conflict. Another upshot of this approach may be to isolate Pakistan further, not only on account of its patronage of the Taliban but also because of what the US State Department in its annual human rights report has called "Pakistan's support of Kashmiri terrorists" and by implication of Pakistan's support of international terrorism. Ultimately, this approach may not pay off, given the organic depth of the relationship between the Taliban and Pakistan, but the Iranian reformists seem determined to pursue the course of dialogue as the best means of dealing with the Afghanistan problem for the time being.

To the south and west of the country, the Arab states of the Gulf Cooperation Council (GCC) and Iraq are mainly ruled either by authoritarian or semi-authoritarian regimes, with Islam providing the basis for political legitimation in various ways. With the exception of Bahrain, which has recently embarked on a process of political liberalization, and Kuwait, which has developed some traditions of political pluralism and parliamentary representation, they all lack, to a large extent, democratic processes of transparency and accountability, as well as mechanisms for electoral political change and meaningful representation. Yet with the oil-based drive for social and economic modernization, the need for wider political participation in policy-making and policy-implementation processes has been growing. The opposition groups, most of which want to operate within the Islamic frameworks of their societies, have been informally critical of their ruling elites for not even attempting seriously to institute an Islamic-based process of democratic change and development.

While the Arab states are predominantly Sunni Muslim and many in their opposition ranks may have little desire to emulate Iran's Shi'ite leadership, some could find the Iranian experiment invigorating and worthy of adoption without its sectarian content. In fact, some reformist opposition leaders and groups have already publicly questioned why their governments have not moved down the same path of reform as their Iranian counterpart. They have expressed deep disappointment at the fact that their regimes have procrastinated at creating the necessary conditions for wider public participation, transparency, and accountability within a framework that would be in accord with both Islam and the needs of modern life. If the Iranian reformation accelerates, it can cause tension in the region, and associated resentment on the part of Arab ruling elites towards Iran. The chances are that just in the same way that the Iranian revolution of twenty years ago inspired a radicalization of Islamic groups in the region, now the Iranian Islamic liberalization, if successful, has the potential to have a similar impact, except this time in the direction of democratization. This impact may have already manifested itself to some extent in the democratic changes that Bahrain has just introduced.

Similarly, these developments are bound to intensify the challenge to the United States' unqualified support of various power elites and to its dominance in the region. They have the capacity to exacerbate Washington's old dilemmas and create new ones for it. Washington has often stressed its championship of democracy and human rights, and voiced a promise to bring democratization to the region, but in reality has done little more than pay lip service to the cause. In the wake of the Gulf war, which reversed the August 1990 Iraqi invasion of Kuwait, Washington declared democratization and elimination of Weapons of Mass Destruction (WMD) as the avowed goals of its future policy actions in the region. Yet a decade later it has very little to show in respect of either.

Shortly after the Gulf War, it abandoned its objective of democratization in favor of building what may be called a "unipolar security" system in the Gulf, which identified Iraq and Iran as the "enemy" and the GCC states as "friends" of the United States. It deliberately promoted the dependence of the GCC on the US and demonization of Iraq and Iran as the source of threat to enforce this dependence. In the process, it relied on the very ruling elites which were to become the subject of its promised democratization to give weight to its new security system, and by the same token helped them to maintain their rule, with little or no change, in perpetuity. It also seriously diminished the possibility of improving relations with Iran, thus letting pass valuable opportunities to secure important leverage in the conduct of its wider regional policy and to enable American companies to secure lucrative business deals with Iran.

Undoubtedly, Washington has, especially in the past three years under pressure from American businesses and international changes, shown some awareness of its mistakes. While abandoning, for all practical purposes, its policy of "dual containment" in the case of Iran and welcoming Khatami's reforms, Washington has increasingly indicated a desire for an improvement in relations. In March 2000, the Secretary of State, Madeleine Albright, even acknowledged the fallacy of America's past intervention in Iran's internal affairs, particularly in 1953, when in a covert operation the CIA succeeded in toppling the elected, reformist government of Prime Minister Mohammed Mossadeq in favor of re-installing the Shah's regime to transform Iran into a client-state. As a gesture of goodwill she announced a partial lifting of the embargo on the import of some Iranian goods. Despite its initial declaration of the measures as too little in view of its conservative opponents' total rejection of them, the Khatami government quietly expressed a willingness to build on them towards an eventual rapprochement. However, it is important to emphasize that this much has so far come about not because of any major policy innovation on the part of Washington but largely because of reform initiatives from the Iranian side, although some in the Clinton Administration may claim that it was America's policy of containment that pressured Iran in the direction of reform in the first place.

For the United States to move beyond this point, it now needs to take a number of further concrete steps. The first is to unfreeze all Iranian assets in the US, which Washington froze in the wake of the Iranian revolution and hostage crisis, resulting from Iranian student militants taking some fifty American embassy workers in Tehran as hostages from 4 November 1979 to 20 January 1981. This should be accompanied by lifting all sanctions against Iran.

The second is to issue a formal regret to the Iranians for America's wrongful intervention of 1953, which has recently been publicly confirmed by documentary revelations from the US Central Intelligence Agency (CIA), and for providing virtually unqualified support for the Shah's twenty-five year long dictatorship. Such a regret may go a long way to achieving two objectives: to defuse the attitude of some of those Iranian Islamic conservatives who have dwelt on America's past behavior to maintain an anti-American rage, and at the same time to assist the reformist camp to overcome its opponents' objections to a normalization of relations with the United States.

The third is to fulfil its promise of promoting democratization and a regime of arms control for elimination of WMD in the region. Success in these areas could have two important results. One is that it will help to generate a participatory system of government in the GCC countries, especially Saudi Arabia whose changes could have profound impact on its smaller partners within the alliance. This in turn could assist the Iranian reformists to proceed with their process of reform without being too concerned about its regional repercussions. Another is that, with the institution of a push for WMD disarmament in the region, the process could alleviate Iran's deepening concern about its own security and prompt it to claw back whatever plans it may have for production of WMD. This would be a development that in turn would help Iran's Arab neighbors to feel more secure in relation to Iran, and thus place greater premium on wider confidence-building measures. However, a success in this area will depend very much on whether Washington will also be prepared to ensure that its approach to the regime of arms control is comprehensive enough to include Israel and involve a major reduction in America's own military presence in the region. Otherwise neither Iran nor, for that matter, any Gulf Arab states will find it justifiable to participate in such a regime effectively.

The fourth is to promote a system of "collective security" to replace its unipolar one in the region. This system would require that all the Gulf states be locked into regional responsibilities, and that the issue of Gulf security be decoupled from the political considerations of resolving the Arab-Israeli conflict. It would also demand that it be separated from US policy toward South Asia, where America's concerns over the nuclearization of Pakistan and India are still linked to the US's interests in the Gulf. The new security system should be based not on the notion of "some against some" but "all against one". It should involve all the states of the Gulf—although with regard to Iraq only at the appropriate time—but exclude outside powers as the central players.

A comprehensive collective security system would succeed only if it were designed to place a premium on security through not only institutionalized processes of confidence-building and conflict resolution, as well as enhanced political, cultural, economic, and military cooperation between all the member states, but also "face-to-face" interactions among the peoples of those states. This is one factor that has constantly remained in short supply in the Gulf. This has been the case not only between Iran and its Arab neighbors, but also among the Arab states themselves. One of the original purposes of the GCC when it was created nearly twenty years ago was to generate wider exchanges and understanding beyond the elite level within the alliance, but this objective still remains by and large elusive. All the GCC states are still information shy, although to varying degrees. The main reason is governments' continued reluctance to institute the necessary political reforms as a condition for accelerating inter-state exchanges without fear of political repercussions.

Furthermore, the system would prove ineffective if there was not a balance within it between Iran and the Gulf Arab states, including also at some point a receptive Iraq. The system should be based on Iran and the GCC counter-balancing one another, so that neither side could challenge the other's position. The balance should be such as to deter any regional power from doing anything within the collective arrangement, which could prove costly to it. As for the role of a major power like the United States in such a system, it should be to mediate between the regional powers, and to help promote respect for national independence, human rights, and democracy within the broad context of regional traditions rather than to exploit regional differences to enforce its own dominance. It is within these parameters of power parity that the parties involved would feel secure enough to seek a resolution of their territorial disputes, particularly in relation to the island of Abu Musa, which has become an issue of dispute between the UAE and Iran. This issue needs to be addressed on the basis of the 29 November 1971 Memorandum of Understanding between Iran and Sharjah—a federate member of the UAE, which was formed in the wake of the British withdrawal in that year. And it can be done once trust is sufficiently built in other areas.

The changes in the region confront the United States with both valuable opportunities and daunting challenges. The question is: does the United States have the will and vision to steer a new course of policy approach? If the past is any guide, American policy actions do not inspire much confidence in Washington's making the right decisions. However, the new Republican administration of President George W. Bush is in a position to make a fresh start. It can use the changes in the region and world politics to its advantage to develop a more prudent Gulf policy, provided that it acts more in the long-term interests of the region than for the short-term gains of the United States. This is a challenge that is worth meeting. Otherwise valuable opportunities will be lost and the Gulf could easily slide towards greater upheaval than ever before. This is not what the regional states or the United States want, and this is what should guide the decision-makers in the region and in Washington.

CHAPTER 5

Saudi-Iranian Relations: Implications for Gulf Security

Saleh Alkhatlan

The present rapprochement between Saudi Arabia and Iran is the most significant positive development in the Gulf during the last two decades. Knowing that Iran is still more or less isolated in the international arena, the current high level of understanding and cooperation with Saudi Arabia can be described as the most important success for Iranian diplomacy in the last ten years. The speed with which ties have improved between the two countries is evidence that Riyadh was all along waiting for a moderate leadership in Iran to re-establish relations.

The dramatic and unexpected speed has also caused a great deal of interest among observers of the region, leaving them guessing as to the causes of the unprecedented level of cooperation between these two countries which were once hostile to each other. It has not just been the scholars who have been overwhelmed by the speed of the improvement of relations, but government officials of the region have also expressed concerns about the potential implications of a high degree of affinity between the two major regional powers.

In this chapter, I will discuss the nature of relations in 1997–2000 and explain the reasons for the course of events. I will then examine various reactions to the rapprochement and finally try to analyze the expected implications of the new relations for Gulf security. My argument is based on the assumption that security and peace in the Gulf cannot be accomplished without some degree of understanding between its major players.

Historical Background

The *founding* act for the rapprochement between Saudi Arabia and Iran was the meeting in Islamabad in 1997 at the Organization of the Islamic Conference (OIC) between the former president

Hashemi Rafsanjani and Crown Prince Abdallah. That meeting was the first high-level contact between the two countries since the Islamic revolution. The two leaders stressed the need for a new beginning in their countries' relations. The meeting laid the ground for a new page in Iranian-Saudi relations. Since then officials at all levels have been frequenting Tehran and Riyadh and repeatedly stressing the necessity of a fundamental transformation in the relations between the two countries. In the series of official visits, we can point to five major ones that have left lasting impact. In historical order these were: Hashemi Rafsanjani's visit to Riyadh, Crown Prince Abdallah's visit to Tehran, Prince Sultan's (Saudi Minister of Defense) visit to Tehran, President Khatami's visit to Riyadh, and finally Iranian Minister of Defense Ali Shamkhani's visit to Riyadh.

Former president Hashemi Rafsanjani's extended visit to Riyadh in February 1998 left a substantial mark on the views the Iranian leadership developed of Saudi Arabia. Rafsanjani came with a large delegation including the ministers of oil, commerce, labor, agriculture, and the mayor of Tehran. During the visit he went to a number of ministries, agencies, and historic places and held extensive meetings with Saudi officials in both the government and the business sector. As the Saudi foreign minister described the visit, "it opened a new chapter in the relations between the two countries."[1] Since then officials from both countries have been in regular meetings.

The visit radically altered Rafsanjani's views of Saudis. He was highly impressed by the level of development and modernity the kingdom had reached. Saudi Arabia was no longer seen as a proxy of the United States controlled by a group of corrupt leaders with a fanatic Wahabi ideology seeking to destroy Shi'ites. The new positive Iranian perception of Saudi Arabia was reinforced by a number of Saudi policies that underscored the country's independent stand. For example, Iran was appreciative of Saudi Arabia's refusal to attend the 1997 Middle East economic conference in Doha, Riyadh's uncompromising support for Syria in the peace process, and more importantly the Saudi rejection of American attempts to implicate Tehran in the Khobar tower bombings.

Notwithstanding that the initial stage in the rapprochement was mainly based on political concerns, commercial, energy, economic, cultural, and military relations have also experienced remarkable rise. In May 1998, Saudi Arabia and Iran signed a comprehensive agreement covering cooperation in almost all areas. The agreement was "evidence that relations between the two countries have become firm and strong, based on solid foundations of mutual trust and respect."[2] The agreement talked about cooperation in industrial, mineral, oil petrochemical, agricultural, livestock, and health projects. It called for visits by economic and trade representatives, diversification of trade, joint investment, exchange of information on scientific and technical research, exchange of experts and professionals, joint training and setting up of centers, research laboratories and cultural conferences, and cooperation among universities and other educational institutes. A joint committee at ministerial level was established to meet annually to oversee the implementation of the agreement and study ways of developing bilateral relations.

Because of improvement in relations trade has rapidly increased and a number of Iranian shops and restaurants have recently opened in Riyadh. During the last two years three large Iranian trade exhibitions were held in Riyadh and Jeddah with the participation of a large number of Iranian companies. Iranian foodstuffs and traditional industries, such as handcrafted carpets, have found the great approval of Saudi consumers. The large number of Saudi citizens attending these exhibitions could be taken as indication of popular support for improved relations with Iran. A similar exhibition for Saudi products was held in Tehran in November 1999. The exhibition was preceded by a visit by the Saudi Minister of Industry and Electricity to Tehran accompanied by a 117-member business delegation.[3]

Over the last three years trade has increased three-fold and Saudi Arabia is expected to become one of Iran's major trade partners in the coming years. Iran exports carpets, cement, fruits, and steel to Saudi Arabia. Today there are twelve investment projects with a total of US$ 280 million invested.[4] SABIC, the famous Saudi industrial company is planning to expand activities in Iran. Its current sale in Iran is about US$ 100 million.[5] During a visit to Tehran by the Saudi Minister of Trade in January 2000, the two countries signed a memorandum of understanding on ways to promote their economic trade ties. In the future, Iranian territories can become a route to transport industrial and consumer products from the GCC countries to Central Asia and the rest of the CIS countries. Finally, we should mention that Iranian flights to Saudi Arabia have been resumed. May 2000 also witnessed the resumption of Saudi flights to Iran, with a Saudi plane in Tehran carrying the Iranian Minister of Defense after concluding his visit, which lasted more than a week. Iranian airlines will soon start to fly to Riyadh after more than fifteen years of absence.

Oil comes at the forefront of Saudi-Iranian relations. The two countries are major producers and leading members of OPEC. Their cooperation brought about last year's agreement to cut production that led to the swift rise of oil prices. However, Iran and Saudi Arabia still have their differences in this area as was seen at the recent OPEC meeting during which oil production was increased. The two countries split into two camps. Saudi Arabia led efforts to raise production while Iran refused to move and accused the US of pressuring OPEC to raise the production level. Last year Iran and Saudi Arabia also clashed over the nomination of a new Secretary-General for OPEC. Iran unexpectedly opposed the Saudi nominee. Thus, oil seems to be an issue that has not seen total cooperation and may in the future cause disagreement if not tension, especially with the current opening up of Saudi Arabia to huge Western investment in the oil and gas sector.

If economic interests constitute the concrete base upon which permanent relations are built, cultural factors play a significant role in deepening such relations. Negative feelings associated with the historical Sunni-Shi'i split have prejudiced the way the elites and publics in both countries have viewed each other. Furthermore, for about fifteen years Saudi Arabia and Iran competed for ideological dominance in the Muslim world and used their financial wealth to lure Muslim minorities in the West. They also published books and financed publications and radio programs that discredited each other. Hence today, in order to rectify years of misperceptions by both parties, a cultural bridge has to be built. The first step toward such an undertaking began with two visits to Saudi Arabia by a group of Iranian scholars. Moreover, last year a number of Iranian scholars participated in cultural activities in Riyadh and Tehran is expected to host a Saudi cultural week. However, for such contacts to be effective they must go beyond the formal level and a genuine and candid dialogue between scholars and intellectuals should begin.

Pilgrimage, which was in the past a source of tension and confrontation, has become a high point in the two countries' relations. During the last two years, Iranian pilgrims have performed their Hajj rituals free of political slogans. Although Hajj is only a few days each year, in the past it was a major, if not the major, source of confrontation between Saudi Arabia and Iran, and was in fact the direct cause for cutting off relations in 1989 (Ahmad 1992). Therefore, what we are seeing as far as this holy occasion is concerned is a great advance. It shows that Iranian foreign policy towards Saudi

Arabia has matured and become a standard state policy instead of a strategy designed to export the revolution.

Furthermore, the number of Iranians coming to Saudi Arabia for the *Ummrah* has increased, reaching about five thousand people each week.[6] This significant improvement cannot be overlooked and should have further positive impact on the overall relations. There is also talk about starting cooperation in the area of judiciary which, if it happens, would mean a profound move in light of the fact that the two countries belong to two different and usually conflicting religious schools of thought. In the area of internal security, Saudi Arabia has agreed to open negotiations with Iran on a bilateral security cooperation agreement on combating drug trafficking, terrorism, and organized crime.

The most important proof of the comprehensive and serious nature of the relations can be found in the field of military cooperation. No one ever thought that Iran and Saudi Arabia, which spent years competing for influence in the Gulf, are now talking about military coordination. The visit of Saudi Minister of Defense Prince Sultan to Tehran in May 1999 marked a turning point in the two countries' relations. During his visit, Prince Sultan reconfirmed the need for continuous cooperation. Furthermore, since 1998 Saudi ports have been receiving Iranian military ships, and there is talk about exchange of military training and expertise. In April 2000 the Iranian Minister of Defense Ali Shamkhani traveled to Saudi Arabia on what many described as a groundbreaking visit. His trip marked the steady improvement in ties between the two countries. He met with the Saudi Minister of Defense, the crown prince and King Fahd. The minister who was accompanied by a large military delegation held talks on Gulf security and reaffirmed the Iranian serious desire for strong relations with the kingdom.

The above discussion shows that relations between Saudi Arabia and Iran are more comprehensive than most observers believe. It also shows that they have gone beyond the point of return, despite the existence of some standing issues, especially regarding the disputes over Abu Musa and Tunb islands with the GCC and oil policy. It must be understood that the current rapprochement is not merely focused on political interests and ties between Riyadh and Tehran have become too attached to split again.

Saudi Arabia made three major initiatives towards Iran that demonstrated its seriousness about establishing permanent relations. To begin with, for the first time in its diplomatic history Riyadh appointed a Shi'ite official, known for his dynamic personality, as the ambassador to Tehran. This was done in spite of negative talks in Saudi Arabia about the move (i.e. talks about whether it meant a rise in the political fortunes of the Shi'ite minority).

Second, the Saudis rejected all attempts by the United States to implicate Iran in the bombing of Khobar towers in June 1996, which killed 18 American airmen. Riyadh endured the combined pressure and criticism of the US Justice Department and the FBI that accused Iran of plotting the bombing and instead insisted that all those involved were Saudi nationals. It was believed in the Kingdom that the US was trying to use the bombing as a pretext to initiate a pre-emptive strike against Iran's nuclear complex at Bushehr on the Gulf. The Iranians praised the Saudi bold stand on the issue and corrected their old misperceptions about the kingdom as being US dependent. In fact, in October 1999 the press reported that Riyadh expressed to Washington that it supported open relations between the US and Iran and offered its good offices to mediate between the two countries.

The third Saudi initiative towards Iran was Riyadh's defense of Iran's right to arm itself. This stand was clearly stated by Crown Prince Abdallah and by the Minister of Defense. In an interview, the crown prince argued, "like any other country Iran has all rights to arm itself".[7] This position presents a major departure in Saudi policy regarding Iran's military buildup.

Moreover, Iranian officials appreciated Prince Abdallah's role in convening the OIC summit in Tehran in December 1997. According to former president Rafsanjani the summit was "successful and effective largely due to the valuable role played by Prince Abdallah".[8] We should also point to Riyadh's successful effort to moderate last year's GCC declaration *vis-à-vis* Iran. The declaration was noted for its moderate and soft language on Iran's policy in the Gulf. The change was personally credited to Crown Prince Abdallah who used his good relations with Sheikh Zayid to persuade the United Arab Emirates of the new moderate stand. Tehran, therefore, is expected to reciprocate those initiatives. This can be achieved by a softening of Iranian position on the islands dispute.

Motives for the Rapprochement

Having concluded this brief description of the current state of relations between Saudi Arabia and Iran, I now turn to the discussion of reasons for such strong ties. I believe that the new stage in Saudi-Iranian relations was the product of a triangle of visions held by leaders in both countries. President Mohammad Khatami, Crown Prince Abdallah and former president Hashemi Rafsanjani are the true makers of the new chapter in Saudi-Iranian relations. They have all contributed to the fundamental transformation of relations between Riyadh and Tehran and were all needed to break the ice between the countries and to set a new beginning after many years of hostility. Unlike many writers and observers conclusions about the start of a Saudi-Iranian axis, I would like to argue that Khatami's coming to power in 1997 was not the driving force behind the rapidly built partnership. In fact, it was a combination of visions held by the three leaders concerning their respective countries' future that brought about the shift. Furthermore, because the rapprochement is vision-driven, and not just a product of concrete short-term considerations, it will eventually have a broad, permanent, and positive impact on the whole region. This is of course assuming that the countries of the Gulf as well as states linked with the region understand it in this way as well.

I start with President Khatami whose visionary views are already known and have been eloquently expressed in his books, speeches, and interviews. The most important element of this vision is his profound belief in the value of dialogue, tolerance of others, and moderation in politics in general. These views were well received in the region as well as in many parts of the international community. Notwithstanding the philosophical dimension of his views, Khatami is also aware that through such positive concepts Iran can break out of its isolation, which was partially self-imposed as a direct result of past revolutionary rhetoric.

Second, Crown Prince Abdallah's increasing role in Saudi foreign policy is visible in his recent historic visits to a number of countries including the US, UK, France, China, Japan, South Africa, Italy, South Korea, and Pakistan. Prince Abdallah has also been recently active in inter-Arab diplomacy, trying to coordinate an Arab position on the peace process. During these visits and on a number of occasions Prince Abdallah has shown keen understanding of the complex nature of the current international politics and the increasing role of economic forces, under the umbrella of globalization, in shaping world affairs. His candid views on foreign policy, investment, oil, water security, and even education are well received in the country. One can also point to the prince's recent decision to ban middlemen from intervening in the new deals with the oil and gas companies investing in Saudi Arabia. This is a very bold initiative given the fact that potential middlemen would have been powerful people in the government. The decision also reflects the crown prince's awareness of the huge commissions the companies would have paid, which would in turn have had negative impact on their overall performance.

The Saudi crown prince has also shown a high level of concern for the country's economic difficulties. These difficulties are caused by the sharp decline in oil prices in 1998, and by the heavy financial price the kingdom has paid for the Second Gulf War. He understands that only a peaceful external environment can help the kingdom to restructure its economy in order to face new challenges. Such a peaceful environment can only be achieved if Saudi Arabia has good relations with all of its neighbors, especially the more powerful ones like Iran. Consequently, rapprochement with Tehran was the most appropriate device to prevent conditions of instability in the Gulf that might lead to the recurrence of more costly confrontations.

Finally, former president Hashemi Rafsanjani, who still plays an important role in Iranian politics, has made a major contribution to the reconstruction of Iranian views of Saudi Arabia. His historic visit to Riyadh in February 1998 led to what can be described as the fall of the ideological wall through which Iranians had looked at Saudi Arabia since the Islamic revolution. Ideology of course played an obstructive role in Iran's relations with the Arab world, particularly with Saudi Arabia because of its leading position in the Muslim world. For more than fifteen years, Iranian foreign policy towards Saudi Arabia was largely determined by a radical ideology that portrayed a very negative and conspiratorial picture of the kingdom and its leaders. Thanks to former president Rafsanjani this view disappeared and was replaced by one that sees Saudi Arabia as a respectable and moderate country, which plays a strategic role in the region.

Reactions to the Rapprochement

Saudi officials at all levels have always asserted that the improvement of relations with Iran would not only serve the interests of both countries, but would also have broader positive implications for the whole region. As the Saudi foreign minister stated during his visit to Tehran in 1998, "the continuing and regular dialogue will inevitably have positive impact, not just on Saudi Arabia and Iran, but on the region".[9] The minister also expressed the larger ambition that bilateral relations would reflect positively on Iran's relations with the Arab and Muslim worlds.

However, in spite of Saudi and Iranian insistence on the good intentions upon which their new relations have been founded, many in the region have negatively assessed the warming of relations between the Riyadh and Tehran. Consequently, reactions to the Saudi-Iranian rapprochement have not been supportive. This was expected although neither Riyadh nor Tehran liked it. It is a natural response because when two regional powers get closer their neighbors become concerned. This is true in any region of the world.

The most outspoken has been the UAE. Officials in the UAE have been concerned that such warming of relations would be at the expense of their dispute with Iran on the three islands (Greater and Lesser Tunbs, and Abu Musa). They have also argued that improvement of relations between the GCC and Iran should be preconditioned on the final solution of the dispute. Saudi officials have tried to convince the UAE leadership that relations with Iran would never compromise Riyadh's stand on the islands, which embraces support for the UAE rights in the islands and calls for settlement through negotiation. The Saudi Minister of Defense stated that he supported "UAE efforts to regain sovereignty over the three islands". He also argued that "in view of the fact that Iran was a Muslim country and a neighbor to the UAE and all the GCC states and that there was no enmity on the part of the UAE towards Iran, it was incumbent upon Iran to look into the issue with fraternal emirates, taking into account what was just and right, and reach a solution either through direct understanding or international arbitration."[10] In fact, Saudi Arabia have repeatedly raised the issue of the islands during meetings with Iranian officials and called for a solution based on principles of international law, including the option of submitting the issue to the International Court of Justice.

The Saudis have also argued that they would use their growing ties to persuade Tehran to reach agreement with Abu Dhabi on the islands. In addition, they have indirectly pointed out the strong trade relations that exist between the UAE and Iran and questioned the reasons the UAE has neither used those relations to influence Tehran on the issue of islands nor frozen them as a means to object to Iran's policy. In fact, for many years Iran has been the largest re-export recipient of the UAE.

Saudi Arabia's belief in negotiation as a means to solve the dispute is reflected in its effort to establish a tripartite ministerial committee. But, despite all assurance from Saudi Arabia, the UAE is still troubled by the rapidly growing relations between Riyadh and Tehran. This was reconfirmed in April 1999 by the visit of the UAE's crown sheikh to Saudi Arabia only a day before the Iranian Minister of Defense Ali Shamkhani arrived in Jeddah. The sheikh's visit appeared to be an attempt reminding the Saudis of the islands issue.

I believe that the UAE has maintained a rational and flexible position on the islands, reflected in Sheikh Zayid's repeated calls for direct negotiations or arbitration. Therefore, Iran ought to reconsider its rigid position and search for ways to end this dispute that stands in the way of complete normalization of relations with the rest of the GCC members, and in fact, with the Arab world in general. It is understood that in light of the high level of mobilization in the Iranian society on the islands issue, it is not easy for the Iranian leadership to modify its position. Nevertheless change has to come in order to close a volatile issue in the Gulf.

The persistence of the islands issue can lead to the reemergence of tensions in the Gulf and may in fact cause confrontation in light of the military buildup in both Iran and the UAE. It is not totally irrational to say that in the future the islands could be used as a pretext to involve the Gulf in a third war. On the bright side, however, the diminishing power of the conservative elements in Iran, as seen in the 2000 parliamentary elections, gives hope for a more conciliatory Iranian position. During last month's visit by the Yemeni president to Tehran, President Khatami offered a moderate position on the islands when he called for negotiations as a means to resolve the dispute.

If the UAE for apparent reasons has not been supportive of the rapprochement, other countries in the region have welcomed the new state in Saudi-Iranian relations. The most obvious has been Oman, which has always played a constructive role in mending relations between Iran and the GCC members. In fact, it was mostly Oman's efforts that brought the restoration of relations between Saudi Arabia and Iran in 1991.

Outside the Gulf, the most noticeable position towards the rapprochement was that of the US. At first, Washington's reaction was not welcoming for it saw the rapprochement as a step toward the ending of Iran's isolation. The US tried to spoil the warming relations by asking Saudi Arabia to implicate Tehran in the Khobar tower bombing. However, Washington later began to understand the Saudi policy of cooperation with Iran. The change of American stand was due to the re-examination of US approach in response to the increasing criticism of its dual containment policy.

In Europe, the United Kingdom, which is an important external player in the Gulf, welcomed the growing relations between Riyadh and Tehran. The British Foreign Ministry announced that it was "very pleased to see the improving relationship between Iran and Saudi Arabia". According to Britain's former Foreign Secretary Malcolm Rifkind, rapprochement between Iran and Saudi Arabia had "profound implications for the Gulf, oil, and US influence in the region".[11]

Implications for Gulf Security

Indeed normal relations between Iran and its neighbors are a basic condition for the stability and security of the Gulf. This is what the Saudis have been arguing since they turned a new page with Tehran in 1998. Iran is a major regional player whose past and present history testifies to the special place it has preserved for the Gulf in its domestic and foreign policies. The preoccupation with the Gulf has existed under the Shah, the revolutionary regime, and the current Islamic state. This may explain the intensity with which the question of security in the Gulf has always been dealt with in Tehran.

Long-established states like Iran tend to be rigid when it comes to issues of security and border disputes. The political and cultural elites of such states rely heavily on their nation's history when forming their views of themselves and the world around them. They see only their nation's great achievements and are inclined not to believe whatever transformations may challenge their people's greatness. These views tend to reflect on the country's foreign policy and are partially responsible for its rigidity. Therefore, it is a blessing when a leader, whose belief system is characterized by such concepts as moderation, tolerance, and dialogue, rises to govern a country with such features.

President Khatami's tenure and the steady rise of the reformists are an opportunity that must be seized by the GCC to begin serious moves towards the establishment of a security regime that benefits all. The Gulf states can contribute to the strengthening of the moderate line in Iran by establishing good relations, which then may be used by Khatami supporters as a winning card in their struggle with the radicals. Notwithstanding its sentimental value, the Gulf has always been used as a card by all political forces in Tehran. In the past, and under strong national and religious feelings, the radicals succeeded in using Gulf issues, such as the American military presence, to mobilize the Iranian public. Today, with a young population tired of conflicts and longing for peace and prosperity, the Khatami government can present the newly restored relations with the GCC as a carrot to win more domestic support. This is what the Saudis hope to accomplish from their continuous positive moves towards Tehran. They themselves are working for stability and security in their immediate external environment that will help them shift attention towards more pressing domestic issues.

Just like the international system the transformation of a regional system is usually a product of either a shift in the distribution of power among its principal players or a major change in the domestic environment of any of the players, consequently leading to substantial modification in its external behavior. Both processes of change have occurred in the Gulf. The traditional regional balance of power has been altered and Iran's political structure and orientation have changed. Hence a new regional system has to be established.

One of the major requirements for the establishment of a security regime in the Gulf is the restoration of the traditional balance of power among its three powers. Since 1990 this balance has been shifting towards Iran due to the continuous destruction of Iraq's military power under UN resolutions and Iran's vast military buildup. Iran's military expansion is not helping to alleviate the concerns of the GCC. The latter is still wary of Iran's growing military arsenal, especially its nuclear plant project at Bushehr on the eastern coast of the Gulf. The Iranian government insists that the plant is for peaceful purposes. However, the sheer existence of a nuclear plant with even the smallest possibility of turning it into military use causes fear and mistrust. Notwithstanding Saudi Arabia's recognition of Iran's right to advance its military capability, Tehran should not underestimate the concerns which its amassing of weaponry is causing. This is the reason why so many in the Gulf see the Iranian foreign policy as vague and contradictory, for while President Khatami calls for dialogue and cooperation, his government is continuing to accumulate weapons that many think go beyond its defense needs.

Therefore, the simple restoration of the balance of power is not enough force for stability and security in the Gulf. It has to be reinforced by common understanding, recognition, and respect of the interests of all eight countries. The outside powers, especially the US, should encourage and support cooperation between the countries and must realize that stability is the only guarantee for Western interests, strategic or economic. As the hegemon of the world and protector of Western interests in this vital region, the United States views in future security arrangements have to be taken into account. The contemporary history of the Gulf affirms the fact that, whether we like or not, world powers, particularly the US, have been important elements of security or insecurity in the region.

Furthermore, for a security regime to persist and be effective it has to be realist, independent, and endowed with a cultural dimension. First, it should be realist in terms of balance of power politics, meaning that it must be inclusive of all eight countries (even Iraq). This necessitates that the Iraq-Kuwait conflict must be resolved before such a regime can be established. What has been done so far is not enough. The Arab countries' passivity is not helping and simple enforcement of the embargo and insistence on Iraq's acceptance of UN resolutions will lead to nowhere.

Second, the proposed security regime has to include an economic component in the form of creating a common market that would benefit all eight states, making their citizens reap the fruit of cooperation, and enhancing their support for the security regime. Moreover the more countries that are interdependent, the less prone they are to fight. This does not mean that disagreements will disappear, but when they happen they would be dealt with peacefully so that common interests are not harmed. Security must be defined as development; meaning that a regime built on traditional concepts that equate security with only military balance will be short-lived.

Third, any security arrangement must take into account psychological and cultural conditions. This is because of the widespread misperceptions among elites and wider publics in all the eight states. The region's modern history, mainly characterized by hostility and clashes, has created a climate of fear, suspicion, and mistrust. The elites in each state question each other's intentions and views, and negative stereotyping heavily influences ordinary people's attitudes. In international politics, misperceptions have been found to play a negative role, complicating relations among states. Thus, it is very important that informal and frequent meetings among intellectuals and scholars should supplement relations between the countries of the Gulf. Borders should also be opened to encourage citizens to travel around and know each other personally. If implemented, these steps should help discard the many negative feelings that may stand in the way of establishing a solid and agreeable security regime.

The Gulf is a vital but volatile region for the whole world and its security and stability is a concern of the members of the international community. History has demonstrated that the effects of instability in the Gulf go beyond its geographical borders and reach areas as far as East Asia and the Western Hemisphere. Hence, all developments towards initiating durable peace must be welcomed. The Saudi rapprochement with Iran is an important step toward such a goal and must be objectively assessed. The extensive nature of relations between Riyadh and Tehran should prove beyond any doubt that the two countries are not only cooperating out of self-interest. The leaders of both countries are also fully aware of the weight of their countries' relations on the whole region in terms of stability and prosperity. As such, if the neighboring countries as well as all states interested in the Gulf objectively and impartially understand the current Saudi-Iranian relations, they would be less apprehensive. The rapprochement should confirm once and for all that the regional actors could act independently of outside influence. This independent will must be further enhanced as a means to establish a lasting security regime in the Gulf.

Notes

1. www.ain-al-yaqeen.com/issue/1998. February 25,1998.
2. *Ibid.* June 3, 1998.
3. www.saudif.com/main.y0761.htm. October 3, 1999.
4. www.iraniantrade.org/NewsUpdates/0000049a.htm. January 21, 2000.
5. *Ibid.* October 10, 1999.
6. Figure reported by the cultural Attaché at the Iranian Embassy in Riyadh, April 22, 2000.
7. www.saudif.com/main/y0327.htm. June 1, 1999.
8. www.saudif.com/main/y0027.htm. February 21, 1998.
9. www.ain-al-yaqeen.com. June 3, 1998.
10. *Ibid.* June 17, 1998.
11. www.iraniantrade.org/NewsUpdates. May 30, 1999.

CHAPTER 6

Territorial Disputes and Security of West Asia

Pirouz Mojtahed-Zadeh

West Asia comprises largely of what was about to become known as the "Greater Middle East", which is meant to refer to a combination of the two regions of the Persian Gulf and the Caspian-Central Asia as well as the Arab Middle East. As is the case for any region, the study of security concerns of West Asia must be cognizant of what might constitute a threat to the economic interests or political function of the region. This is wholly dependent on the way the region might define its economic interests and/or political function. The two regions of the Persian Gulf and Caspian-Central Asia are poised to function as the two main energy-supplying regions of the early decades of the 21st century with an interconnected geopolitical and geostrategic role in the emerging world order. Any issue of security in these two regions will consequently be of major interest to the regional and global players alike. Furthermore, it is from the strategic concerns of these two regions that the concept of a new "heartland" could materialize (Kemp 1997). Sandwiched geographically between the Persian Gulf and Caspian-Central Asia is Iran. If the Middle East and the Persian Gulf were to be connected geographically to the region of Caspian-Central Asia, this connection can be possible only through Iran, which is the only Middle Eastern and Gulf country with actual geographical presence in the region of Caspian-Central Asia. This is what the United States finds extremely difficult to fit in its global security designs of the so-called "New World Order". This geopolitical and geostrategic situation forms the foundation upon which varying Iran-US security concepts clash and overshadow bilateral relations between the two, which in turn constitute the main sources of threat to the security of the whole of West Asia.

For too long Iran was considered by the superpower on her northern flank as a land barrier to be surmounted for access to the warm waters of the south, namely the Persian Gulf and the Indian Ocean (Khrushchev 1974, 297f). The collapse in the 1990s of the bipolar global geopolitical system brought the United States to the regions of the Persian Gulf and Caspian-Central Asia where security has become an issue of supreme global and regional concern. This changed world order of the 1990s and early-21st century has influenced West Asia and its strategic priorities beyond recognition. The region of Caspian-Central Asia has been freed from the clutches of the former Soviet Union. And the priorities in the Persian Gulf have changed from concerns about Soviet threats to tensions arising from geographical conflicts within the region. There are many areas of territorial differences, some potentially as explosive as that of the Kuwait crisis of 1990–91. While geographical differences are, at present, thought to be the main source of insecurity in the Persian Gulf, security in Caspian-Central Asia is more threatened by the geopolitical and geostrategic games played by various regional and global players. These security concerns are subjects of closer scrutiny in the following pages.

Security Matters in the Persian Gulf

With the collapse of the bipolar global system after the dismemberment of the Soviet Union and Warsaw Pact in the early 1990s, security concepts changed in the Persian Gulf almost beyond recognition. These concepts changed from outside threats through the Strait of Hormuz to the sharply increased territorial disputes within the region. For instance, the Kuwait crisis of 1990–91 brought the big power military presence in the region for security protection while the prolongation of this military presence may be considered by some in the region as a potential source of tension and insecurity therein.

The changing world order works as an impulse necessitating regional groupings to facilitate the emergence of a multipolar geopolitical world. At the same time, national interests in the regions function as imperatives dictating regional integration for the survival of regional policies in the new political world. As such the settlement of territorial disputes is the prelude to achieving regionalism of the kind that fits the new global geopolitical pattern. Here I only list the most noticeable instances of territorial differences in the Persian Gulf, which in general terms can be classified into two main categories: inter-Arab disputes, and Arab-Iranian territorial differences.

Inter-Arab Disputes

Of this category, the following areas of differences are of security concern:

- The Kuwait-Iraq territorial disputes, which were settled by the United Nations Boundary Commission in 1993, at least temporarily. Although Iraq did not agree totally with the terms of the settlement, it had to accept it however grudgingly. This settlement still leaves the issue of maritime division and boundary differences unsettled.
- Having averted an all-out war in 1986, Bahrain and Qatar have referred their territorial and maritime disputes to the International Court of Justice for adjudication. This dispute is highly complicated as it involves the Hawar archipelago of 17 islands, two shoals, and the seabed and continental shelf areas between the two states (Mojtahed-Zadeh 1994 & 1999). The ICJ delivered its judgement on this issue in March 2001.
- The long-standing border disputes between Saudi Arabia and Qatar, which led to border clashes between these two members of the Gulf Cooperation Council in late 1992. Riyadh and Doha have since decided to delimit and demarcate border areas with the assistance of a French legal firm specializing in such a task. Nevertheless, Saudi Arabia's unsettled territorial disputes in Buraimi, Liwa regions and Shoibah oil fields with Abu Dhabi, and its unclear access corridor in Khor al-Odaid affects border relations with Qatar.
- Saudi Arabia and Abu Dhabi (UAE) have been involved in border and territorial disputes in the Boreimi areas since the turn of the 20th century. This highly complicated dispute involves the sultanate of Oman and its continuation in the Liwa and Khor al-Odaid regions involve Qatar as well. Several border settlements mediated by the British and American interests in the first half of the 20th century failed to solve the dispute completely. A bilateral agreement between Saudi Arabia and Abu Dhabi in 1974, whereby Abu Dhabi granted Saudi Arabia a corridor of access to the Persian Gulf in the Khor al-Odaid bay at the foot of Qatar Peninsula, has further complicated the issue. Territorial complication in the Shoibah Saudi oil fields near Abu Dhabi borders, which affects exploitation and exportation of oil from this region by Saudi Arabia, attracted some attention in Spring 2000. But the two states have in the recent decades tried to give a low profile to these disputes.

- Saudi Arabia and Yemen began their territorial and border disputes in a vast area involving the three provinces of Assir, Jizan and Najran in 1934. These disputes brought the two neighbors to armed conflict on several occasions, including border clashes of 1994. The two countries however, succeeded in settling this dispute in 1995 as a result of withdrawal by Yemen's present regime of claims to the said three provinces. The border settlement agreement of 1995 delimits and demarcates the 25,000-km boundaries between the two countries.
- There are a number of less significant territorial and boundary disputes among the Arab states of the Persian Gulf. These disputes include the Kuwaiti-Saudi Arabian disputes over the two islands of Qaruh and Umm al-Maradim in the offshore areas of former Neutral Zone between the two countries; the territorial disputes between United Arab Emirates in the Diba region on the Arabian Sea; and the Ras al-Khaimah border dispute with Oman in the Persian Gulf.

Arab-Iranian Disputes

In this category, there are two major areas of territorial disputes between Iran and the Arab states of the region:

- The Iran-Iraq territorial and border disputes which began several centuries ago and ended in the eight-year war of the 1980s. These disputes have been used extensively for political purposes by both parties as well as by the outside powers. Iran used the issue of Iraqi Kurdish movements (a peripheral issue in the two countries' disputes) in the 1970s to establish its supremacy in the region. The United States used this dispute in the 1980s to arm and encourage Iraq to invade Iran in order to "contain the spread of Iran's Islamic revolution to the rest of the region", as admitted on 17th March 1998 by US Secretary of State Madeleine Albright. And Iraq used the actual territorial and border disputes with Iran to forge a leadership role in the Arab World. In the second half of the 20th century, Iraq saw itself as one of the most eligible contenders in the rivalry for Arab leadership. But, given the fact that hostilities with Israel was the most decisive factor in reaching the position of leadership in the Arab world, the Iraqi leaders found their ambitions frustrated by countries situated on the frontline with Israel, such as Egypt, Jordan and Syria. To turn this geographical deficiency into an advantage exclusive to Iraq, the leaders in Baghdad concluded that they needed to create a new common enemy for the Arabs with whom Iraq would be the only frontline Arab state. Not only was Iran the natural choice, it was also the only choice. It was a country with a long history of rivalry with the Arabs, was suspected in the 1960s and 1970s of political or economic cooperation with Israel, and its territorial and boundary disputes with Iraq provided the latter with the best excuse for conflict. These disputes were presented as the symbol of Iran's ill intentions towards the "Arab lands". Extensive planning of a propaganda campaign against Iran included attempts to change the historical names of geographical entities such as the Persian Gulf, despite the fact that Iran refused to seriously consider similar undertakings. For instance, the river separating Iran from Iraq is still referred to in Iran as Shatt al-Arab. With the success of the Islamic revolution in Iran in February 1979, relations deteriorated with the Arab neighbors. This was mainly because of the perceived threat in the region and in the West that Iran was attempting to export the Islamic revolution to the neighboring countries. The neighboring countries were also worried about Islamic uprisings in the countries of the region inspired by the Iranian revolutionaries (Mojtahed-Zadeh 1994). These developments together with active encouragements from the United States enticed Iraq unilaterally to abrogate the Algiers Accord of 1975 with Iran, and to champion the slogan of "defending the Gulf Arabs against Iran's revolutionary threats". Hoping for a quick victory over the Iranian defense forces, which were largely disoriented by the revolution, Iraq waged a war of attrition against Iran, lasting from 1980 to 1988. As is well known, Iraq failed to achieve its declared war aims of annexing the entire Shatt al-Arab as well as parts of the Iranian province of Khuzestan. Accordingly Iraqi president Saddam Hussein wrote on 14 August 1990 to the president of the Islamic republic of Iran confirming that Iraq was prepared to negotiate border and territorial settlements with Iran on the basis of the Algiers Accord of 1975. Most of the lands held by the Iraqis in Iranian Kurdestan and Khuzestan was also released to the Iranians as a result of the withdrawal of the Iraqi troops to the boundaries pre-dating September 1980.

- The Iran-UAE territorial dispute over the islands of Tunbs and Abu Musa, which was launched by the United Arab Emirates in 1992, 21 years after a negotiated Anglo-Iranian settlement returned these islands to Iran. While in its position paper of 27 October 1992 to the United Nations the UAE claimed that these islands belonged to the emirates since the dawn of history, the Iranians maintain that the UAE did not exist before 1971. Therefore, it cannot claim ownership of any territory since the dawn of history. They also argue that the emirates forming the federation did not have territorial dimension until early 1960s when the British divided among them various territories in Musandam areas, which were lately in their actual possession. The Iranians have also argued that these islands, like many other islands situated in the northern half of the Persian Gulf, have always belonged to Iran as dozens of official British maps and numerous other historical documents prove. The UAE, on the other hand, speaks of documents from the Qasemi (Jawasim) rulers of Bandar Lengeh verifying Ras al-Khaimah's ownership of the Tunb islands. In response, the Iranians insist that the position of the Qasemi family in Bandar Lengeh and dependent islands in the 19th century as Iranian officials, governing the district on behalf of the central government, did not amount to any territorial right to them or their tribal cousins of Musandam (Mojtahed-Zadeh 1995). Recently uncovered documents, however, disclose that a secret meeting at the British Foreign Office in 1902 decided that in anticipation of Russian encroachment into the Persian Gulf, the strategic islands at or near the Strait of Hormuz should be occupied.[1] The British sanctioned in July 1903 the occupation of Greater Tunb, Abu Musa and Sirri islands by the Qasemi rulers of Sharjah (Lesser Tunb was occupied in 1908).[2]

In 1904 Iran's director of customs of the South visited Abu Musa and was surprised to see Sharjah's flag flying there. He replaced it with the Iranian flag and installed Iranian custom guards. Although the British swiftly reinstated Sharjah's occupation of the islands, the Iranians continued protesting against the occupation for the next 68 years, even succeeding from time to time in interrupting this occupation.

Having secured restoration of sovereignty on Sirri Island in 1962, Iran resumed an open campaign for the recovery of the two Tunbs and Abu Musa islands in late 1960s. The British, however, would not come to the negotiating table with Iran in spite of many warnings by the Iranians that they would take the islands by force should a negotiated settlement prove to be impossible. But what made the British begin talks with the Iranians on the subject were not these threats of the use of force. It was the emergence of an impasse in 1970 regarding the creation of the federation of Arab emirates in the wake of the termination of pax-Britannica in the region. All three major regional powers—Iran, Iraq, and Saudi Arabia—declared that they would not recognize the emerging federation, each for reasons of its own. The British, thus, concluded that the creation of a union of small emirates without the good will of the regional powers would put this feeble union in danger. It was the realization of this situation that forced the British to abandon their 68-year policy of deferring negotiations with Iran on the issue. Acting on behalf of the emirates of Sharjah and Ras al-Khaimah in these negotiations, the British pursued a strategy of putting Iran in a tight corner by prolonging the negotiations and playing for time. Ultimately Iran accepted the British formula of unconditional return of the two Tunb islands to Iran, and recognition of its rights of sovereignty in parts of Abu Musa island through the enforcement of a memorandum of understanding between Iran and Sharjah.[3]

Arab reaction to this development was mixed. Moderate Arab states preferred prudence since many of them, including the ruler of Abu Dhabi, were kept closely informed of the nature and progress of the Anglo-Iranian negotiations on the settlement of the dispute. Radical Arab governments, on the other hand, adopted vociferous policies both domestically and in the United Nations. Algeria, Iraq, Libya, and former South Yemen took their complaint to the UN Security Council, which met on 9 December 1971 and decided, unanimously, on the recommendation of the representative of Somalia, a member of the Arab League, to lay the case to rest.[4]

No claims to the islands came to the fore for twenty one years after the United Arab Emirates came into existence on 2 December 1971, two days after these islands were returned to Iran and one day after British rule over the emirates ended. Tehran has misgivings about the reasons and the way the claim came about in 1992. This was right after the US military presence in the Persian Gulf was established in the wake of the Kuwait crisis of 1990–91 and after the so-called dual containment policy of the United States against Iran and Iraq was in full swing in the region. An incident in the Abu Musa Island in 1992, described by the Iranian foreign ministry at the time as a "misjudgement by junior Iranian officials",[5] prompted the United Arab Emirates to claim sovereignty over the whole of Abu Musa. The UAE also "demanded" the "return" to that country of the two Tunb islands, situated off Iranian shores.

The contemporary history of the Tunbs and Abu Musa islands illustrate the volatility surrounding the boundary issues in the Persian Gulf. In its position paper of 27 October 1992 to the UN, the UAE confirms the legality of the 1971 Iran-Sharjah MOU by asking Iran to adhere to the text and spirit of that document on shared sovereignty in Abu Musa. But Abu Dhabi now claims sovereignty over the whole of that island and the two Tunbs. More controversial is Abu Dhabi's open campaign to politicize and internationalize the issue of its claims to these islands. This intention became abundantly clear when other members of the Gulf Cooperation Council, the Damascus Declaration (6+2) and even the Arab League were dragged in by the United Arab Emirates, repeatedly issuing communiqués in support of the UAE efforts. Yet, there has been no real commitment to this course of action from any member of the said Arab organizations save for Iraq. Thus the UAE's hope to make the issue a *cause celebre* at the Middle Eastern regional level, reflecting "US-Arab resistance to the spread of Iranian influence in the Persian Gulf", seems to have been dashed by the increasing Arab-Iranian rapprochement and cooperation. Despite having signed various GCC or 6+2 statements in support of the UAE claims, most Arab members of these organizations, especially Syria, Saudi Arabia, Oman, Qatar, Bahrain, and Kuwait, routinely reaffirm their dedication to the expansion of Arab-Iranian cooperation for peace and stability in the region. This was particularly evident in the spring of 1999 when the Saudi Arabian Defense Minister openly criticized the UAE stance *vis-à-vis* Iran and the three islands. To compensate for the UAE's growing frustration, the GCC decided in its foreign ministerial meeting of Spring 1999 to form a tripartite committee of foreign ministers of Saudi Arabia, Qatar, and Oman to facilitate direct negotiations between Iran and the United Arab Emirates. Tehran has on several occasions announced that it is willing to negotiate with the UAE on the subject provided that Abu Dhabi is prepared for real negotiations. The realization of a direct and peaceful negotiation on any territorial and boundary disputes requires that the claimant observes proportionality of claims, depoliticizes the issue of the claim, and demonstrates true desires for the settlement of the claim. Ultimately, however, the settlement of Iran-UAE territorial disputes must be sought through the expansion of Arab-Iranian cooperation with the view that this cooperation would result in the expansion of the goodwill between the parties, which is the prerequisite for the settlement of geographical differences.

Security Matters in the Caspian-Central Asia

Unlike the Persian Gulf in which geographical issues are the main source of threat to regional security, the only geographical matter that may influence security in the Caspian-Central Asian region is the issue of the legal regime of the Caspian Sea. In this region the main destabilizing factor is geopolitical: the geopolitics of access to the outside world, and the geopolitics of oil and gas pipelines.

The Caspian region may be seen as the vast expanse stretching from the Caucasus in the west to Central Asia in the east. The region is both divided and connected by the Caspian Sea. As such, for the purpose of this study the Caucasus, the Caspian, and Central Asia are amalgamated into one geopolitical region that can be referred to as the region of "Caspian-Central Asia". Numerous factors of regional geography and human environment support this approach, providing a much-needed term of reference in studying regional matters related to this vast geographical expanse.

The Geopolitics of Access

All former Soviet republics in the Caucasus, Caspian, and Central Asia are landlocked with no direct or easy access to international maritime trade. Kzakhstan, Turkmenistan, and the Republic of Azerbaijan, along with Iran and Russia, border the Caspian Sea. This particular geography is conducive to the development of maritime trade among the said five littoral states. Such a development will not, however, solve the problem of lack of maritime access to the international markets. A practical solution to this problem can be sought in the idea of linking all these republics and Afghanistan to the Persian Gulf and Gulf of Oman by road, railway, and pipeline networks.

In December 1991 Kzakhstan and Iran signed an agreement providing for the Central Asian republics to extend their railway networks to the Persian Gulf across Iran. Another agreement signed in the same year between Iran and the waning Soviet Union permitted freedom of cross-border travel up to 45 miles on either side of the Iran-Azerbaijan, Iran-Armenia, and Iran-Turkmenistan borders by ethnic Azeri and Turkmen peoples respectively. In June 1995 Iran, Turkmenistan, and Armenia signed a tripartite agreement providing for expansion of overland trade among the three. March of that year witnessed inauguration of the linking of the Central Asian railway networks to those of Iran. These railway networks were hooked up in March 1996. Leaders of many regional countries and/or their representatives attending the inauguration ceremony acknowledged Iran's geographical situation as the main bridge of access between Caspian-Central Asia and the outside world. At the same time, Iran can facilitate direct access of the oil producing Arab countries of the Persian Gulf to the Caspian-Central Asia, a region that is becoming a rival to the Persian Gulf in the global energy markets. Similarly, as a land bridge connecting Caspian-Central Asia to the Indian Ocean, Iran may prove pivotal to India's commercial undertakings in that region. Presently, Indian ships use Georgian and Ukrainian ports, as well as negotiating hundreds of kilometres of roads through Russia in order to reach Central Asia. Iran has suggested that India should fund a 700 kilometre railway connecting Bafq to Mashhad, thereby shortening the Central Asia-Persian Gulf connection by several hundred kilometres. This would give India a competitive edge over Pakistan in Central Asia.

The Geopolitics of Oil Pipelines

From an economic point of view, piping Caspian oil and gas to the outside world through Iranian territories is unquestionably the most practical way of making this region's oil and gas exports competitive in the international markets. This route will offer the shortest, safest, and cheapest alternative for the export of energy commodities of the region, especially as far as Caspian oil and gas exports to the ever expanding energy consuming markets of Indian Subcontinent, Africa, and the Far East are concerned. Moreover, Iran's wealth of manpower skilled in petroleum industries, developed transportation and shipping infrastructure, existing refineries and port facilities, and existing network of oil and gas pipelines offer a considerable technical and logistical advantage. None of the alternative routes that might be considered for the export of Caspian-Central Asia oil and gas can match any of these. Iran's pipeline network is connected to the Republic of Azerbaijan and is situated within a short distance of Turkmenistan. A pipeline connecting Kzakhstan and Turkmenistan to this network will be, at least, four times shorter in length and cheaper than any alternative destined to the Black and Mediterranean Seas through harsh terrain and insecure regions

The all-round advantage of an Iran-bound pipeline network for the export of oil and gas from the Caspian-Central Asia is known to all concerned. Several agreements for the utilization of this route have been signed to export Caspian oil and gas to the Indian Subcontinent,

China, Far East, Europe, and Australia via Iran (Mojtahed-Zadeh 1998b). The overland transportation of some Turkmen oil through Iran and Turkey to the Mediterranean Sea has already begun. Furthermore, Turkmenistan and Kzakhstan have begun exporting some of their crude via swap deals through Iran even when the US geopolitics of neutralizing Iran's geographical position in the energy trade of Caspian-Central Asia has worked against the utilization of this most economically viable route. The position of the United States regarding Iran's role in the region is premised on the categorical and *a priori* notion that any idea of an Iranian involvement in the affairs of Caspian-Central Asia is not to the liking of the United States and her Turkish and Israeli allies.[6] Furthermore, the United States' geopolitics of diverting the export of Caspian-Central Asian oil and gas from its natural route seems to be dictated not solely by the idea of benefiting the Turkish ally and thus establishing some sort of strategic control over the lines. It is also guided by the notion that Iran's geographical potentials, as the only country connecting the two main energy-supplying depots, provide her with the possibility of playing a major role in the global geopolitics of the 21st century. As such the potentials will have to be kept in check in order to safeguard US perceived regional and global security.[7] These openly anti-Iranian US geopolitics are being pursued in the region despite the process of democratization that is taking shape in Iran and the fact that "national interests" are replacing ideological considerations in her foreign policy.

Beyond the geopolitics of oil and gas in the Caspian-Central Asia, by signing numerous contracts for investment in the region, the US has been able to claim real interests in that region. This, in turn, has provided the possibility for Washington to fill the geopolitical gap left behind by the Soviet Union as a means to have the final say in regional affairs. It is on this basis that the United States seems to be gradually moving towards security arrangements by preparing for NATO's eastward expansion as far as Caspian-Central Asia. It is worth noting that in the past few summers the United States has staged joint military exercises in Central Asia with the participation of all Caspian-Central Asian countries except Iran. These exercises have occurred with the participation of Turkey, which is a NATO member but without geographical links to the Caspian-Central Asian region. This creeping geostrategic alignment was accompanied with the US announcement in January 1999 of moving its military base from Ancelic in Turkey to Abshorun in the Republic of Azerbaijan in the Caspian Sea. The announcement on 20 February 1999 by the

President of the Republic of Azerbaijan that his country is ready to join NATO followed. Together these activities leave little doubt that the United States without any regional rationale is contemplating militarizing the region. Meanwhile, in a public statement in Georgia in January 2000, the President of Turkey suggested the formation of a regional security arrangement for the Caucasus in view of insecurity caused by the Chechen civil war. While instances of local insecurity in that region can and have been successfully dealt with by regional players, Turkey's suggestion for a regional security arrangement involving NATO members and excluding regional players like Iran, can only reinforce suspicions of NATO's creeping advances towards Caspian-Central Asia. This is an eventuality that can only undermine current strategic balances and promote insecurity in that region.

Conflicts in Historical Perspective

In the Persian Gulf, the bulk of Arab-Iranian territorial differences do not exceed in volume or complexity those that existed among the British, the French, and the Germans for a long period of time. If these European nations have learnt to give their common interests priority over their mutual differences, surely the Arabs and the Iranians can also learn to do the same.

The Arabs and Iranians have in recent years faced a barrage of propaganda in the region, accusing regional states of entertaining ill intentions towards each other. As a result salvation has been sought in extraregional domination of the affairs of the region at the expense of regional integrity and self-reliance. The question that needs to be raised here is whether extraregional powers have done anything to help regional countries to solve their differences and create a regional arrangement for peace and cooperation. Or have they constantly been engaged in promoting political and territorial disputes in order to create and maintain justification for their continued military presence and political interference in the region. Answering these questions requires the examination of three periods in recent history during which alternatively foreign powers managed affairs of the region, the littoral states managed their own affairs, and foreign powers returned to take control of the affairs of the region.

The Era of Pax-Britannica

During their colonial presence in the Persian Gulf the British approached issues of territoriality and states relationships with a great deal of inconsistency. The natural outcome of such an inconsistent approach could not have been anything but numerous territorial and boundary disputes in the region. British researchers of contemporary times argue that this was because of variations in British interests over time. They also believe that the British treatment of territorial disputes in the Persian Gulf was based on a policy of leaving the matters alone as long as they caused no problem. This might have been the case but the reality is that siding with one party at one time and with the other at another effectively divided the parties and made British rule easy. It also provided the British with regional justification for the continuation of colonial rule.

The Post-Colonial Era

The January 1968 British announcement of withdrawal of pax-Britannica from east of Suez by 1971 created a sense of urgency in the Persian Gulf, which necessitated Arab-Iranian cooperation. An added factor was the atmosphere of goodwill created by the meetings of Saudi and Iranian leaders in 1965 and 1968, when they decided on extensive cooperation among regional states. Contrary to negative propaganda in the West against this period of regional domination of regional affairs, many complex border issues were settled. Two of the most complicated territorial disputes settled in this period were those of continental shelf settlement of 1968 between Iran and Saudi Arabia which involved two islands, and the 1971 understanding between Sharjah and Iran on the Abu Musa island. These were followed by a number settlements such as: Qatar-Iran continental shelf boundary settlement of 1969; Iran-Bahrain maritime boundary settlement of 1971; the 1975 Iran-Oman boundary delimitation in the Strait of Hormuz; and the river and inland boundary settlements between Iran and Iraq in that same year. Maritime boundaries were also settled between Iran and Dubai and between Qatar and Abu Dhabi in that period. Other manifestations of Arab-Iranian understanding and cooperation in the period 1968–78 include Iran's internationally praised withdrawal of historical claim to Bahrain and her swift and highly effective response in 1973 to Oman's call for assistance in defusing the Marxist-separatist threat against her territorial integrity. Similarly, Arab-Iranian cooperation in the Organization of Petroleum Exporting Countries (OPEC) placed the Persian Gulf region at the heart of the global geopolitics of the 1970s. It effectively tipped the balance of political influence in the international political system in favor of the Gulf region, that is to say the Arabs and the Iranians.

The Wars and the Onset of Pax-Americana

Iraq's invasion of Iran brought the US naval fleet into the region on the pretext of escorting Kuwaiti ships. Iraq's occupation of Kuwait provided the necessary excuse for the establishment of a permanent American military presence in the Persian Gulf. Resembling the colonial policies of "divide and rule", these developments coincided with the rapid changes taking place in the global geopolitical system, increasing the significance of Western control of the Persian Gulf in the 21st century. This is a new status quo, the continuation of which would need to feed on continued disputes among regional states.

Arab-Iranian rapprochement has begun once again and it seems that the experience of the 1970s is being repeated but this time with greater mutual confidence. It is important to recognize that the Iranians and Arabs succeeded in realizing regional balance and cooperation in the 1970s mainly because both sides enjoyed, at the time, the goodwill and friendship of the United States. This goodwill was premised on the Nixon doctrine of non-interference in regional conflicts and the policy of leaving regional security around the world to friendly regional powers. As before, it is important to realize that in the emerging regional geopolitics, the West has legitimate interests in the continued safe flow of oil and gas from the Persian Gulf. As such, a return to the period of understanding and cooperation within any framework will need the goodwill of the West, attained by a reassurance that these legitimate interests will be safeguarded. Also important is regional goodwill as the requisite condition for solving differences. Promotion of disputes at the expense of goodwill and cooperation in the region, the way the United Arab Emirates, for instance, is doing at present, will of course be counterproductive. It can only result in the continuation of regional justification for extra-regional domination and insecurity. Should the UAE truthfully wish to settle its territorial disputes with Iran, it has to treat the issue in dispute as a technical matter to begin with. This means that Abu Dhabi must first and foremost depoliticize the issue of its claim to the islands in question, and then try to consider the proportionality of the extent of the claim so that it could be acceptable as a factual geographical and legal claim worthy of attention.

As more international attention is being given to the security of the Persian Gulf and Caspian Sea, the significance of Iran's unique geographical position between these two regions, and the inevitability of its natural influence on issues of regional security becomes more evident. Despite this central role and the fact that Iran is gradually addressing itself to the new realities of global geopolitics, the United States still seems to prefer the continuation of its confrontational approach towards Iran. Washington's persistence in this approach goes against conventional wisdom that regional security is best preserved by integrating all regional players. This is why US-Iranian relations must be considered as the key to safeguarding security in West Asia as well as solving Iran's economic and strategic concerns.

Contrary to the existing perception in the West and in the Arab World, the issue of Iran-US relations is very much in the public domain in Iran largely because of two factors. This is due to the expansion of popular political participation as well as recent public statements on the subject by the US political leaders. The following could be counted as the main factors influencing Washington's recent overtures towards Iran:

- Iran's unique geographical situation between the Persian Gulf and the Caspian Sea, and the fact that Iran has the capability of connecting her northern geopolitical depth to her southern geopolitical depth. This can be done by allocating one of its many ports on the Persian Gulf to each one of the landlocked states of Caspian-Central Asia for their exclusive and autonomous use within the framework of Iran's sovereignty and rule of law. This undertaking will turn Iran's unique geographical situation into a unique geopolitical position in the global order. It will also provide countries of Caspian-Central Asia with direct and easy access to the international trade routes and will provide the countries of the Persian Gulf with direct and easy access to assuming a role in the energy business of Caspian-Central Asia. This is a situation that the United States can hardly afford to ignore forever, especially considering the fact that the many attempts to divert oil and gas routes away from Iran have met with little success.
- Iran's democratization process suggests that Washington is no longer dealing with the Ayatollahs alone. At the same time, in Iran some of us have been promoting the idea that the country cannot live in isolation forever and needs to expand its relations with the outside world, including the United States.
- Political pressure exerted upon US administration by domestic and international players such as Saudi Arabia, Kuwait, Qatar, Oman, and Bahrain played a role in encouraging the former Democratic administration to repair its relations with Iran. These

> players see Arab-Iranian cooperation in the Persian Gulf as the main source of stability and security in that region. This policy of safeguarding regional security through regional integration is sustainable only when it is not confronted by the single superpower under current Republican administration that wants to have the final say in the security affairs of the region. The European Union sees major economic opportunities in assisting the settlement of US-Iranian differences. On the domestic front, oil companies and other industrial establishments as well as a growing number of political personalities like Cyrus Vance and Richard Murphy, have actively criticized Washington for failing to solve the problem of its relations with Iran. They urge the administration should come to terms with Iran and its new political identity.

Ordinarily normalization of relations between two belligerent states is possible only by going through three phases: a) Declaration of détente; b) Implementation of confidence-building measures; and c) Establishment of diplomatic relations. On the issue of confidence building measures, it is noteworthy that US administration's pretension of being concerned about democracy and human rights for the people of Iran, and considering the same people as **terrorist** by banning their entry into the United States can hardly represent a position of sincerity. The current US administration has intensified animosity towards Iran since late 2001 for no plausible reasons. US sources have made it patently clear that all those involved in the September 11, 2001 terrorist atrocity were of the Saudi, Egyptian, and Jordanian nationality. Yet, George W. Bush accused Iran on January 29, 2002 of being a partner in his so-called ***axis of evil*** with Iraq and North Korea. Moreover, while the West has acknowledged that all members of the Taliban and Al-Qaedah terrorist organizations were Pakistani, Afghan, Saudi and Egyptian nationals, US Government has banned entry into the United States of Iranian nationals in order to prevent 'terrorism' in that country. This patently discriminatory and highly offensive treatment of Iran and the Iranians by current US administration leaves little doubt that the policy persuaded by this administration is only designed to please a group of fanatically anti-Iranian who holds power in Israel. This intensification of tension between the two countries, however, has elevated threats to the security and stability of West Asia and needs to be addressed seriously.

Should the two sides decide to bridge the gaps between them, Iran would be expected to speed up the process of integration in the global political system, while the United States might be expected to consider the implementation of the following confidence-building measures:

- Abandoning the geopolitics of diverting the Caspian-Central Asian oil and gas pipelines away from Iran and allowing economic imperatives to guide the course.
- Freeing Iran's assets in the United States, and agreeing to a serious and fundamental review of the arbitrary use of these assets in favor of its citizens and companies.
- Abandoning the so-called D'Amato extraterritorial sanctions law against Iran and its people.
- Lifting all economic sanctions and embargos against Iran.

Should the United States fail to implement these measures, there will only be one conclusion left for Iranians and others in the world to draw. This failure suggests that the United States wants to restore relations with Iran on its own terms with no respect for Iran's independence, national interests, and natural rights in the region. This can only amount to lack of regard for the principle of "mutual respect", which has been the guiding norm in international relations and should prevail in this instance as well. Whatever the nature of political development in Iran, it is doubtful that the Iranians would wish to become subservient to any other country.

Notes and References

1. Confidential Memorandum by Sir T. Sanderson, 14 July 1902, FO 416/10.
2. Government of India to Broderick, Enclosure in No. 130 of 16.4, 1904, FO 416/17, 191.
3. For full text of the MOU see Mojtahed-Zadeh (1995), Appendix III, 227–233.
4. UN Monthly Chronicle 9, 1 (January 1972): 48.
5. *Iran Focus* 5, 11(November 1992).
6. Remarks by Glen Race, US Department of State, at a seminar on the Caspian Sea in London on 24 February 1995, as appeared in "Iran most logical route to export Caspian Oil," *Ettela'at International*, 27 February 1995.
7. Remarks by John Wolf, US Energy Envoy in the Caspian Region, in the Seminar on The Political and Economic Prospects in the Caspian Sea Region, London, Wilton Park Conference, 6–9 March 2000.

Additional References

a) N. Khrushchev, *Khrushchev Remembers – The Last Testament*, Translated into English and edited by Strobe Talbott, London 1974, p. 297f.

b) Pirouz Mojtahed-Zadeh, *Security and Territoriality in the Persian Gulf*, Section III, Qatar – Bahrain Territorial and Boundary Disputes, Curzon Press, London 1999, pp. 115 to 158.
c) Pirouz Mojtahed-Zadeh, *A Geopolitical Triangle in the Persian Gulf*, The Iranian Journal of International Affairs, IPIS Publication, Vol. VI, Nos. 1 & 2, Spring/Summer 1994, pp. 47–59.
d) Pirouz Mojtahed-Zadeh, *The Islands of Tunb and Abu Musa*, CNMES/SOAS University of London publication, 1995.
e) Pirouz Mojtahed-Zadeh, *Iranian Perspective on the Caspian Sea and Central Asia*, in Iwao Kobori and Michael H. Glantz ed. *Central Eurasian Water Crisis*, United Nations University Press, Tokyo 1998, pp. 105–124.

CHAPTER 7

A Russian Perspective on West Asian Security

Vitaly V. Naumkin

The Gulf is one of the pivotal parts of the Middle East region strategically. In the last two decades, it was the scene of the two most dramatic armed conflicts in the world. The first was the Iran-Iraq War, which claimed the lives of almost 1.5 million people, while the second between Iraq and Kuwait prompted an intervention of the entire international community. The current security environment of the subregion is marked by the presence of overlapping conflicts and asymmetrical relations among its states in many respects.

In analyzing the level of conflict, it is useful to distinguish between the objective and subjective conflict-generating factors. As to the objective factors, among them one may, for instance, note the disproportion in the provision of security, the unsettled state of borders, territorial and other disputes, grave differences in approach and position towards the main political problems among the states of the region, competition over resources, demographic and migration processes (e.g. the growing share of foreign workers or migration pressure on a number of states), great gaps in standards of living, social status and amounts of rights enjoyed by various population groups, and the dependence of many state economies on oil production. The subjective conflict-generating factors include the claims and ambitions of individual states and their leaders, the tradition of resorting to violence as a means to resolve disputes, the absence of visible progress in the democratization of societies, the logic of "zero-sum games", by which the protagonists in disputes and conflict situations are still guided, and other factors.

The countries of the subregion, many of which fear and distrust each other, today provide for their security needs through a variety of means. Some rely on their own capacities (Iran), others depend on collective mechanisms (GCC countries, although that organization is not geared to tackling security issues), and some do it on a treaty basis with foreign partners (mostly the US). At the same time, it is clear that genuine peace, security, and stability in this subregion may only be adequately assured within the framework of a subregional or regional (i.e. Middle Eastern) security regime. Given the character of existing threats, challenges, and risks such a security regime must be based on comprehensive cooperative security, implying guarantees for the defense of the state, nation, and individuals against external attacks and internal challenges.

As suggested by the discussions in the SIPRI Expert Group, designing the concept of a regional security regime in the Middle East involves at least two other issues besides military security. These issues are "social cohesion within states and the region as a whole; and the growing demographic problem and its attendant impact on the resources and environment of the region" (Jones 1998).

On the whole, one may safely assume that the differences and contradictions existing in the region bear a predominantly bilateral character. Some of them—the "softest" contradictions—may find a solution in the framework of an effectively operational organization such as the Gulf Cooperation Council. But at the same time, as Tariq Ahmad al-Haidan, a prominent UAE diplomat, points out in his dissertation written in Russian, the Arab countries of the Gulf may encounter quite a few difficulties in resolving their territorial and interstate disputes with Iraq and Iran. These states generate serious challenges to regional stability not only in terms of territorial claims but also in the economic and political fields. It is a framework of a subregional or regional security zone—within the zone of the Arabian Peninsula and the Gulf or the entire Middle Eastern region—that may possibly ensure the solution to antagonisms between member-states of the GCC, Iran, and Iraq. Some analysts even speak of an expanded Middle East in which the states of Central Asia and the Trans-Caucasus are also included. No matter how extensively or limited the region is defined for security purposes, however, the point is that not only Iran and Iraq, but also Yemen must necessarily be included, even if we are dealing with a subregional variant.

Of course, it should be taken into account that the GCC member-states are striving to resolve the disputes amongst themselves either through efforts of their organization, or on bilateral bases, preferring not to submit the discussion of disputed problems to international organizations. But progress towards the formation of a regional security system will not mean a renunciation of bilateral arrangements, which will be incorporated into a common system to ensure joint, cooperative security. A regional or subregional framework will help neutralize existing asymmetries, conferring on all Gulf states a responsibility for maintaining stability and peace.

Many politicians and experts have repeatedly voiced the need for the creation of an organization for security and cooperation in the Middle East akin to the European one. The path to this is seen as the development of broad international cooperation in the region, dialogue among all parties, including those in conflict, and the creation of various networks to contribute to the resolution of these tasks. Dialogue should not be confined to security issues, which are the hardest of all. At the same time, joint measures directly related to security, such as coordination of border control, joint monitoring of the observance of the rules of navigation, and cooperation in the search and rescue in emergency situations may be discussed at the initial stage. In certain situations, joint peacekeeping cannot be ruled out either. World experience testifies that the states that are not allies at all and have sharply divergent interests and positions may take part in joint peacekeeping activities through an international mandate.

Along with the discussion of possible joint actions, pertaining to the "easiest" category, the parties have to identify common threats, challenges and risks, and establish basic security needs and interests. Naturally, the initial success of actions will depend on the accuracy with which the participants assess all the particular features of the situation in the region, among which, to sum up the aforesaid, one may notably identify the following:

- Discrepancies among states, interests and political goals, and security needs.
- Negative historical memory, particularly in the states that have been involved in bloody armed conflicts.
- The role of pre-existing institutions and alliances, first and foremost the Gulf Cooperation Council.
- Reliance of regional states on external forces, particularly the US, in guaranteeing their security.
- The major overlapping conflictive relationships (Iran-Iraq, Iraq-Kuwait), as well as minor cases (The operation of the Turkish armed forces in the north of Iraq) and unresolved territorial disputes (UAE-Iran, Saudi Arabia-Yemen, etc.).
- The special role of international organizations in monitoring, guarding, patrolling, and implementing the international sanctions regimes against certain states.

In recent years, Russian diplomacy has exerted great effort to resolve the question of improving the enforcement of international sanctions. UN Deputy Secretary-General and Director-General of the UN European headquarters in Geneva, Vladmir Petrovsky, noted in a message to an international conference on sanctions held in Moscow on 4 April 2000 that the present-day practice of enforcing compulsory measures in relation to individual states does not always yield expected results and takes a heavy toll on the mostly civilian population. His fact-finding missions to Libya in 1992 and 1997 led to a report submitted to the UN "citing clear and inconvertible proofs that the sanctions are in essence selective. By striking against the economic and social sectors of the society, they affect above all the most vulnerable groups of population. All this has strengthened my conviction that the international community has to transform its instruments in a way to ensure the observance of a minimal 'humanitarian threshold'. This threshold is the line beyond which the final political aim of using such means can no longer justify the extent of human suffering it causes." Enlarging the idea in the same sanctions conference, Russia's Foreign Minister Igor Ivanov said, "in enforcing any sanctions regime, it remains the most important task to provide the essential commodities for the civilian population. It must be assured of an untrammeled and indiscriminate access to humanitarian aid. In turn, the international humanitarian organizations must not fall within sanction-based restrictions, which could hinder their work in countries on which sanctions are imposed."

Russian politicians and strategic analysts also strive to make their contribution to the idea of creating a collective security system in the Middle East, which has a direct bearing on the Gulf subregion. A. Baklanov, a Russian diplomat specializing in the Middle East proposes to examine confidence-building measures (CBMs) in terms of different dimensions, which include the sphere of application, the extent of legal entrenchment, and functional design.[1]

Since this proposal, which was published in Moscow, comes from an official in the Russian Foreign Ministry, it is worth dwelling upon it in greater detail. In terms of application, the author believes it is appropriate to speak of two main categories and, correspondingly, interpretations of CBMs. The first category concerns the declarative and politico-legal confidence-building measures. The declarative CBMs are statements made by states, which "strictly speaking, do not bear an international legal character and, as a rule, represent a list of the most general principles and norms of behavior of nations in the field of security." These politico-legal CBMs are "called upon to bolster the declared intentions (principles of behavior) of the parties by the creation of a corresponding system of commitments with a view towards 'leading' the CBMs to the level of international legal norms."

The second category includes CBMs of a technical-organizational and functional character, "creating a specific operational environment for practical implementation of the negotiated security regime". These are the various ways of ensuring transparency (like exchange of data on military doctrines, budgets, concrete military activity, notification on troop movements, the holding of maneuvers, missile launchings etc.), the creation of special security regimes (zones), etc. As the Russian diplomat writes, decisions in the domain of organizational guidance determine "which joint body of states will be carrying out the negotiated 'set' of CBMs and in what form." If we are, however, to speak of other kinds of measures—those of monitoring and control, "they mostly determine the practical, including technical, aspects of monitoring, control over fulfillment of the decisions taken, as well as the range of organizations and persons that are entrusted to perform these functions".

In general, this classification is inspired by the corresponding experience of the European continent of the Cold War era. This experience led to the creation of the CSCE (then OSCE) and now many politicians are proposing to extend it both to the entire Middle Eastern region and to its component part, the Gulf. Often ignored in the process are both the miscalculations contained in the European experience and the difficulties involved in transferring any experience from one region to another. Besides collective security systems in areas lying beyond Europe, notably in Latin America and Southeast Asia, they also have many positive elements requiring examination and careful study in devising an appropriate regime for the Gulf states. Characteristically, regional regimes markedly differ from each other. Thus for the ASEAN an important principle is strict non-interference in each other's affairs, presupposing a renunciation of the forms of pressure practiced in other regions. The European experience, including in CBMs, is peculiar in that it was born in conditions of severe bloc confrontation and, on a broader scale, general global bipolarity.

This does not mean that Europe's valuable experience is not applicable to other areas. The essence of the matter, however, consists in the necessary differentiation between the universal features of this experience (say, the entire classification of CBMs and the worked-out mechanism of its application) and those elements that have an apparent regional context. The realities of the epoch and the region make us refrain from any mechanical transfer of the entire architecture and individual structural elements, of even the most successfully functioning regional security system, to another region (in this case, the Gulf which possesses many rich singular features in addition). They warn us against copying particular institutions and mechanisms, without rejecting the universality of approaches, goals, tasks, and functions bolstered by globalization.

Correction of experience is necessary in view of a dual set of circumstances: geographic and historical. Let us assume that an exchange of information on the activities of territorial groups as an important CBM reflects the specifics of a region in which there are grounds to speak about the sources of such danger for a number of states. Given terrorism's threat to present-day international security, exchange of information on these groups addresses a global concern as well. In principle, the clear-cut identification of risks and threats to security for the Gulf should underlie the approach towards ensuring security, both on the national and regional levels. This said, for a number of Gulf states one may identify a number of risks and threats, especially of a non-traditional kind, which, for other countries, do not play a significant role or are totally absent. By way of example one may cite reliance on a foreign work force as a risk factor.

Going back to the ideas voiced in the Russian press and stemming from the Russian Foreign Ministry, one can reduce the options and patterns for changing political geography with a view towards building security safeguards for the Middle Eastern states to three:

1. "Drawing" the countries of the region closer to the already existing extraregional security patterns and military-political structures.
2. A "selective" system of mutual guarantees and checks (the formation of various kinds of "axes", "triangles", and so forth).
3. The creation of a regional security system on a universal basis (that is, for all).

One can hardly doubt the numerous advantages of the third option. However, in order to bring it about one should overcome many obstacles and difficulties of both the objective and subjective kind. To surmount the objective obstacles, one has first of all to ensure that the states of the region and global actors become interested in the creation of such a system, and then provide reliable security safeguards. To remove the subjective obstacles, one has to build first and foremost an atmosphere of trust.

In the 1990s, the Russian leaders repeatedly put forward initiatives dealing with security of the Middle East in general and the Gulf in particular, demonstrating continued interest in the affairs of the region despite changes in the system of Russia's foreign policy priorities compared to that of USSR. It is useful to recall Moscow's activity in the last year of the USSR's existence with respect to the Iraq-Kuwait crisis and its attempt to play an independent role in the settlement of the conflict. Among the initiatives in recent years one may note the proposal of Russia's Foreign Minister of the day, Yevgeni Primakov, expressed in his visit to Cairo in October 1997. The Russian minister proposed the adoption a code of behavior in the domain of security for the Middle East, which would be premised on the following assumptions:

- Lasting and enduring security of each state in the region can only be ensured with a peaceful settlement in all the negotiating avenues of the Middle Eastern peace process.
- The national security of any state in the region cannot be ensured by purely military-technical means.
- The security of some cannot be based on the infringement on the security of others.
- Given the direct or indirect involvement of the countries of the region, the security of conflicting parties cannot be "locked in". It is necessary to get Iran, Turkey, North Africa, the Arab countries of the Persian Gulf, and also Iraq involved in the "Middle East security zone".
- The security of the Middle Eastern countries cannot be based on the opposing strategic alliances and groupings, which rely on outside forces and structures.
- International legality is the foundation of security and stability. What is necessary is commitment and continuity with respect to the bilateral and international treaties and agreements.
- There has to be resolute combat against all forms and varieties of terrorism and extremism for whatever reasons, religious included. Peace must not be hostage to terrorists.
- A renunciation of weapons of mass destruction and the eventual creation of a WMD-free zone.
- Mutual cutbacks on military budgets by the regional states with resources to be channeled towards the needs of development, including multilateral regional economic cooperation. Peace

with neighbors is cheaper and more profitable than the upkeep of first-class armies.

- Unconditional mutual respect towards the unique cultural and religious heritage of any people, freedom of denomination for all confessions, and the provision of untrammeled access of the believers to the holy places in Jerusalem and other parts of the region.
- A just solution to the humanitarian problems of the region, including the settlement of the refugee problem acceptable to all sides.
- Development of regional economic cooperation and the creation of an integrated economic system for the Middle East.

The Russian diplomacy views the adoption of such a code of behavior as a path towards the next stage. This next stage would include the holding of bilateral and multilateral consultations with the aim of working out a general and comprehensive model of Middle Eastern security for the 21st century. The final step would be the entrenchment thereof in a politically and legally binding document—a charter or treaty for Middle Eastern security.

Examining these proposals by the Foreign Minister at a later date, A Baklanov of the Russian Foreign Ministry suggested the possibility of including other questions. Notably, he suggested a conception of defense sufficiency in conformity with the realities of the region, the achievement of agreements on weapons ceilings, and a register of the parties' concrete commitments in the context of the creation of a zone free from WMD. The notion of code of behavior echoes the ideas contained in other conceptions of regional security for the Middle East. Thus a document drafted by the SIPRI Middle East Expert Group speaks of the necessity to elaborate "a set of guiding principles for a regional security regime" (Jones 1998). A great amount of work in that direction was done in the framework of the Arms Control and Regional Security Working Group of the multilateral talks of the Middle East peace process. Such principles are also contained in quite a few other fundamental international documents, starting with the UN Charter. Summarizing them, the SIPRI document mentions the following guiding principles:

- Equal rights for all peoples and recognition of their right to self-determination;
- Non-interference in the internal affairs of others and respect for the sovereign equality of states;

- Settlement of disputes by peaceful means, including the renunciation of the use of threat or threat of use of force to settle disputes;
- Recognition of the right to legitimate means of self-defense within an overall commitment to ensure that military establishments are kept to the lowest level consistent with purely self-defense needs; and
- Commitment to the principle that weapons of mass destruction should be abolished.

As far as the Russian politicians are concerned, the desire to rely on the mechanisms of bilateral and multilateral consultations in the framework of preparatory measures to create a security system is clear. This desire was reflected in the measures taken by the new Russian leadership at the beginning of 2000 to launch the mechanisms of multinational negotiations. The Middle Eastern format of collective security obviously differs from the Gulf format. However, an approach towards the security of the Gulf may be based either on a conception of an autonomous system or a conception that incorporates the Gulf into the Middle Eastern system. From this perspective, the proposals worked out by Russian diplomacy incorporates the Gulf states either through their entry into the Middle Eastern system, or through the extension to the Gulf of the same measures and mechanisms that have been proposed for the larger system.

In this connection, one may still address another concrete idea lodged in the above-mentioned program, namely that of "intermediate" forms of leading the region towards the formation of a collective security system. Here a "useful role", writes Baklanov, "might be played by the holding, possibly under UN aegis, of an international forum on questions of security, confidence-building measures, and lowering the level of military confrontation. A specific feature of such a forum might be the participation in its work of both governmental and non-governmental organizations, as well as the leading experts in the field of regional security. An open, informal character of such a gathering might facilitate the involvement of representatives of such states which until recently had a negative or sceptical view of the idea of forming mechanisms of regional security for building stability and peace in the region. The convocation of the forum could also make it possible to identify and apply the ideas and proposals of specialists from various countries, which might help in finding an optimum working model."

In conclusion, it must be said that the implementation of confidence-building measures, the repudiation of violence as a means to resolve disputed issues, and commitment to methods of peaceful dialogue and cooperation are priority steps in the creation of a comprehensive collective security regime in the subregion. Russia could play a part in designing and implementing these measures, providing international security guarantees to the states of the region, and the subsequent monitoring and international control over the observance of the understanding reached. As one of the permanent members of the UN Security Council, Russia carries a special responsibility for the maintenance of international peace and stability.

Note

1. Baklanov's view on CBMs in the Middle East can be found in articles in 1998 and 1999 issues of *Mezhdunarodnaya Zhisn*. All the quotations in this text from Baklanov are drawn from these issues.

CHAPTER 8

American Perspectives on Gulf Security

Stephen Zunes

In the decade since the Gulf War, the United States—with the support of Great Britain—has thrown its immense military, diplomatic, and economic weight behind the monarchies of the Persian Gulf. Though they make up less than 10 percent of the Arab world's total population, they control most of its wealth and some of the most strategically important territory in the globe. Prior to the war, it was difficult for the United States or Great Britain to engage in military exercises or even arrange a port call without asking for permission months in advance. This is not the case anymore. While American and British military personnel wear civilian clothes so as not to offend the local population, they are difficult to miss in the hotels, marketplaces, and restaurants of the Gulf states. The Anglo-American military role is based on a desire to fill in a perceived strategic vacuum, as a staging ground for combat training, and to strengthen military ties with the Arab states. Underlying this is the assumption of both the United States and Great Britain that these countries have an obligation to meet the security needs of the six allied Arab monarchies, which make up the Gulf Cooperation Council (GCC). Underlying this presence is the perceived threat to the Gulf posed by Iraq and Iran, the two largest countries in the region.

This post-Gulf War system led by the United States has given the GCC states an unprecedented role in Middle East security and diplomacy, surpassing the League of Arab States as the leading inter-Arab organization and effectively putting any pretense of pan-Arabism to rest. This has heralded a long-sought triumph for US policymakers who wanted to divide the oil-rich monarchies and their allies from the potentially radical nationalists of the poorer Arab countries. To some, this is a realistic and pragmatic recognition of the end of the Cold War realities resulting in the rise of a single superpower and the primary threat of Iraq and Iran. To others, particularly in the Middle East, it is a return to the divide-and-rule tactics of Western imperialism.

Given the great scope and expense of the Anglo-American military presence in the region, it is surprising that the underlying assumptions of the ongoing role of these outside powers has been subjected to so little debate. This chapter examines the question as to whether such a military role by the United States and Great Britain actually enhances regional security. Both Great Britain and the United States have long seen the Gulf region as the great strategic prize of the 20th century. American oil interests, particularly in Saudi Arabia, increased US involvement in the region, as did the close US relationship with the Shah of Iran after the CIA restored him to the throne in 1953, supplanting Great Britain as the primary outside power in that country. Still, Gulf security was primarily seen as a British responsibility until Prime Minister Harold Wilson announced in 1969 that Britain would withdraw most of its security commitments from areas east of the Suez. The United States felt a need to fill in what was seen as a potentially dangerous power vacuum. However, in the midst of strong anti-interventionist sentiment among the American public at the height of the Vietnam War, a more overt military presence was not politically feasible. The Nixon Administration had had some success in curbing anti-war protests through its "Vietnamization" program, leading to an increased fighting role by South Vietnamese conscripts and an escalated air war with reduced American troop strength, fewer American casualties, and smaller draft rolls. In 1971, President Richard Nixon announced the establishment of what became known as the Nixon Doctrine. Also known as the Guam Doctrine (where the policy was announced) or "surrogate strategy", this approach instituted Vietnamization on a global level, with the US arming, training, and providing logistical support for the armed forces of an allied regime, which would do the actual fighting. The Gulf became the first testing ground for such a policy, with Iran's Shah, who owed his throne to the United States, with lots of petrodollars to purchase weapons, and a sense of megalomania to feed, playing the willing surrogate. Throughout the 1970s, the United States sold over $20 billion in advanced weaponry to the Shah (with an additional $20 billion on order), sending thousands of US advisors to turn the Iranian armed forces into a sophisticated fighting force capable of counter-insurgency operations. This policy was successfully implemented when

Iranian troops—with American and British support—intervened in support of the Sultan of Oman against a leftist rebellion in the Dhofar province in the mid-1970s. This policy came crashing down in 1979, however, with Iran's Islamic revolution, which brought a stridently anti-Western regime to power.

At this point, the Carter Doctrine came into being. The United States would no longer rely on potentially unstable allies but intervene directly through the Rapid Deployment Force, later incorporated into the Central Command. An agreement was reached with the Saudi government whereby, in exchange for the sale of an integrated package of highly sophisticated weaponry, the Saudis would build and pay for an elaborate system of command, naval and air facilities large enough to "sustain US forces in intensive regional combat". For example, the 1981 AWACS sale was to be the linchpin of an elaborate communications system comparable to that of NATO. According to a *Washington Post* report at that time (then denied by the Pentagon), this sale was part of a "grand defense strategy for the Middle East oil fields" that included "an ambitious plan to build surrogate bases in Saudi Arabia, equipped and waiting for American forces to use" (Armstrong 1981).

Such intervention would come quickly and with overwhelming force to make the casualty ratio favorable and the length of fighting short (preferably within the sixty days before the War Powers Act would come into effect) enough so that public opposition would not have time to mobilize in a disruptive manner. This, in effect, was what happened during the Gulf War against Iraq, though the exact scenario in which US forces would be deployed could not be predicted at the time.

During the Iran-Iraq War in the 1980s, the US cynically armed and supported both sides in an attempt to insure neither gained dominance. When the Clinton administration came to office in 1993, the policy was shifting to that of "dual containment", seeking to isolate both countries, labeling these nations as "rogue states" and seeing them as potentially dangerous and destabilizing. As defined by US national security managers, rogue states are those that possess substantial military capability, seek the acquisition of weapons of mass destruction, and violate what are seen as international "norms". According to former national security advisor Anthony Lake, "our policy must face the reality of recalcitrant and outlaw states that not only choose to remain outside the family [of nations] but also assault its basic values … [and] exhibit a chronic inability to engage constructively with the outside world." Lake argues further that just as the US took the lead in "containing" the Soviet Union, so it must now also bear the "special responsibility" to "neutralize" and "contain" these "outlaw states" (Klare 1994, 625).

It is noteworthy that a number of US allies in the region—including Israel, America's chief partner in the region and the world's largest recipient of US economic and military support—would also fit this definition by some accounts. Yet rogue states have a clear function in US foreign policy independent of any objective criteria.

While US and British concerns about Iran and Iraq's human rights record and violations of international norms are not without merit, neither country is unique in the region in such transgressions. What makes Iran and Iraq so important to the United States and Britain is that they are the only two countries in the region that combine a large population, adequate water resources, and oil wealth to be major independent players. As such they have a reasonable chance to challenge Anglo-American hegemony in the region. Indeed, prior to the current regimes being perceived as so antithetical to American and British interests, these countries engaged in large-scale military procurement and other practices to become major strategic players. What makes these countries "rogue states" in the eyes of American and British policymakers is their failure to accept the post-Cold War order, which rests upon US global leadership with Great Britain as the leading junior partner. The difficulty in justifying this essentially imperial world order in an era of liberal internationalism, however, forces British and American policymakers to defend their hostility towards these countries in the name of collective security and other liberal ideals. The radical nature of these regimes and their history of aggression and subversion against their neighbors make such rationalizations for ongoing Western hostility easier. However, a critical analysis of Anglo-American policy in the Gulf reveals that concerns over the security of allied Gulf monarchies from potential hostile actions by either Iran or Iraq are greatly exaggerated. The very assumption that both Iran and Iraq pose serious threats to the security of GCC states, and thus the free flow of oil, needs to be questioned. For example, both countries, which are also dependent on the sale of oil for their own prosperity, would seem to have little incentive to do so. Furthermore, the strategic balance in the past decade has swung decisively in favor of the GCC and the West, placing the pro-Western monarchies in a more comfortable strategic position than thought imaginable even a little more than a decade ago. Yet, US strategy continues to be based on a notion that Iran and Iraq pose an immediate threat to their security.

Virtually all of the Arabs of the Gulf and their leaders felt threatened after Iraq's seizure of Kuwait and therefore supported the US-led war against Iraq. At the same time, there is an enormous amount of cynicism regarding US motives. They cannot shake the sense that the war was not fought on the grounds of international law, self-determination, and human rights as the Bush administration claimed, but simply to protect US access to oil and for the US to gain a strategic toehold in the region. It is apparent that a continued US presence is welcomed only as long as there is felt need for a foreign military presence for protection. Many Gulf Arabs suspect that the United States may find a need to exaggerate the threat from Iran and Iraq in order to justify its ongoing military presence and encouragement of arms sales.

The tendency to exaggerate the security threat is used repeatedly by US and British officials to justify the ongoing presence of foreign troops and continued arms purchases. For example, the US successfully lobbied the Saudis to allow US troops onto Saudi Arabian soil in August 1990 by telling them that they had evidence that Iraqi occupation troops were preparing an assault into northeastern Saudi Arabia. It has since been revealed that satellite footage at the time indicated no such aggressive designs; indeed, Iraqi forces were digging into defensive positions just south of Kuwait City.[1] According to former crown prince Hassan of Jordan, this Saudi decision scuttled a tentative agreement he had made with Saddam Hussein to withdraw from Kuwait (author interview with HRH Hassan, Royal Palace, Amman, Jordan, Jan. 8, 1991).

It is significant that the US-led military offensive against Iraq in 1991 went well beyond what was necessary to rid Iraqi occupation forces from Kuwait. Indeed, the US appeared to want war, rejecting a series of peace overtures and announcing its refusal to lift sanctions even if Iraq withdrew from Kuwait, thereby giving the Iraqis little incentive to comply with UN Security Council resolutions demanding their withdrawal. The US concern was that, without a war, Saddam Hussein's regime would remain with its military assets intact, free to sell its oil, popular among some segments of the Arab world's population and able to threaten its neighbors. As a result, the US—with the support of Britain and some other Western countries—was determined to inflict a devastating blow to the country's infrastructure with the heaviest bombing in world history. Even the regime's most strident critics in the Gulf were offended at the level of overkill, particularly what was inflicted upon the civilian population, unwilling conscripts, and non-military infrastructure. Indeed, in the weeks before the launch of the bombing of Iraq on January 16, talk in Washington of a "nightmare scenario" was in reference to an Iraqi withdrawal without war.[2]

Iraq's Potential Threat to Gulf Security

Great Britain established control over Iraq following the fall of the Ottoman Empire more than eighty years ago, essentially creating the country from parts of various Ottoman provinces. A nationalist coup in 1958 overthrew the pro-British monarchy, limiting both the British and American influence in the country. Recognizing its importance in the regional balance of power, Great Britain and the United States maintained a largely cooperative relationship, much to the chagrin of human rights advocates in their respective countries. Upon Iraq's invasion of Kuwait in 1990, however, the United States and Great Britain have been at the forefront of international hostility toward Saddam Hussein's regime.

British and American warplanes have been bombing Iraq on average every three days since late 1998. None of the Gulf states that the US and Britain claim to be protecting have supported the bombing campaign. More significantly from a humanitarian point of view, the sanctions regime pushed by the United States and Britain has resulted in enormous human suffering for the civilian population in Iraq. According to UNICEF, hundreds of thousands of preventable deaths—primarily of children—have resulted from the sanctions due to the difficulty in importing medicines, foodstuffs, and spare parts necessary to rebuild the country's infrastructure (such as water treatment plants) destroyed during the Gulf War. While the GCC states support maintaining a strict arms embargo, sanctions that primarily harm the civilian population are highly controversial. The GCC states observe how the sanctions actually strengthen Saddam Hussein's regime by making the population more dependent on the government for its survival, by deflecting anger from the government to the West, and through the destruction of the middle class—traditionally the group most likely to press for change—which has immigrated or been reduced to penury. Indeed, the fear of the regime's brutality, the secret services which penetrate virtually every aspect of the armed services, and the well-paid Republican Guard and corps commanders in the army probably makes any British and American hopes of a successful coup attempt in the foreseeable future misplaced.

The American and British obsession with Iraq's potential threat to the region during the past decade is rather ironic, given that Iraq's military, including its potential and existing weapons of mass destruction, was significantly stronger in the late 1980s. Iraqi dictator Saddam Hussein then had his full complement of medium-range missiles, a functioning air force and a massive stockpile of chemical and biological weaponry and material. Yet successive US and British governments dismissed any potential strategic threat to the point of coddling Saddam's regime with overt economic subsidies and covert military support. Since then, the 1991 Gulf War and the subsequent inspection regimes have destroyed virtually any aggressive military potential by Iraq. UNSCOM has reported destroying 38,000 chemical weapons, 480,000 liters of live chemical-weapons agents, 48 missiles, six missile launchers, 30 missile warheads modified to carry chemical or biological agents and hundreds of related equipment with the capability to produce chemical weapons. In late 1997, UNSCOM director Richard Butler reported that they had made "significant progress" in tracking Iraq's chemical weapons program and that 817 of the 819 Soviet-supplied long-range missiles had been accounted for. There were also believed to be a couple of dozen Iraqi-made ballistic missiles, but these were of questionable caliber.[3]

Iraq's armed forces are barely one-third their pre-war strength. Even though they have not been required to reduce their conventional forces, the destruction of their weapons and their economic difficulties have led to a substantial reduction in men under arms. The Navy is virtually nonexistent, and the air force is just a fraction of what it was before the war. Military spending by Iraq is barely one-tenth of its levels in the 1980s (Cordesman 1999, 27). Why then, beginning in early 1998, when Iraq had only a tiny percentage of its once-formidable military capability, was the United States suddenly portraying Iraq as an intolerable threat? It is no surprise, under these circumstances, that so many Americans, rightly or wrongly, suspected President Clinton of manufacturing the crisis to distract the American public from the sex scandal surrounding his office.

Neither the British nor American governments has ever publicly presented any credible evidence that Iraq currently has biological weapons or other weapons of mass destruction, though in the past Iraq has certainly produced both chemical and biological agents and may continue to do so, albeit at a greatly reduced capacity. UNSCOM inspections have revealed evidence of the production of large amounts of biological agents, including anthrax, and have charged that Iraq had vastly understated the amount of biological warfare agents they had manufactured. In response, UNSCOM set up sophisticated monitoring devices to detect chemical or biological weapons, though these were dismantled by the Iraqis in response to the four-day Anglo-American bombing campaign in 1998.

More important, there are serious questions as to whether the alleged biological agents could be successfully dispersed in a manner that could harm troops or the civilian population, given the rather complicated technology required. For example, a vial of biological weapons on the tip of a missile would almost certainly be destroyed on impact or dispersed harmlessly. Frightening scenarios regarding mass fatalities from a small amount of anthrax assumes that the Iraqis have successfully cultivated the rare strain lethal to human beings (an anthrax bacillus is usually fatal to animals but rarely to humans), and have developed the highly sophisticated means of distributing them by missile or aircraft. To become a lethal weapon, highly concentrated amounts of the spores must be inhaled and then left untreated by antibiotics. Similarly, the winds would have to be just right, no rain would fall, the spray nozzles would be not clogged, the population not vaccinated, and everyone would have to stay around the area targeted.

It is also hard to imagine that an Iraqi aircraft, presumably some kind of drone, would somehow be able to penetrate the air space of neighboring countries, much less far-off Israel, without being shot down. Most of Iraq's neighbors have sophisticated anti-aircraft capability. Similarly, as mentioned above, there is no evidence that Iraq's Scud missiles and launchers survived the Gulf War. Indeed, UNSCOM reported in 1992 that Iraq had no launchers for their missiles or even any engines. Israeli military analyst Meir Stieglitz, writing in the Israeli newspaper *Yediot Ahronot*, noted, "there is no such thing as a long-range Iraqi missile with an effective biological warhead. No one has found an Iraqi biological warhead. The chances of Iraq having succeeded in developing operative warheads without tests are zero."[4]

In accusing either an individual or a nation of a crime, or even of the potential for committing a crime, the accuser should be willing to make a plausible case about what would motivate the criminal. Neither the British nor American governments have been able to make a plausible case about what Iraq would gain by attacking its neighbors with biological weapons and what risks it would take in doing so. Indeed, the Israeli government has been quite explicit that it would be willing to use nuclear weapons against

Iraq in retaliation. The fact remains that Saddam has far more to gain by creating an ongoing crisis with the United States and Great Britain and thereby increasing his popularity with the Arab masses than engaging in a suicidal attack with biological weapons against another country. Despite a great deal of evidence documenting Iraq's intention to produce anthrax bacillus, there has been no plausible scenario as to how or why the Iraqis would deliver these to other countries. Indeed, during the Gulf War, Saddam still had a large arsenal of chemical and biological weapons as well as scores of ground-to-ground missiles and aircraft. In the course of that conflict, with his nation being attacked in the heaviest bombing raids in history by the largest multinational armed force ever assembled, a situation where a leader would be most tempted to use such weaponry, he did not do so. Neither the United States nor Great Britain has been able to make a convincing case as to why Saddam would suddenly be motivated to make such an attack now, when not even provoked. The GCC states do not feel particularly concerned.

This raises another question regarding who would be the potential victims of such an Iraqi biological weapons attack. Even if we were to assume that Iraq had the motivation and capability to launch such an attack by air, these weapons would certainly be no threat to the United States or Great Britain. In addition, virtually none of Iraq's neighbors within range of Iraqi missiles believe that the ongoing air strikes and punitive sanctions against the civilian population are the most appropriate response. The only real exception is Israel, which has a nuclear deterrent against such potential attacks as well as substantial conventional weapons capability with which to launch massive pre-emptive strikes against Iraq if it deemed necessary.

A far more likely scenario for an Iraqi distribution of such biological agents would be through terrorists smuggling them clandestinely into targeted countries. Such a possibility requires aggressive counterintelligence efforts by the United States, Great Britain and other potentially targeted nations, but they are not the sort of contingency that sanctions and bombings would prevent. Indeed, such policies would more likely encourage rogue elements of Iraqi intelligence or an allied terrorist group to engage in such an attack as an act of revenge for the heavy Arab civilian casualties.

Though US and British air strikes have continued since late 1998 and more sporadic bombing raids have taken place prior to that, none of the GCC states has ever requested such military action on its behalf. Indeed, during Operation Desert Fox in December 1998 and the September 1996 raids following Iraqi incursion into Kurdish areas, the Saudis would not even allow US air force jets to leave their territory to take part in the raids. This forced the US to rely on Navy jets based on aircraft carriers.

Regarding conventional forces, Iraq not only had much of its equipment destroyed, but has never had an effective system of support, sustainability or supplies for its military outside of its now blocked dependence on foreign imports. Though there are certainly international demands to liberalize the current sanctions regime on humanitarian grounds, there are no serious calls for ending the military embargo. As a result, there is little reason to believe that Iraq would pose a credible threat to its neighbors in the foreseeable future. Most of the Gulf states which the US and Great Britain claim to be protecting are aware of this and therefore question why continued sanctions against the civilian population and the ongoing low-level bombing campaign continues.

As a result of US policies, the Gulf War coalition built by the Bush administration is in tatters. The US and British credibility has been further compromised in the international community in general and in the Arab world in particular. And Saddam Hussein's standing in Iraq and throughout the region has been enhanced. Meanwhile, problems that threaten the stability of the region far more than the Iraqi dictator—the breakdown in the Israeli-Palestinian peace process, uneven economic development, and the militarization of the region—continue to grow, in part due to US and British policies.

Thus far, the United States has given Iraq little motivation to cooperate within its international obligations. For example, Madeleine Albright declared in March 1997 that the United States would veto any UN Security Council efforts to lift sanctions, even if Iraq finally came into full compliance with UN Security Council resolutions.[5] Only if Saddam Hussein no longer ruled Iraq would the United States allow for the sanctions regime to end. President Clinton reiterated this position later. This not only goes far beyond the original UN mandate, it gives the Iraqi government no incentive to cooperate. Saddam might be willing to make further compromises on issues of weapons production and inspector access if that would result in lifting the sanctions. This would not be the case if sanctions would remain intact anyway. Furthermore, no one expects that Saddam would give up power voluntarily. Indeed, Saddam's harassment of UN inspectors is based largely on the realization that he has nothing to lose as long as the United States blocks the lifting of sanctions even if he complies fully.

For sanctions to work, one needs a carrot as well as a stick, something which the United States until recently has failed to recognize. What the United States, in consultation with other members of the Security Council, needs to do is to offer specific promises for lifting non-military sanctions. This should be done in return for compliance with inspections and other outstanding issues of UN Security Council Resolution 687. The US also has to be specific as to what positive responses could be expected for what specific improvements in behavior.

Furthermore, the United States must pledge to enforce other outstanding UN Security Council resolutions, and not simply single out Iraq (and other hostile Arab states like Sudan). As long as the United States allows allied regimes like Turkey, Morocco, and Israel to flout UN Security Council resolutions, any sanctimonious calls for strict compliance by the Iraqi government will simply be dismissed as hypocritical and mean-spirited, whatever the merit of the actual complaints. This is particularly important since recent Iraqi violations have been largely of a technical nature. They also fall under a resolution unprecedented in its level of interference in areas traditionally considered a country's sovereign rights. The aforementioned cases of ongoing military occupations of neighboring countries are, in contrast, direct contravention of the UN Charter.

In a similar vein, the United States must support a more comprehensive arms-control regime for the region. This would mean the establishment of the Middle East as a zone where all weapons of mass destruction are banned. This would necessarily force the United States to end its practice of bringing nuclear weapons into the region on its planes and ships as well as force Israel to dismantle its sizable nuclear arsenal. A more holistic program of non-proliferation might also include, for example, a five-year program where not just Iraqi missiles, but Syrian, Israeli, and other missiles would also be phased out. As with its highly selective insistence on the enforcement of UN Security Council resolutions, the double standards in US policy make even the most legitimate concerns about Iraqi weapons development virtually impossible to pursue successfully. As described above, UN Security Council Resolution 687, which was the basis of American complaints against Iraq, explicitly states that the disarmament of Iraq should be part of a longer-term program for the abolition of weapons of mass destruction throughout the region. Iran, Iraq, and all six GCC states are on record supporting a comprehensive ban of weapons of mass destruction. The US refusal to support such a regime raises serious questions regarding the US commitment to regional peace and security.

Iran's Potential Threat to Gulf Security

Iran—with its strategic location, 60 million inhabitants, and control of as much as 15 percent of the world's oil reserves—continues to be a major concern to those who formulate American and British foreign policy. The British played a major role in what was then known as Persia for the latter half of the 19th century and early-20th century. The US government has had contacts in Iran since early in the century, and major US involvement dates back to 1953 when the CIA organized the overthrow of the country's constitutional government. Over the next 25 years, the US armed and trained the military and secret police of Shah Mohammad Reza Pahlavi, one of the most brutal dictators of his era. Following his overthrow, radical students, backed by the government, seized more than fifty American hostages at the US embassy in late 1979 and held them for 444 days, creating a major crisis in US-Iranian relations that has yet to heal. Ironically, US strategic cooperation with Iran was highest in the years that followed the hostage crisis, during the time when the revolutionary government reached its most radical and repressive stage. From 1981 to 1986, the US shipped arms clandestinely to the country. By helping to shore up the Iranian military, these shipments were part of the US policy to promote the mutual destruction of Iran and Iraq. Parts of the secret arms transfers were also channeled to anti-Soviet Afghan Mujahedin. The US also passed on names of Iranian leftists to government authorities, resulting in the deaths of hundreds of dissidents.

Despite this limited cooperation, the US generally sided with Iraq during the eight-year war that began in 1980 when Saddam Hussein's forces invaded western and southern Iran. While the US tolerated widespread attacks by Iraq against Iranian oil tankers during the war, the US Navy intervened to protect Iraqi and Kuwaiti oil shipments from Iranian retaliation. This led to a series of armed engagements between the US and Iran. Following one such encounter in 1988, a US missile shot down an Iranian airliner on a regularly scheduled flight over international waters, killing 280 people.

Since May 1995, the US has used its economic clout to isolate Iran, prohibiting all trade, trade financing, loans, and financial services to

Iran. In August 1996, President Clinton signed a law that imposes a secondary boycott on foreign countries investing more than $40 million in Iran's oil and natural gas industry. This law provides for an array of sanctions, including banning the sale of products of culpable firms in the United States. In addition, Congress has authorized $18 million for the budget of US intelligence agencies to be spent on covert actions to undermine the government of Iran, once again making covert action a major facet of US policy toward Iran. Despite subsequent election victories by moderates, various sanctions and other restrictions by the United States are still stricter now than during even the darkest days of the mid-1980s. In January 2002, in his State of the Union speech, President George W. Bush claimed that the increasingly pluralistic Iran was part of an "axis of evil" along with the totalitarian regimes in Iran and North Korea.[6]

Great Britain and most European countries question ongoing US hostility towards Iran, particularly in light of the election of a more moderate president and parliament in recent years, citing the fact that efforts to isolate and overthrow the Iranian government are not based on legal grounds. The US has avoided urging the UN to support its sanctions, because Washington knows there is no legal basis for such actions and it would thus fail to get any support. Unlike international sanctions against the former apartheid government of South Africa or the current military junta in Burma, sanctions against Iran are not predicated on significant legal or moral imperatives. As with similar extraterritorial efforts regarding Cuba, US attempts to pressure other nations to get tough with Iran have alienated even America's strongest allies, who consider such efforts to be in violation of World Trade Organization principles. Similarly, US efforts to subvert the Iranian government are contrary to international legal conventions that recognize sovereign rights and principles of non-intervention. They also directly counter the Algiers Declaration of 1981, under which the US unequivocally pledged not to intervene politically or militarily in the internal affairs of Iran. In addition, the US is obligated under the Nuclear Nonproliferation Treaty to allow signatory states in good standing (like Iran) to have access to peaceful nuclear technology, which the United States has gone to great lengths to try to limit.

Throughout the Cold War, the US sought to place the blame for violence and internal unrest in the Middle East (and in the Third World in general) on the Soviet Union rather than on the failures of its own allies to govern fairly. This same pattern soon emerged regarding Iran, with the US blaming the Islamic Republic of Iran for unrest in several Middle Eastern countries. The US also sought to link Iran with acts of terrorism throughout the region and beyond, both through its own agents and through local groups, and accused Iran of launching military threats and acts of subversion against Arab Gulf monarchies. Even Arab states suspicious of Iran's intentions, however, were concerned about the American tendency to define "Iranian-backed terrorist groups" so broadly as to include the Lebanese guerrillas fighting Israeli occupation forces in their own country.

The Clinton administration was unable to show any evidence to suggest an upsurge in Iranian-backed terrorism to justify its increased efforts at isolating Iran early in 1994. Although Iran has certainly trained, funneled arms, and offered financial support to extremist Islamic groups and to the repressive government in Sudan, US charges of direct Iranian responsibility for specific terrorist acts against Israeli and American targets remain highly dubious. The United States exerted enormous pressure against the Saudi government to implicate Iran in the Khobar Tower bombing, even when Saudi investigators found no such link. Indeed, Iranian support for such groups had declined significantly in the preceding years. Iran's terrorism beyond its borders has always been primarily directed at exiled dissidents, not against the US or Israel.

Similarly, Iran's potential as a nuclear power has been greatly exaggerated, with the Clinton administration even overruling the more modest conclusions of its own agencies. The foreign diplomatic community in Tehran and the president of the International Atomic Energy Agency appear to agree that Iran's motivations in building a nuclear reactor are entirely peaceful. Indeed, American companies—with the blessings of the US government—helped initiate Iran's nuclear program in the 1970s.

Iran's immediate post-revolutionary zeal to export its ideology was short-lived as internal problems and outside threats deflected the attention of its leadership. In addition, Iranians are culturally and religiously very different from the Sunni Arabs who dominate the Gulf region and much of Middle East, particularly regarding the hierarchical structure of Shi'ism, which limits the revolution's appeal as a model for other Middle Eastern states.

There is little evidence to suggest aggressive Iranian designs in the Gulf either. Iran has not threatened—nor does it have any reason for provoking—a confrontation over sea-lanes, and it is at least as dependent as its neighbors on unrestricted navigation. Iran would be hurting itself by closing the Straits of Hormuz, since the lack of pipelines for its southern oil fields makes it far more dependent on tanker shipping. Iran has been dramatically reducing its military spending due to financial problems. Additionally, despite increased Iranian procurement of sophisticated missiles, Arab Gulf States have similar missile capabilities, serving along with the US Navy as an effective deterrent force. The US and Britain have cited Iran's occupation of three islands claimed by the United Arab Emirates as evidence of Iranian aggressive designs in the Gulf, yet Iran—then under the rule of the Mohammad Reza Shah—seized the islands in 1971 with American and British encouragement.

Iran's military procurement relative to the GCC states is far less than it was during the 1970s, when the United States and Great Britain were actually promoting arms sales to Iran. In addition, Iranian military spending is barely one-fifth of what it was during the 1980s. Much of Iran's naval capability was destroyed by the United States in the tanker war. Iran lost a large amount of its ground weaponry during Iraq's 1988 offensive; indeed, as much as half of Iran's inventory of major land-force weapons was destroyed in the course of the war (Cordesman 1999, 82). While Iran's defensive capabilities have improved somewhat, there is little to suggest that they pose any kind of realistic offensive threat to the Gulf. Indeed, their number of tanks and planes is substantially less than in the 1970s.

Motivations Behind US Policy

Since the United States has taken the lead in Anglo-American policy in the Gulf, it is useful to examine the motivations behind such policies.

There are a number of domestic political forces in the United States pushing US policy in this direction. One comes from mainstream-to-conservative Zionist groups and their supporters, a long powerful lobbying force in the United States, which have used these supposed threats against Israel as the chief rationale for continuing large-scale military and economic aid to the Israeli government. There are several problems in this rationalization, however. First of all, Israel is separated from Iraq and Iran by distances of hundreds of kilometers and the land in between consists of countries that are formally at peace with Israel and openly hostile to these regimes. The Israeli air force is more than capable of protecting Israel's border against any combination of these opponents. Surface-to-surface missiles have been cited as a possible threat, yet adequate missile defense systems would cost only a fraction of the more than $4 billion in economic and military aid sent annually to Israel from the United

States. Furthermore, there are serious questions as to whether—despite the frequently bellicose rhetoric these countries have directed towards Israel—they really have such hostile intentions even if they were capable. Saddam Hussein, whose war-making capability was largely destroyed in the Gulf War, will likely not be a threat to anyone (besides his own people) for a long time to come. Finally, it is highly unlikely that Israel would have armed the Ayatollah Khomeini's government throughout the 1980s if the Islamic Republic of Iran was actually considered such a threat. Still, these rogue states are useful excuses to continue taxpayer subsidies for the Israeli government and the US military contractors that send the Israelis their wares. With Egypt, Jordan, and the PLO formally at peace with Israel, Syria reducing its military and absent of a great-power sponsor, Lebanon as weak as ever, and with the Gulf states focused on Iraq and Iran, Israel is in a far stronger position militarily than it has ever been. Similarly, with the demise of the Soviet Union, Israel is no longer of use as a Cold War asset. As a result, having Israel portrayed as both a potential victim of and potential bulwark against Iraq and Iran allows for ongoing high levels of US aid to Israel. Of course most of this aid comes back to the United States to the coffers of American military contractors and American banks as interest on previous military loans.

Another reason for the current US obsession with Iraq and Iran is broader domestic political considerations. It is a time-honored tradition for political leaders to maintain their popularity at home by manipulating public opinion to believe that there is some kind of external threat from which the public needs protection. Indeed, critics from across the political spectrum cited this as a possible motivation for President Clinton ordering a series of air strikes against Iraq just two months prior to his re-election in 1996 and again on the eve of his impeachment in 1998. With the United States having among the most secure borders in the world and no longer faced with a superpower rival, Iraq and Iran are among the few international scapegoats available against which a politician can build a reputation for toughness. Unlike US conflicts with Nicaragua or even Vietnam, there is virtually no domestic support for the other side. Peace groups and left-wing movements in the United States are often as critical of the Iranian and Iraqi regimes as is the US government, despite frequently taking issue with specific policies towards these countries. In addition, it has traditionally been less damaging politically for a policymaker to take what is perceived to be a hard line towards an unpopular government overseas than to take a line that is perceived as too soft. As a result, targeting these governments is not unpopular with the public or detrimental to one's political ambitions.

The most important function of Iraq and Iran, however, is the role in maintaining public support for high levels of military spending. With the end of the Cold War threatening to result in a dramatic reduction in military spending, the Bush administration embarked on a "regional strategy" based on the prospect of periodic clashes with emerging Third World powers. The result was the adoption of a military posture, essentially confirmed by the Clinton administration in their 1993 review, which argued that the United States must maintain enough force to fight two simultaneous major regional wars on the scale of the 1991 war against Iraq. This was to be in response to surprise attacks from rogue states with no allied forces to support the American side. To fight such a war, it is argued, requires standing combat personnel totaling 1.4 million and the air, naval, and land equipment to support them. While most independent observers see such a scenario as extremely unlikely if not completely ludicrous, it has been adopted as the basis for maintaining these high levels of military spending for more than a decade. Pentagon planners who had a vested interest in maintaining a large military establishment developed the scenarios under the Bush and Clinton administrations. It is these rogue states of the Middle East, along with North Korea, for which the United States justifies a military budget of more than $300 billion. This is a figure higher—even counting for inflation—than the level of military spending for most of the Cold War, including the final military budgets of such Republican presidents as Dwight Eisenhower, Richard Nixon, and Gerald Ford. Both the US administration and Congress pledge the figure will grow dramatically in the coming years.

The traditional arguments against close military cooperation among the Gulf states have little merit. Barring a big drop in oil prices or petty squabbling between rulers, the Gulf countries are quite stable politically. The economic prosperity and the majlis system of direct petitioning to royalty has essentially co-opted most of the population. Human rights violations against citizens are relatively minor compared to Iraq, Syria, or the Israeli-occupied territories, though abuse of foreign nationals continues. All of the Gulf states appear ready to recognize Israel once Palestinian rights are also recognized, so there is little risk that US arms would be used against the Jewish state.

But allied Middle East governments are frequently dismayed by American double standards on such issues as nuclear proliferation and terrorism as well as the use of such punitive actions against the so-called rogue states. In addition, such policies feed popular anti-Americanism in the region. Not only do such policies drain the US budget and take money away from its neediest citizens in order to feed the military establishment, it focuses attention away from more pressing foreign policy concerns. These concerns include the deterioration of the global environment, the economic disintegration of Mexico, right-wing nationalism in Russia, expanding trade, growing international economic inequality, and other issues.

There are domestic critics within the United States and Great Britain over their policies in the Gulf. Perhaps more than any recent foreign policy issue—with the exception of those challenged by mass popular movements, such as the Vietnam War—elite opinion is sharply divided. In the academic community as well as among leading former foreign policymakers, there has been widespread criticism of the dual containment policy as ineffective. Particular criticism has been expressed regarding US policy towards Iran, but even prestigious establishment journals like *Foreign Affairs* have stated the cynical but probably not inaccurate observation that "if Saddam Hussein did not exist, we would have to invent him" (cited in Al-Shayeji 1997). This is not surprising to the Gulf Arabs, who also see the policy as not working. What it does is to re-enforce the sense that the US policy is not actually geared towards its stated aims but to justify a continuation of a domineering US role in the region for the exclusive promotion of American interests. This concern is particularly evident among Islamist and nationalist circles, particularly among intellectuals. They see the growing dependency on the United States for security as a means by which the US can expand its economic and cultural hegemony and push the Gulf states into an alliance with Israel.

Another problem is that no Gulf state agrees with the US perception that Iran and Iraq are equal threats. The UAE and Qatar see Iraq as a potential ally in their border disputes, whereas states such as Kuwait see Iran as a potential ally against Iraq. Oman, meanwhile, has pursued a more traditional balance of power approach towards the two powers.

It is becoming increasingly apparent that the most serious offenses by Iran and Iraq in the eyes of US policymakers are not in the area of human rights, terrorism, nuclear ambitions, subversion, or conquest, but in daring to challenge American hegemony in the Middle East. It is these regimes that are preventing the United States from exercising its political dominance over this crucial region. The overthrow or control of these regimes, the American policymakers hope, will create the kind of environment which would give the US unprecedented leverage in shaping the future direction of the Middle East.

In diplomacy, as in military engagement, however, it is important to be engaged with the enemy. Not only has the United States refused to engage in serious dialogue with Iran and Iraq, it has actively discouraged its Gulf allies from engaging in such dialogue as well. Stability requires the integration of all major parties into a structure, which can sustain peace and security. Yet the US has made that virtually impossible.

There is a tendency in the Middle East to overstate the level of political pluralism in the United States in regards to the development of US policy, most evident in the often-exaggerated view of the power of the pro-Israel lobby. Conversely, there is a dangerous tendency in Washington and London to discount the importance of public opinion in Middle Eastern countries. And US/British policy is breeding enormous dissent among the West's closest Arab allies. The ongoing US-led militarization of the region, rationalized to counter these rogue states, severely retards economic development and political liberalization. Most GCC countries are more threatened by potential internal instability than external attack. Cabinet-level officials of two of these countries have acknowledged this in my presence. The highly visible military role and the US-promoted militarization and its deleterious economic impact encourage dissent, often by radical and destabilizing elements. In effect, adherence to an American-defined security doctrine may actually threaten the security of these regimes, which are squandering their nations' wealth on weapons to the detriment of education, health care, housing and employment for their rapidly growing populations. One need only look at Iran in the 1970s.

However, as long as the ongoing tensions remain with the Iraqi and Iranian regimes, the United States can maintain its base and pre-positioning rights in Saudi Arabia and other Gulf states, keeping a major military presence in this strategically and economically important region. It also sends a signal that any adversary regime that possesses even the potential for creating a credible military challenge to US prerogatives in such strategic regions as the Middle East will be destroyed.

Strategic analyst Michael Klare has labeled this myopia as the "sole-superpower syndrome", which he describes as "a sense of nearly godlike power derived from the absence of any balancing forces in the international system." Klare goes on, in reference to US plans to attack Iraq, to say that "with no curbs on American adventurism, US leaders are undeterred from engaging in impetuous and ill-conceived actions" (Klare 1998).

Though it is easy to see US Gulf policy as conspiratorial, it may simply be a result of the arrogance of power. Quite a number of diplomats in the Gulf have complained about the way US officials have lectured their officials—at times in public—about their policies in the region and have "overstepped the boundaries of diplomacy" and demonstrated an "arrogance and disdain for others" (Al-Shayeji 1997). Another example comes from almost a decade of deadly but futile military actions against Iraq. The United States may give an ultimatum to Iraq, expecting the Iraqi government to capitulate, and when it does not, the US feels obliged to follow through with some kind of military action to preserve its credibility. This is despite the fact that even US officials realize that the response will not have the desired effect. Indeed, American and British actions in the Gulf seem almost to be a kind of foreign policy by catharsis rather than based on any rational strategic calculation. There is enormous anger and frustration at not getting their way against upstart regimes in a post-Cold War New World Order in which the assumption is that a level of authority should be respected.

Thus, there comes a final irony. Serving as an impediment to such American ambitions, these regimes gain a kind of credibility and legitimacy that they would not otherwise receive from large numbers of Middle Eastern peoples. Resentful of such foreign domination, this dynamic strengthens these regimes' rule at home as well as their influence throughout the Middle East and beyond. It is the Anglo-American role in the Gulf that is what makes the US and Britain the enemy in the eyes of millions of Arabs. A less visible and less militarized role would likely mean improved relations and greater security.

Conclusion

There is a tendency to define security in terms of a given country's strengths and interests. With the United States as both the world and the region's dominant political, economic and military power, it is not surprising that Gulf security has been defined in ways that promote American interests. This has been the case even if these interests may be at odds with the interests of the countries of the region itself, including the United States' allies. There is also a broader general phenomenon—certainly not unique to the United States—to define security principally in terms of military hardware. From the American perspective, if it is US military hardware, all the better. While the economic imperatives promoting the arms trade are probably not the primary motivator of US policy, the political and economic power of American arms exporters does make it difficult to challenge these assumptions. Indeed, it is rather striking how arms transfers to the Gulf have taken place without any consistent strategy or basic mission priorities and with little regard for coalition warfare (Cordesman 1999, 85).

It is striking that Gulf policy is formulated largely through the US National Security Council and the Department of Defense, with relatively little input from the State Department, non-governmental organizations familiar with the region, or Middle Eastern scholars and experts, including a large number of Arab-American and Iranian-American intellectuals. A similar pattern exists in Britain, though—except for policy towards Iran—the British government simply appears to be willing to take the United States' lead.

Yet, the current situation is untenable. The stronger the US military presence and the stronger the US strategic ties are with GCC countries, the more likely Iran and Iraq will feel threatened. Hard-line elements in Iraq and Iran will point to these ties to depict GCC countries as puppets of American imperialism. Ongoing close strategic ties between the US and the GCC provokes both a genuine fear and a convenient excuse by Iran and Iraq to continue their quest for further militarization and discourage Iraq and Iran from pursuing a regional security regime.

The blame, however, does not rest exclusively with the United States and Great Britain. Clearly, France, among others, is very much involved in promoting the regional arms race through large scale arms sales to GCC states. More importantly, there are certainly elites within the GCC who support such large-scale arms transfers for their own reasons of career-enhancement, ideological precepts, and/or personal financial gain. Meanwhile, there are elements within Iraq and Iran that draw upon their regimes' revolutionary heritage to promote militarism, nationalism and hostility to foreign powers. However, given the strong incentives of the United States and Great Britain to maintain the status quo, neither country can be relied upon to develop a security regime that will promote the best interests of the region as a whole or even of its closest allies. The United States does not want war, but is unwilling to support a peace where perceived US interests are not given primacy. In short, US policy in the Gulf could be summarized as not war, not peace, but Pax Americana. British policy appears to play little more than a supporting role.

When any government spends years demonizing another country and exaggerating its threat, it is extremely difficult to reverse course, even when there is consensus within the government that it is in the national interest to do so. It has to convince its population that peace and compromise is possible with a supposedly intractable enemy, and this opens the government to accusations by opportunistic opposition of weakness, appeasement, and surrender. In many respects, Middle Eastern countries have historically had an easier time at reversing such perceptions. Indeed, there have been growing calls for reconciliation with Iraq and Iran by parliamentarians, journalists, intellectuals, and others in GCC countries, but there are far less initiatives of this kind in the United States or Great Britain.

Another reason it may be difficult for the United States to shift course comes from the perception that rewarding partial reforms or concessions could lead to enormous political embarrassment, such as what occurred in the Iran-Contra scandal. The affair was depicted as an effort to promote moderate elements within Iran. This was despite the fact that the American contacts during the clandestine arms sales in the 1980s were actually very hard-line elements. These elements were willing to work with the Americans in areas of mutual concern, such as supporting the Afghani Mujahedin, eradicating remnants of the Tudeh Party, and dealing with the Lebanese Hizbullah, who were holding American hostages. Still, the experience has given US policymakers little willingness to pursue a policy with more nuances.

Even if the US and Great Britain did put forth a balanced proposal for regional security which did not have on an overbearing US role, neither Iran nor Iraq would accept a security regime put forth by these two countries. Given the history of US and British policy towards their countries, it will still be assumed to be based on American and British strategic priorities and contrary to their own interests. Within the GCC states, meanwhile, leaders will have to defend the arrangement to sceptical segments of their population who will assume that it merely institutionalizes their dependency on outside Western powers. Therefore, any security regime must grow out of initiatives from within the region itself, with facilitation limited to non-governmental organizations or minor powers.

This could be difficult. Indeed, the United States and Great Britain have systematically undermined efforts by Yemen, Jordan, the PLO, the Soviet Union, and France to negotiate a settlement, which would have led to an Iraqi withdrawal from Kuwait prior to the Gulf War. The hostility to any Arab or European-led negotiation to the crisis over Iraq's occupation of Kuwait may be an indication of an Anglo-American reaction to such efforts to establish a region-wide security regime.

In many respects, the GCC states have already demonstrated a greater determination to pursue peace and security than their American allies pledged to protect them. UN Security Council resolution 687 calls for Iraqi destruction of weapons of mass destruction capability within the context of ridding the entire region of weapons of mass destruction. The Gulf states support that broader conception of disarmament, which would include Israel. The United States, however, rejects it, preferring a kind of nuclear apartheid where the US and Israel can maintain their nuclear arsenals in the region, but Iraq and other Arab states are barred from developing such weapons of mass destruction. Another positive development is that, much to the chagrin of American and British arms exporters, there has been a decline in the rate of new arms purchases by GCC states in the past few years.

To develop regional security and a sustainable peace, it is imperative to integrate all major actors into a process of consultation and negotiations in areas of mutual concern. Yet US policy explicitly excludes two of the most important parties. This raises a fundamental question: does the US really care about the interests of the Gulf states or are the Gulf states essentially being used to advance an American agenda? Indeed, there is a growing perception in the Gulf that sees American policy simply as a cover for a permanent American military presence and profits for arms exporters. It may be that the only hope for the establishment of a sustainable security regime may have to come from the Gulf states themselves, perhaps with the support of non-government organizations. Unless that can occur, the Gulf states will continue to be dependent on an American military presence which most of them distrust.

Based on the experience of the Contadora process in Central America, GCC states should anticipate the possibility of scepticism, discouragement, and even hostility and pressure from the United States to reject any regionally-based mutual security agreement. If accepted, as was evident in the Arias Peace Plan for Central America, the US will likely put forward a one-sided implementation policy which will strengthen hard-line elements in Iran and Iraq, who will see the process as rigged against them, as well as hard-line elements in the GCC who will think they can get away with less than full implementation. The challenge for all eight littoral states is to resist such pressure. Should a Gulf-initiated security regime be established, it is important that the US is not sought out as a guarantor. The guarantor of regional security should not be a power that tends to be more inclined to exaggerate the security threat and more inclined to use force than the countries that it is trying to protect. As with Central America, perhaps the United Nations could play an active role, since ultimately, longstanding principles of collective security would need to be maintained as a further deterrent to aggression.

The successful peace agreements in Central America in the face of US opposition came despite the enormous dependency, close historic ties, and geographic proximity these countries had with the United States. As these were primarily internal conflicts, the peace agreements were also forced to address complex issues of class, ideology, political structures, economic policies, land tenure, ethnicity, and a host of related concerns. By contrast, in the Gulf, the strategic concerns in this inter-state conflict are more straightforward and easily resolvable. Furthermore, the relative wealth of the Gulf states compared with the impoverished nations of Central America may also make such a peace agreement easier. In short, if the Central American nations can do it, so can the states of the Gulf. What needs to take place is both some bold initiative from the Gulf States themselves and a willingness by the United States and Great Britain to allow their allies to define and pursue their own security interests.

Notes

1. Jean Heller, "Photos Don't Show Buildup," St. Petersburg Times, Jan. 6, 19??, p. ??.
2. For example, see House Armod Series Committee chairman Les Aspin, "Gulf Diplomacy Needs Arms Threat to Succeed," Center for Strategic and International Studies, Dec. 21, 1990.
3. Institute for Policy Studies, "Iraq's Current Military Capability", Feb. 1998.
4. Meir Stieglite, cited by Rep. Cynthia McKinney, "News Hour with Jim Lehrer," Public Broadcasting System, Feb. 10, 1998.
5. Madeleine Albright, lecture at Georgetown University, March 26, 1997.
6. President George W. Bush, State of the Union address, Jan. 29, 2002.

CHAPTER 9

Oil, US Interests, and Gulf Stability

Richard W. Murphy

This chapter examines how the stability of the Middle East may affect oil production, investment, and access to Persian Gulf oil. The emphasis will be on conditions in the states bordering the Persian Gulf.

We should of course begin with the earlier definitions of US national interests in the Gulf. One, which is now clearly out of date, was the familiar assertion that we had a vital national interest in the freedom of movement of Gulf oil. In the light of the past decade of international sanctions on Iraqi oil which, until December 1999, set strict limits on the level of its export as well as America's unilateral sanctions on Iran, we cannot seriously argue that Washington stands today for freedom of movement of Gulf oil in general. Of course, we cannot even maintain that in Washington's latest confrontation with oil producing states in and outside of OPEC, the United States showed itself to be the world's leading defender of market forces and free trade. A more honest formulation of our national interest is that it is vital for America and for much of the rest of the world to have access at reasonable prices to the Gulf's energy sources. To assure this interest Washington today keeps land, air, and naval forces in the Gulf region with a total strength of some 20,000 servicemen and women.

Some senior American observers, including the present commander in chief of the US Central Command, have argued that the most likely threat to Gulf stability, or perhaps I should say to the status quo, will not be the Iraqi military attack on Kuwait in 1990 or an Iranian move to close the Strait of Hormuz. Those observers say that the more likely threat will stem from the combination of soaring birth rates leading to increased demand for government services and the emerging demand for broader political participation in government decision making. The Gulf states have some of the highest birth rates in the world. The demographic profile of all these states bulges dramatically with the majority of their populations in the 15 to 30 year bracket. For example, the current population of Iran of 72.5 million is double what it was at the time of the 1979 revolution.

The social and political pressures are already having an impact in Iran and several states of the Gulf Cooperation Council (GCC). Up to now all of the GCC governments have been able to deflect pressures for change in the traditional power structures by meeting popular demand for services through generous and adroit allocation of patronage and financial largesse. However, the low oil prices in 1997–98 caused budget shortfalls, leading to a cutback in services. This in turn stimulated widespread debate, normally in private, over the quality of their political leadership. There was pointed criticism of the heavy expenditures made in weapons purchases. There was also considerable soul searching on how to redirect these economies away from their near total dependence on oil revenues. These domestic challenges have created a degree of political ferment in the GCC states as well as in Tehran. Each government must devise its own responses to these challenges. A foreign protector cannot deal with such issues.

Of course, we do not dismiss altogether the possibility of a repeat of the 1990 aggression. The reality in the Gulf is that regional power dynamics have periodically produced instability. The readiness of a strong external power such as the United States to intervene will be needed for many years ahead. The US is not going to delegate that responsibility to any other power external or internal to the Gulf.

In the last two years there have been several instances of smooth transfers of power in the GCC, one caused by the death of the Bahraini Amir and another by the move in Qatar by the then crown prince to replace his father as the ruler. In Saudi Arabia the agreement within the Saudi royal family to shift authority to Crown Prince Abdallah with King Fahd remaining in office, plus its consensus over the eventual succession from Fahd to Abdallah, promises further transitions without political upheavals.

As a general proposition, I foresee no lessening in the desire of all Gulf states to maximize their oil exports as long as they can receive a price in the range of US$25 a barrel. But the overall situation is not static. Domestic changes in Iran and the lack of them in Iraq promises that the relative calm, which allowed Washington to pursue largely unchanged policies it had developed towards Iran and Iraq over the past decade, will not indefinitely endure. I will devote the rest of remarks on external threats to the Gulf states to which the US can respond.

I predict that the United States policymakers will continue to plan on deploying a substantial military force in that region. Recognizing that we will be in the game of assuring Gulf security for the indefinite future, the present administration and its successor must improve on the job of educating the American public and Congress as well as the international community about the open ended nature of the US security mission in the Gulf. Our military presence, ashore and afloat in the Gulf, requires a constant expenditure of both diplomatic and military resources even though compared to our long standing investments in NATO and Korea the actual financial outlay may be small. What are the challenges to the American security role in the Gulf? I see four:

- How to keep Iraq contained over time, even after the end of Saddam Hussein's regime;
- How to improve relations with Iran but not fuel nuclear and regional ambitions;
- How to maintain US forces in the region without causing serious domestic political troubles for our regional partners, few of whose people are comfortable with a significant alien presence on their soil; and
- How to plan for and operate a post-proliferation environment, where we have to intervene militarily without any assurance that a conflict will remain at the level of conventional arms.

There is little prospect of improving relations with Iraq under Saddam and I foresee no significant improvement under his likely successor. In regards to Iran, there are more chances for improvement. The administration should maintain its posture of willingness to improve ties when Tehran is ready but not risk falling on its face by leaning too far too soon.

American policy on Iraq has come under increasing challenge on humanitarian grounds, both from the human rights community and our UN Security Council partners. The Clinton Administration has basically followed the Bush Administration, using economic sanctions, weapons inspections, and military reprisals as stopgap measures, awaiting the day when Saddam is no longer in charge. To contain Iraq over the long run, Washington needs to modify its approach in order to maintain as much international support as possible. Our habit of pointing the finger at Saddam as the one responsible for the suffering of his people is no longer persuasive. Washington's assertion that the current situation will not persist smacks of political spin and wishful thinking and invites unpleasant comparison with our policy toward Castro's Cuba. However, once Saddam has gone American policymakers will immediately find themselves in a serious dilemma. Washington has so personalized the problem of "Saddam, the second Adolph Hitler" that we can expect intense pressure—even from close allies—to abandon quickly all sanctions on Iraq.

The American vote to approve Security Council Resolution 1284 in December 1999 was a vote to expedite delivery of food and medicine and begin to provide for a broader rehabilitation of Iraq's economic infrastructure, so that we would no longer be regarded as the villain opposed to the welfare of the Iraqi people. The resolution removed any ceiling on the amount of oil Iraq could export and promised additional spare parts for the oil sector. It also called for the creation of a new inspection mechanism, the United Nations Monitoring and Verification Commission or UNMOVIC, which is still under formation. The timetable for the Security Council to pass judgement on UNMOVIC's work, which could lead to the suspensions of sanctions, was effectively pushed back into 2001.

Given its obsession with Saddam's leadership, the administration has slighted some longer-term problems for which its own policy bears partial responsibility. First, the prolonged standoff with the Baghdad regime feeds Kurdish aspirations for independence, threatening the territorial integrity of Iraq, a matter of deep concern to the Arab as well as Turkish governments. Second, it serves to deepen the popular hatreds and divisions between Iraqis, Saudis, and Kuwaitis, with the latter seen as American agents on sanctions. This will add to the difficulties inherent in Iraq's eventual peaceful reintegration into the region.

Saddam did misjudge American intent and especially our ability to keep sanctions in place, while simultaneously engaging in a low-level war of attrition against him. However, for UNMOVIC to start its work in Iraq requires Iraq's acquiescence and Saddam's iron grip can keep international inspectors at bay and even out of his country altogether. At the same time American policymakers have been broadcasting their support for the goal of the Iraqi opposition to overthrow Saddam. Trying to ride both these horses, which head off in opposite directions, is self-defeating.

The debate continues about what will constitute an effective restraint on Saddam's program for weapons of mass destruction. For domestic political reasons, the White House and State Department pronouncements on the topic of inspections have undergone amazing transformation. First, there was a tone of hysteria, which prevailed when inspections were interrupted for weeks in 1998. But this was followed by infrequent and increasingly muted comments during the eight months of Security Council negotiations in 1999. Today Washington is relatively silent as UNMOVIC struggles to be born. Interestingly, our arms control community appears readier, if need be, than America's political leaders to accept a flawed inspection regime, such as UNSCOM. Arms control experts recognize that Saddam will probably revive his familiar attempts at cheating the inspectors but this, they argue, is better than having no inspections at all.

Meanwhile the degradation of Iraqi society continues and Saddam, while operating from a smaller power base, wields great power in central and even in southern Iraq. It is time for the international community to agree on more drastic remedial measures. Despite the formidable difficulties involved in bringing Washington to accept it, I want to suggest an amendment to Resolution 1284, which would galvanize Iraq's economic recovery. It assumes continuation of UN financial controls over Iraqi oil revenues but has the potential to achieve earlier job creation and rebuilding of the Iraqi middle class. I propose that the timing for the re-entry of international oil companies into Iraq be separated from the timing of suspension of sanctions provided in Resolution 1284. That resolution makes clear in paragraph 37 that the companies must await Security Council approval, which would be given only after UNMOVIC and the International Atomic Energy Agency have reported that "Iraq has cooperated in all respects with UNMOVIC and the IAEA in particular in fulfilling the work programs in all aspects … for a period of 120 days after the date on which the Council is in receipt of reports from both UNMOVIC and the IAEA that the reinforced system of ongoing monitoring and verification is fully operational."

The potential benefits of proceeding in this manner are:

- It would kick-start the multi-year process of restoring the Iraqi oil industry. The slow and piecemeal moves we have approved to date authorizing spare parts for the oil sector will not have the same galvanizing impact on the industry and through it on the Iraqi economy as a whole.

- The world oil market would more quickly gain access to a larger reserve of oil stocks.
- It would enhance the transparency of operations of the Iraqi oil industry, thereby perhaps constraining the regime's ability to smuggle oil out of the country.
- It would make available to the United Nations a much larger fund to be used for countrywide economic rehabilitation.
- Permission for the oil companies to invest now could create a large number of well paying jobs, treating Iraq as an investment opportunity and its demoralized people as other than welfare recipients.

Of course, to assure benefit to the workers they would somehow require assurance that they get the full benefits of working with the international companies and not be forced to hand most of their wages over to the regime. That would require monitoring of the energy sector by UNMOVIC or another instrumentality of the Security Council. This proposal is also premised on the assumption that Baghdad is ready to welcome international oil company investments under arrangements such as the ones the Kuwaiti government has been discussing with the international oil companies or as Iran has done in its "buy back" contracts. At the same time, any modification in Resolution 1284 will be difficult for Washington to accept particularly in this election year. But if the UN continues its financial controls over Iraqi revenues, including the escrow account, it might just be possible to work this modification out within the Security Council. For its part Baghdad will resist any continuance of financial controls.

On Iran, it is clear the wounds left behind by previous American interventions and the 1979 hostage crisis still throb. Passions and politics rather than interests are still the most important drivers of policy on each side. Early in his first term president Clinton approved the policy of "Dual Containment" and mandated secondary sanctions against Iran's commercial partners under the Iran-Libya Sanctions Act. This act was renewed in the summer of 2001. In the meantime international oil companies, other than American, will have the monopoly on working in Iran. Only with President Khatami's election in 1997 did Washington find it possible to begin to create an atmosphere in which our relations could improve. Clinton deserves credit for consistently articulating a desire to improve ties. But even today, the future status of American-Iranian relations and Khatami's reform program remain hard to predict. He has spoken little about foreign policy. How much authority he can win over Iran's foreign or security policies, despite his followers' remarkable success in the recent parliamentary elections, also remains to be seen.

Complicating matters further will be the American response to Iran's programs for weapons of mass destruction and missiles. We are a major supporter and beneficiary of the global nonproliferation regime, which we want to protect and strengthen. We have a major interest in slowing or blocking the acquisition of destabilizing weapons systems by any regional actor, particularly given the dilemma this would constitute for our own forces in the Gulf. I do not assume that Iran has opted for nuclear weapons but, given nuclear weapons developments in Israel, Iraq, Pakistan, and India, it would be surprising if Tehran was not seriously considering the pros and cons of doing so. This is the best argument for early and official American engagement with Iran. We need to share the hard lessons of nuclear responsibility learned from the US-Soviet confrontation in the Cold War. It should not be beyond our ability to persuade Tehran that we have a common interest in nuclear arms control, especially since Iran shares our interest that Iraq not develop its WMD programs.

In sum, there is volatility in aspects of our Gulf policies as there are in the broader Middle East. That said, the United States clearly intends to remain involved in the complex effort to maintain Gulf stability and assure a high level of oil exports, an interest shared with all Gulf producing states as well as the rest of the world.

CHAPTER 10

The Curse of Oil

Amir A. Alanbari

Oil is often a blessing particularly in developed countries where it often generates a variety of related industries and products. In developing countries, the case is different. It could be a blessing of course but a curse as well. In the long run the latter could be far more serious than the former.

To begin with, oil discovered and extracted in developing countries is not actually produced. It is not the outcome of productive processes through which something produces more valuables than the factors used for its production. In fact oil produced in such countries is nothing but part of their existing assets.

Consequently, oil revenues are not earned revenues. They are not the outcome of productive works and patents. Such revenues, like gambling money, tend to be used loosely thereby burdening the economy with as many non-productive but operationally costly projects. Thus instead of speeding up its economic development it actually slows, and even hinders such development.

On the social side, people in oil societies tend not to work to generate income but depend on oil money to meet their financial requirments. Without productive work and productive ethics, the society fails to achieve a healthy integration and viable social institutions.

But oil is a non-renewable natural resource which is bound to go through a gradual decrease and eventual depletion no matter how great the oil reservoirs are. Paradoxically the greater the reserves are and the longer a society depends on it, the more dire their social and political consequences.

Perhaps worse than any of the above curses is the fact that oil is an indispensable source of energy in the industrialized world. As such it attracts the attention and "protection" of developed countries. For this reason the latter countries seek to ensure safe access to oil and oil products at prices they deem reasonable. As often as not these concerns and interests provide a cause for, indeed encourage, intervention by the industrialized countries in the internal affairs of the oil producing countries which in certain cases leads to military intervention or military coups. Moreover, to keep oil-producing countries dependent on their oil revenues, the industrialized countries seek various ways and means to prevent or make difficult and expensive for the oil producing countries to diversify their economies.

Consequently the oil-producing countries must coordinate their policies and cooperate to protect their vital interests in such a way as to preclude the intervention in their internal affairs and to weaken the role of the industrialized countries in affecting the price structure to the detriment of the producing countries. Indeed OPEC was established just to ensure the above objectives. Yet the terms of the OPEC Charter are not always sufficient to guarantee them. The requirement of unanimity is one obstacle as it gives marginal producers a veto power that might jeopardize the long-term interest of OPEC and the major producers whose vital interests require that oil remains a major source of energy in the industrialized countries.

Another defect in the present charter of OPEC is the absence of an efficient mechanism ensuring that all member countries abide by OPEC resolutions and decisions.

A third fault is the absence of any reference, let alone a mechanism, for joint production from joint fields or for swapping crude oil according to the respective market of each producer.

These defects can best be remedied by bilateral or regional arrangements that take into consideration the unique situation facing each country. Thus cooperation need not and should not be limited to collective and comprehensive collaboration. Such common collaboration is of course necessary but simply not enough for it is usually addressed to the common problems of all member countries. Bilateral and regional cooperation would address itself to the problems and issues with which common cooperation does not deal. Such cooperation could also provide examples for other cooperative agreements between two or more member countries.

Part Three:
FUTURE VISIONS

CHAPTER 11

Eliminating Weapons of Mass Destruction: The Persian Gulf Case[1]

Shahram Chubin

The Persian Gulf presents a particularly difficult challenge for the control of weapons of mass destruction (WMD), and the future use of WMD on a calamitous scale in the region cannot be excluded. Iraq employed chemical weapons during the first Gulf War (Iran-Iraq War of 1980–88) and threatened to use them in the second Gulf war (1991) against the US-led coalition and Israel. Numerous UN inspections conducted since Iraq's defeat in 1991 have revealed the existence of an ambitious, well-advanced, clandestine nuclear weapons program as well as extensive biological weapon program. While constrained by international controls today, Iraq's WMD and long-range missile programs could pose a threat again in the future if the controls are lifted, particularly since the country remains unchanged. Iran, Iraq's adversary in the first Gulf War, also remains an uncertain factor in regional politics. Resentful and ambitious, Iran is recovering from the consequences of the extended war, digesting the lessons of recent conflicts, and looking to play a more important role in the region.

Because of the region's structure, maintaining a balance of power in the Persian Gulf has proven elusive. With the longest coastline and a population three times that of Saudi Arabia and twice that of Iraq, Iran dominates the region demographically and geographically, and has a tendency to be hegemonic whether by policy or by virtue of its simple existence. Iraq, which has only a tiny outlet to the Gulf's waters (some 40 km of coastline), has sought parity with its larger neighbor, while remaining openly contemptuous of its Arab brethren in the Gulf region. Even when at odds with Iran, Baghdad has inspired little trust in the smaller sheikhdoms. This is due in part to differences in ideology (Ba'thist, secular, republican versus traditional Islamic monarchists), and in part to geopolitical factors, for, as demonstrated in 1990–91, Iraq's activism in Arab politics expressed ambitions and energy that can be channeled south as well as west or east.

The Kingdom of Saudi Arabia, the largest state in the region, acts as the "natural" protector of the smaller littoral states—Kuwait, Bahrain, Qatar, the United Arab Emirates, and Oman. Although Saudi Arabia's motives for playing this role are not exclusively altruistic and its attitude, and at times, its behavior are a source of some resentment to others, Riyadh managed in May 1981 to circumvent these tensions and organize these states into a potential defense grouping known as the Gulf Cooperation Council (GCC). Both the Iran-Iraq War and the crisis of 1990–91, however, showed the limited contribution that regional cooperation on this scale could make in dealing with major security threats.

In theory, cooperation between the GCC and *either* of the two major states, Iran or Iraq, would be enough to create a stable balance. In practice, however, as the first Gulf war showed, even this is not enough. With no indigenous balance in the region, a compensating foreign presence, led by the United States, has been substituted. The GCC states have come to rely on this presence and plan their security around it. Iran and Iraq resent and feel threatened by the role of foreign interference in the region and work to reduce it.

A discussion of WMD in the Persian Gulf must focus primarily on Iran and Iraq. The parallels and contrasts between these two states are important. They border on one another and have experienced war and defeat; they harbor resentments and grievances; they are ambitious regionally, which pits them against Israel; and they are hostile to the West, particularly the United States, and its presence in the Gulf. Both states are concerned above all with regime security, which takes precedence over national security. In contrast to the governments of some states in the Middle East, such as Egypt and Syria, both Iran and Iraq are run by civilians and neither regime trusts, nor has developed, a truly professional military.

In other ways, the two states are politically dissimilar. Iran has a relatively decentralized system of power and authority that allows for some play of factional politics. Islamic Iran is less driven by reliance on force and internal schisms than by revolutionary message and its impulse, the quest for legitimacy. Iran is populist and less centralized than Iraq. In its search for status and equality and in its frustration and sense of past injustices, Iran demonstrates continuity in its policy orientation, is open to bargaining, and its policies are subject to reversal. Policies are thus not set in stone, identified with, or dependent on, one person. The Islamic republic and its perception of the world and quest to extend its values, is not the only inevitable system in Iran, any more than the government is, itself, immutable. A different regime might see the world differently, be less ideologically oriented, and pursue other policies in the region and toward weapons of mass destruction.

Iraq, on the other hand, is a fractured society dominated by a Sunni minority and an authoritarian leader ruling by fear and reward. Iraq's reliance on force, terror, and image (coercive and symbolic power) for the maintenance of domestic order also characterizes its conduct of foreign relations. Blunt, confrontational, and territorially revisionist, Saddam Hussein's Iraq is an exaggeration of, rather than departure from, Iraqi strategic culture. Iraqi political culture is one of pervasive insecurity, in which reliance on superior power for survival begins at home.

Iraq's system is more centralized and personalized than that of Iran. It bears clearly the distinctive marks of Saddam's personality, but it does not represent a radical change from previous Iraqi and especially Ba'thist regimes. Because of a strong Iraqi belief in military preparedness and the perception that Iraq should lead the Arab world in scientific and technical advancement, there is no assurance that where mass destruction weapons are concerned, any successor would necessarily be radically different.

The scope of change in policies related to WMD is thus probably marginally greater in Iran, which has a wider set of options than Iraq. The latter has seen more intimate connection with, and continuity between, a repressive domestic order and a correspondingly querulous and aggressive foreign policy. While Iran's choices are those made by the regime, options by Iraq spring from the fissiparous nature of the society and the expedients used by its rulers to keep it under control.

Both states are absorbing the lessons of recent experiences and defeats: Iran is rearming and Iraq is likely to do so in the future. An inevitable component of the rearmament process for each state will be an examination of the policies of the smaller Gulf states, Israel, and the West. This process of rearmament already resembles an arms race, in which states make their procurement (and doctrinal) decisions with the decisions of others in mind. Given the distances involved, the inflow of advanced arms to the GCC states inevitably affects the calculations of Iran and Iraq, while the rearmament progress of these two countries, even if nominally aimed at each other, in turn cast a shadow over the other littoral states. Similarly, missiles and aircraft in the Gulf can be further afield, activating Israel's security concerns and linking the Persian Gulf into a single broad theater of Middle East politics.

Consequently, the politics of the Persian Gulf do not correspond to a simple model of Arab Gulf states versus Iran or Iraq, or Iran *and* Iraq. The area is characterized by multiple axes and crosscutting cleavages and alliances. This means that the dominant conflict at any one time may be linked to, or superseded by, another conflict.

Moreover, the crisis of 1990–91, in which Iraqi missiles hit both Saudi Arabia and Israel, showed that strategic linkages connect the Persian Gulf with the broader Middle East region politically and affect actions and decisions accordingly. Thus discussions about WMD in the Persian Gulf must necessarily address Israel, because proliferating states invoke Israel as a motive/justification for developing WMD and because Israel is itself concerned with, and reacts to, WMD capabilities in the Gulf.

Four distinct categories of conflict are possible:

- Iran–Arab (e.g. Iran–Iraq War, 1980–88)
- Intra-Arab (e.g. Iraq–Kuwait/coalition war, 1990–91)
- Arab–Israel (involving Iraqi WMD and missiles)
- Iran–Israel

In the near term, the key variables affecting the proliferation of WMD in the region will be the lessons drawn from recent events by the current regimes in Iraq and Iran, the availability of resources and access to suppliers, and the costs and penalties incurred by clandestine WMD programs. In the longer term, the evolution of Arab-Israeli relations, the stability (and orientation) of the GCC states, and the future of the regimes in Iran and Iraq will be important factors as well. Even without Israel, Iraq and Iran would have each other as principal justifications for the pursuit of WMD capabilities, it is more difficult to envisage Iraq renouncing such weapons than Iran; for while Iraq seeks to offset its neighbor's size with advanced or unconventional weapons, Iran can afford to dispense with them, provided there is a guarantee that Iraq is similarly disarmed.

Because the motivations for acquiring WMD are diverse, arms control measures must encompass all key categories of arms; cover the broader region, including Israel; and take into consideration that within the regimes in each region, decisions in favor of weapons are political as much as military. The kind of regime and corresponding leadership are important ingredients in the overall mix of factors increasing or decreasing the impulse toward WMD in the region.

The Role of WMD in the National Policies of the Persian Gulf States

WMD played a prominent part in both the Iran-Iraq War and the Persian Gulf War. In the first conflict, both chemical weapons (CW) and missiles were used extensively to considerable effect. In the coalition war, Iraq used missiles against Israel and threatened the use of CW without ever implementing its threats. After the war, Iraq was found to have a large stockpile of CW and an advanced nuclear weapons program as well. Iran is also suspected of seeking to develop a chemical and biological (CBW) program and of actively pursuing a nuclear weapons capability. Current WMD capabilities among the Persian Gulf nations, combined with the use of chemical weapons and missiles in the Iran-Iraq War and the threats of CW use made in the 1991 Gulf War, suggest that future use of such weapons in the region cannot be discounted.

The View from Tehran. The lessons drawn from Iran's first and painful encounter with modern war will dominate Iranian defense practice for some time. Iraq's aggression, in Iran's view, was launched with Western connivance. The "tanker war", Iraq's expansion of hostilities to the Gulf, was not punished, while Iran was subject to an increasingly tighter arms embargo. Iraq's use of CW in the war, amply though timidly verified by the UN, was not condemned unequivocally, and the UN Security Council was deafeningly silent on the matter. Iraq's extensive use of over two hundred missiles in the "war of the cities" likewise passed with little condemnation. Finally, while Western states added to Saddam's arsenal, Iran had to scramble for arms on the international arms market. The list can go on, leading the Iranians to pose the question of whether Iraq would have hesitated to use nuclear weapons if it had them, and whether Western protestations and assurances could be believed given the West's recent record.

From its experience during eight years of war, Iran derived several clear-cut lessons:

- Prepare for the worst and emphasize deterrence
- Prepare against "surprises" by missiles and CW, which are best deterred by the threat of in-kind retaliation.
- Avoid any kind of foreign dependence in the arms area; cultivate self-reliance, diversify arms sources, stock supplies, and develop indigenous capabilities to produce arms.
- Do not put much stock in international organizations or fair play; selective indignation and discrimination in the application of principles is standard procedure.
- In brief, prepare for the worst militarily and diplomatically.

Iran justified its own nuclear program with reference to the need for access and exposure to modern technology. Iran is determined to exploit atomic energy and technology in peaceful ways for its growing electricity, agricultural, medical needs. Western concern for non-proliferation is thus seen as a pretext for the denial of technology. Iran's belief that it must keep abreast of all technologies, including those relating to WMD, has led to similar policies in the areas of chemical, biological, and nuclear *industry*. Since Iranian officials deny any intention of acquiring nuclear weapons, insisting that they are neither usable nor moral weapons, it is impossible to be sure whether nuclear weapons are in fact viewed any differently from other categories of mass destruction weapons. Inferences can be made based on the logic of the Iranian geopolitical situation and its leadership goals, but not much more. Thus, while Iran may see CBW as deterrents with little value in terms of military utility or prestige, it may view nuclear weapons as all-purpose weapons—primarily as deterrents—but also as weapons that enhance Iran's global status. Iran may see nuclear weapons as substitutes for inadequate conventional arms, and as means to project influence in regional politics and to buttress the legitimacy of the regime at home.

Several factors may play a role in pushing Iran toward the acquisition of nuclear weapons. Iran may hope to deter US intervention in the Persian Gulf, a prime security motive today. Iran also may have regional goals that it feels nuclear weapons help to achieve, including Israel's monopoly on nuclear possession, deterrence of Iraq, and providing Iran with leverage on regional and Islamic politics. Even in the absence of pressing security threat, the memory of the war with Iraq, in which Iran stood alone, may dictate the acquisition of a suitable all-purpose deterrent. The latter incentive might be all the stronger if Iran was unable to find a reliable source of supply for conventional arms, or felt deprived of its legitimate defense capability in comparison to its over-armed neighbors.

Regarding Iran's policy on CBW, if they are intended as deterrents, Iran would have reason to be sceptical of efforts to limit them unless it could be assured that arms control would be fully effective. Iran, in any case is not an enthusiastic supporter of any attempts to limit activity in these fields. The overlap between commercial and military applications of these technologies is indistinct and ambiguous. Although a signatory of the CWC, Iran has sought to limit the intrusiveness of the inspection regime being set up to monitor compliance. It argues that arms control should not become a pretext under which the developing states are denied technology.

Concurrently with its efforts to develop WMD programs, Iran has pursued a missile program. Western analysts have argued that, given their inaccuracies, missiles are not the optimum means for delivery for conventional (high explosive) warheads. Many observers therefore have inferred that the warhead of choice for missiles is biological or chemical. This may not be the case. Iran sought missiles in part to substitute for an aging air force whose redevelopment was proving costly and time-consuming. The difficulties in maintaining a functional air force led Iran to favor developing a missile program, which is relatively easy to maintain and which is likely to communicate a message of readiness to the state it is intended to deter, or against which missiles might be used. Iran's interest in missiles may be to intimidate smaller neighbors in the Gulf, or to balance the massive conventional arms supplies of its neighbors.

Iran will continue to treat missiles separately from biological, chemical, and nuclear weapons. As they become accessible, indigenously produced, and recently improved, missiles will be touted as signs of technological advances for domestic audience. With their appearance of modernity and their attraction of simplicity, they give their possessor a sense of having an equalizer. Missiles will not be steadily or readily renounced. Nor, in Iran's case, are they necessarily or primarily intended for use with WMD warheads.

The View from Baghdad. Iraq is an extreme case of a state that equates military industrialization and arms industries with economic modernization. The siege mentality of the Iraqi Takriti clan, together with Ba'th ideology and the hardship associated with the war with Iran (especially between 1982–87), reinforced a predisposition to leave nothing in the future to chance. Iraq ended the war with more troops at the front than Iran, which had three times its population. Iraq outgunned Iran in every area: aircraft 7:1, tanks 2:1, artillery pieces 3:1, and missiles, probably 10:1. Not content with these advantages, Saddam's Iraq continued to pour resources into military industrialization, which led to much of the debt run up between 1988–90. This resource drain then necessitated the next step, the seizure of more resources, namely, Kuwait.

Like Iran, Iraq drew lessons regarding the utility of WMD from its recent military conflicts. The two Gulf Wars would appear to underscore the following propositions:

- Chemical weapons deter other chemical weapons. Thus, against a foe with equivalent capabilities, chemical weapons merely cancel each other out, leaving other levels of force at play. Therefore, chemical weapons can be pressed into service against a similarly equipped and conventionally superior foe only at the risk of inviting reprisals.
- Chemical weapons cannot be of much use against nuclear weapons. Attempting to blur the threshold by threatening a chemical weapons response to nuclear weapons use lacks credibility for the following reasons. First, the conditions under which a state like Israel is likely to consider using nuclear weapons will be so extreme to make the fear of a chemical weapon response relatively tolerable. Second, however terrifying and indiscriminate, chemical weapons are not comparable to nuclear weapons in destructive power and hence as a deterrent.
- Attempting to use chemical weapons as an umbrella for conventional aggression (to deter Israeli involvement or to respond to a particular act of aggression) would appear to be risky. To make such a doctrine credible, Iraq would have to consider how it would emerge from such a scenario.
- Finally, even as a terror weapon, chemical weapons are of possible utility only if used with surprise and if the target is not able to respond in kind. The Iranians, for one, will not be caught unprepared a second time.

If these are the broad implications of recent events, what specific lessons about the effectiveness of chemical and other classes of weapons in specific scenarios might Iraq have learned from its experience? These might possibly include:

- Chemical weapons by themselves cannot substitute for either conventional or nuclear weapons when there is a lack of parity on these other levels of arms.
- Only nuclear weapons will deter a future humiliation like the one suffered in 1991.
- Nuclear weapons may be the only way to deter an Israeli attack.
- Nuclear weapons may impress non-nuclear weapon states, but against nuclear weapon states they have limited use. In this case, they have value principally for deterrence of threats against core interests.

Like Iran, Iraq's attitude toward missiles and nuclear weapons technology is likely to be conditioned by the regime's view of these weapons as militarily and politically useful and as technologically necessary. Both missiles and nuclear weapons are sources of status and domestic prestige, and a case can be made for them as a part of the general industrialization process that the country must undergo. Industrialization and status are less plausible as justifications for Iraq's CBW programs, however. These programs are likely to be influenced less by such considerations and more by military power factors. Nevertheless, Iraq is sensitive to attempts to limit transfers of these technologies, or to devise intrusive inspections that might be disadvantageous to the country's industrial development.

Whether Iraq makes a moral distinction between conventional weapons and WMD is not at all clear. Judging from past behavior, Iraq, unlike Iran, seems less likely to make such a distinction *a priori*. Rather, it is more likely to make this distinction only when forced to by practical considerations such as the balance of overall power and Iraq's own vulnerability.

Iraq's interest in WMD, in particular, stems in part from both its geopolitical location and its political goals. Concern about Iran's superior size demographically and in terms of strategic depth has led Iraq to search for a strategic equalizer. Similarly, in its bid for Arab and regional leadership, the Iraqi leadership was determined to confront Israel. For both these reasons—strategic inferiority and regional ambition—Iraq thought it was necessary to find something more than a "relative deterrent". Iraq therefore sought a "qualitative" edge to compensate for the strategic asymmetries with Iran. Iraq could compensate for its situation with Israel only by matching Israel's capabilities on every level, while maintaining two advantages: a larger standing army and leadership of an Arab coalition. Whereas Iraq's adjacency to Iran was involuntary and inescapable,

Iraq's leaders chose to position Iraq against Israel. The answer to both "threats" was to seek technology to compensate for existing asymmetries.

The conception of nuclear weapons as symbols of modernity and equality is not unique to Iraq. The view that nuclear weapons could act as a strategic deterrent is surely not controversial either. Where Saddam *appears* to be different is his belief (insofar as we can infer it from the logic of his actions and past behavior) that nuclear weapons could be used to intimidate Iraq's neighbors, thus freeing its conventional forces for operations in the region. Not content with overwhelming conventional superiority over his neighbors in the Gulf, Saddam persisted with an arms program that operated at many levels at once: conventional weapons, including a super gun for the long-range projection of missiles; many types of missiles (both indigenous and co-produced, and of varying ranges); a large air force; a version of an early warning and command and control aircraft (airborne warning and control systems—AWACS); vast stocks of artillery pieces, tanks and tank transporters, and WMD.

Whether Saddam distinguished between chemical and biological weapons—and between these weapons and nuclear weapons—cannot be known. His investment in each type of weapon was relatively large. It seemed that he viewed all three types as parts of a seamless progression, making little practical distinction among them. Each symbolized progress and science, but nuclear weapons were the ultimate weapon, and as such would be the most desirable and the least dispensable. Iraq's experience since 1991 would surely reinforce this proposition, with the qualification that CBW, though less useful militarily against strong states, still holds some attractions, not least because they are more readily attainable. Chemical and biological weapons may thus serve as shortcuts, substitutes, and symbols for more usable power. These weapons will have some attraction for an Iraq that feels wrongfully punished, and has had its capabilities constrained and its natural role as regional leader subverted.

The View from Riyadh. The Saudi regime and the GCC states as a whole have felt vulnerable to subversion, intimidation, and coercion by their stronger neighbors, Iran and Iraq. Since the Iran-Iraq War, and particularly since the Desert Storm, the GCC states have increased their visible dependence on the United States as the guarantor of their security. Reliance on the West for defense against predatory neighbors is, for the moment, satisfactory. The United

States' policy of "Dual Containment" serves the GCC states' interests and the foundation of a cooperative relationship with the United States, in particular, as well as with Britain, France, and Russia appears dependable. This security relationship, however, cannot be a long-term strategy. First it costs too much for both the GCC and the West. Second, the arrangement depends on a continuing commitment by these distant states, and on their ability to arrive in time or to sufficiently deter the local forces—neither of which can be guaranteed in the long term. Third, the continuing reliance on outside powers, along with the encouragement of policies that exclude the major local states, prevents or retards dialogue among the GCC states, Iran, and Iraq, and must therefore be considered ill-judged if prolonged, particularly as it provokes Iran and Iraq's resentment. The GCC thus may be pursuing policies that, if continued, will contribute to the pent-up anger in the more powerful states of the region.

If the GCC states together are unable to assure their own security and reliance on the West increases enmity of Iran and Iraq, what are their other options? An Arab conventional force would lack credibility and would create its own problems, hence the failure to put life into the largely symbolic and declaratory Damascus Declaration. Appeasement of Iran and/or Iraq also looks dangerous. What may be a more attractive alternative is the creation of a local non-conventional deterrent that goes some way to deterring, or at least inflicting costs on, a regional aggressor. It should be emphasized, however, that the GCC could not afford to alienate the United States and the West by seeking WMD openly. The costs of do so would certainly be greater than any possible benefits.

A more durable solution might be the acquisition of a nuclear weapon *option*, meaning an indirect, attenuated nuclear weapon capability, which appears to have been what Saudi Arabia sought in its cooperation in the early-1980s with Iraq. Saudi Arabia's acquisition of the DF-3 missile from China is revelatory in this regard. Negotiations to acquire the DF-3 missile started in 1985, well before the missile "war of the cities" between Iran and Iraq in March 1988. The US was not informed of the purchase and only discovered the transaction by accident two years later. Saudi Arabia's overall weakness on the ground and its efforts to compensate by building an advanced air force suggest that these long-range missiles were acquired with a strategic purpose in mind. Their value with a conventional warhead is limited, and they are of doubtful effectiveness as a deterrent against Iran and Iraq and may invite pre-emption in a conflict. With unconventional warheads (nuclear or chemical), the missiles' deterrent value and cost-effectiveness would be considerably enhanced.

Saudi Arabia and the other GCC states will find it difficult to continue to acquire advanced weapons systems at the pace of recent years. The rapid acquisition rate will no longer be feasible for financial reasons, and for practical reasons it is inadvisable, as there are limits to the arms that can be assimilated by states with small population bases. There is also a phenomenon of diminishing returns; even when money is not the limiting factor, deterrence cannot be enhanced appreciably by even greater expenditures on the military. At the same time, the GCC states, after the past decade of conflicts and crises, have become more aware of the nature of *military* (as opposed to domestic/subversive) threats to their security.

The GCC states, led by Saudi Arabia, are not about to jeopardize their security relationship with the US, however, by pursuing WMD. Nevertheless, these states will almost certainly seek to leave this option open and pursue it to the extent that they feel is possible without endangering ties with the US. The future of such weapons in the GCC states depends on the state of relations with the United States, on the evolution of WMD in Iran and Iraq, and on developments in regional arms control.

Eliminating Weapons of Mass Destruction

The elimination of WMD in the Persian Gulf is complicated by enmities, disparities in size, and uneven access to conventional arms. Asymmetries between Iran and Iraq in terms of their security requirements and between these two and the smaller states of the Gulf are further problems. The issue of linkages with Israel is clearly another obstacle, as is the question of whether it is possible to constrain any category of arms without reference to others.

Where WMD in the Persian Gulf is concerned, Iran and Iraq are of prime interest, the former for its potential and the latter for its recent record and programs. In light of its recent experience, Iran has powerful reasons to develop chemical and biological weapons capabilities. Given a reliable system of arms control, however, Iran may be more willing to forgo these weapons than others. Iran is less likely to dispense with its missiles, because it perceives missiles as providing self-reliance and substituting, to some extent, for an air force. Similarly Islamic Iran is most unlikely to renounce its program to acquire nuclear weapons, which it sees as necessary instruments for its security and status. Since its motives for acquiring nuclear weapons are global and diffuse as well as specifically security related, they will be harder for the international community to address. Greater effort to meet Iran's legitimate interests, to give it a stake in the system, and to absorb and smother it in a web of interdependence, however, could facilitate arms control and lessen Iran's desire to obtain nuclear weapons. Iran's quest for independence, equality, and self-expression need not lead it inexorably toward WMD. There is nothing in Iran's political/strategic culture that impels it in this direction, and its declarations about the immorality of such weapons have the ring of authenticity rather than public relations. If it felt less threatened by the United States, lacked urgent regional incentives to develop WMD, and was assured access to technology and conventional weapons, Iran's security needs could be met without a need for nuclear weapons. Arms control could then be used to roll back all WMD programs in Iran. Less besieged and more integrated, Iran would have fewer reasons for seeking such weapons.

Iraq is weaker and presents no immediate threat. On arms control, no Iraqi regime is likely to accept controls applied only to Iraq; rather, any future regime will most likely insist on parity across the board with Israel and Iran. Israel here is both *pretext* and *cause*. Iraq needs to be reassured and integrated and its capacity for mischief reduced if it is not to become a threat again. If sanctions are lifted or softened, Iraq may come to pose a major threat, especially in biological weapons, which may be the most accessible and hence the most quickly developed. WMD are the logical endpoint of a quest for a qualitative edge *vis-à-vis* Iran and Israel. If Iraq were less inclined to confront its neighbors, it would have fewer incentives for such weapons. This implies, however, diminished or more reasonable regional goals, which seems likely only in the event of a new regime and assumes a radical discontinuity with the past. While a change in political culture of the society will not come overnight, if encouraged by the rest of the world, a new regime that combines moderation at home with negotiation of differences regionally will facilitate progress in this area. Although the chances of such a regime emerging anytime soon are somewhere between uncertain and unlikely, only such a regime could transcend the politics of fear and confrontation that have been the distinctive hallmarks of Saddam's Iraq.

The primary obstacles to limiting WMD in Iran and Iraq stem from a combination of the nature of political leadership and regime and the circumstances prevailing in the region. Different regimes in

Iran and Iraq might be less ambitious regionally and less confrontational *vis-à-vis* Israel, and might also define national security differently and set about its attainment in a manner less disruptive to regional stability. On the other hand, any regime in either country is likely to consider nuclear weapons exclusively in the hands of Israel, or arms control and technology-denial selectively applied, as reasons to seek compensatory or matching weapons systems. In short, a change in regime might change Iran and Iraq's perspectives on WMD, but it would not alter the sense of resentment at policies that the regimes feel are clearly discriminatory. Arms control that seeks limits only in the Persian Gulf, and thus maintains Israel's arms superiority, or that demands adherence to restrictions only by states other than Israel, are deeply unpopular, resented, and unlikely to be accepted by any regime in either country. Regional arms control regimes in the Persian Gulf should be limited geographically and by item (CW/BW first, then missiles, then nuclear weapons). In addition, the Persian Gulf and the Arab-Israeli zone should be treated separately but in parallel, with an eventual linkup.

Progress toward resolution of the Arab-Israeli conflict, including the conclusion of peace treaties and territorial agreements between Israel and its immediate Arab neighbors, would reduce the incentives of Iran and Iraq to acquire WMD. An Iraq more integrated into the Persian Gulf and an Iran less resentful or more accommodated internationally would also generate fewer pressures for such weapons.

The GCC states, in contrast to Iran and Iraq, are not the prime movers for WMD in the region and may come to see WMD as a distinct threat to their own security. For reasons of Arab solidarity, however, it will remain an article of faith that Israel's denuclearization should take precedence over any discussion of other WMD. The expression of this demand may be tempered by the GCC states' need to rely on the US in the short term. For the GCC states, the threat of WMD is more real in the immediate Persian Gulf region than in the broader Middle East. In buying and stocking arms, holding their neighbors at arms length, and eschewing any dialogue, these states, relying on distant powers for their security, have at times been less prudent in their treatment of their larger neighbors. Over time, the GCC states need to find a means of coexisting with Iran and Iraq that includes cooperation as well as deterrence. If Iran and Iraq are to play less active "regional" roles in the Middle East, they will probably be more present in the Gulf. The smaller states will have to live with this situation, rather than simply pretend that these two large states do not exist.

The conditions for reducing the multiple incentives of the Persian Gulf states to acquire WMD can be met only by change on several levels. Political change in Iran and Iraq is one area of potentially favorable change. It would be a mistake, however, to believe that only rogue regimes resent inequalities in access to arms or selective discrimination in the application of arms control. If the Middle East sees the advent of more Islamic or populist regimes, these equity issues will become more important. Greater diplomatic interaction among regional states may lay the foundation for limited arms control measures and should be encouraged. Progress in the Arab-Israeli process, which sees the substitution of a normal political relationship for an adversarial one based on worst-case assumptions, could make the linkage between these two regions—which has so far been destabilizing—work in reverse, to positive effect.

Note

1. This chapter is a shortened version of the Occasional Paper No. 33 written in March 1977 for the Henry L. Stimson Center. It is printed here with the kind permission of the Center. Extensive footnotes as well as detailed discussion of the current status of WMD in the region can be found in the original document.

CHAPTER 12

Towards Cooperative Security in the Persian Gulf

Bjørn Møller

Both the name and the boundaries of the region to which this chapter is devoted are contested. In the following I shall use the term "the Persian Gulf Region", yet without prejudice for the standing dispute over whether labels such as "the Arab Gulf", "Southwest Asia" or simply "the Gulf" might be more appropriate. Even though a case could be made for including states such as Yemen, Turkey, Afghanistan or the new states of Central Asia, I shall define the region narrowly, as encompassing Iran and Iraq plus the states belonging to the Gulf Cooperation Council (GCC), i.e. Bahrain, Kuwait, Oman, Qatar, Saudi Arabia, and the United Arab Emirates (UAE). In addition, the list of relevant actors also includes various non-state actors such as the GCC itself, the Arab League, The Organization of the Islamic Conference (the OIC), and the United Nations, as well as several external powers, above all the United States and, until recently, the Soviet Union. Russia still plays a certain role in some respects, as do countries such as Britain and France, India, Israel, and Turkey.

In the following, a brief account shall be provided of why the region thus defined is unstable, followed by a set of general proposals for stabilization. Even though the main problems are political, the focus is placed on the military domain, as problems in this field may, at the very least, hamper political solutions to political problems. For dealing with these military problems the contents of a "toolbox" is described. It includes a panoply of political, arms control and confidence-building "tools" that have worked in other parts of the world and which might therefore (*mutatis mutandis*) also prove useful in the Persian Gulf region.

From Conflict Formation to Security Community

That the Persian Gulf region is unstable, perhaps even war-prone, may both be attributed to relations between states and to the nature of the states of the region.

Stable regional dynamics presuppose states which are strong in the sense of possessing internal socio-political cohesion, based on a well-defined "idea" of the state, as well as the appropriate physical basis and institutional expression of statehood. Without such foundations, security policies tend to be driven by a "securitization" of domestic political agendas (ethnic or religious cleavages, for instance) which often spread to neighboring states, thereby destabilizing the region as a whole, perhaps even to the point of war (Wæver 1995; Brown 1996; Lake & Rothchild 1998). Unfortunately for the stability of the Persian Gulf region, all its states fall into the category of "weak states", even though some are weaker than others. All of them are new states (with the partial exception of Iran); most of them have religious or ethnic minority problems; most have unresolved border disputes with their neighbors; and none of them even approach the standard of "stable democracies". The region thus lacks most of that kind of stability, which a mature "Westphalian system" might offer in the form of mutual recognition of sovereignty and the accompanying norm of non-interference in domestic affairs (Bull 1977; Krasner 1999).

On the other hand, the region is almost a textbook example of another, less appealing, feature of the Westphalian system, namely international anarchy, in the sense that there is no political authority over and above the states. Even if one allows for a "conjugation" of anarchy (from "raw" to "mature") one would have to characterize the Persian Gulf as a rather raw anarchy—i.e. a "conflict formation" where the use of force by states against each other is far from excluded (Väyrynen 1984). As evidence of this might surely count the plethora of wars and other major armed conflicts in the recent history of the region, including the Iran-Iraq War (1980–88) and the 1990 Iraqi invasion of Kuwait and its aftermath, lasting until the present day in the form of a low-intensity US and British war against Iraq.

Traditional balance-of-power mechanisms are unlikely to provide stability. The region is open and multipolar with three poles, namely Iran, Iraq, and Saudi Arabia. Not only is the balance of power between these regional great powers tenuous and "delicate"; it is also highly asymmetrical. While Iran is clearly in the lead in terms of population (i.e. mobilizable military manpower), followed by Iraq, Saudi Arabia surpasses both in terms of wealth (i.e. ability to purchase military hardware) as well as allies. While temporary alignments between any two poles against the third are conceivable, it strains the imagination to envisage durable alliance ties. Saudi Arabia certainly fears Iraq, but not enough to produce any stable alignment with its enemies, as Iran is also a viewed as a threat; Iraq fears both Iran, Turkey, and almost everybody else, but is unlikely to be able to forge any alliance around itself; and Iran fears everybody else, but perhaps especially Iraq. The present tripolarity thus seems unlikely to evolve into bipolarity, and much more likely to produce shifting patterns of *ad hoc* alignments, perhaps interrupted by hot wars. Furthermore, the regional balance-of-power will almost certainly be open-ended rather than self-contained, *inter alia* because all three states also have to guard against threats from other directions, e.g. from Israel, Turkey or the United States.

Neither do international organizations hold much promise of being able to stabilize regional dynamics. There are simply no organizations worthy of the label "regional", as their membership is either too broad or too narrow, or both. Either they include non-regional states (as the Arab League or the OIC) or they exclude important regional states, as is the case of the GCC, designed primarily to provide the Gulf monarchies with defense and deterrence against Iran and Iraq.

Moreover, not only is the general level of armaments in the region high, but the region has also seen a general arms build-up through the 1990s until quite recently. The rich oil-producing members of the GCC, especially, have been purchasing large batches of quite sophisticated aircraft and other hi-tech weaponry. Moreover, both the Iran-Iraq War and the subsequent defeat of Iraq in 1991 have dramatically affected the regional balance-of-power, as summarized in Table 12.1. Not only do such rapid and profound changes hamper a realistic assessment of strength; they also provide declining powers (Iran and, even more so, Iraq) with a motive for preventive war and rising ones with incentives to accelerate their ascent by means of war.

If the build-up continues, the region may end up in a situation where each of the three great powers is in a position to hurt everybody else, but unable to defend itself against a determined surprise attack: a "mutual offensive superiority" stance, where the only stabilizing factor will be each state's ability to retaliate, i.e. some form of reciprocal deterrence.

Table 12.1. Balance of power

	Military Expenditures (Constant 1997 US$)				Armed Forces (1000)				Arms Imports (Constant 1997 US$)			
	1987	%	1997	%	1987	%	1997	%	1987–90	%	1991–97	%
Iran	9,350	13	4,730	13	350	24	575	43	10,044	14	6,226	7
Iraq	35,000	48	1,250	4	900	63	450	33	21,212	30	0	0
GCC	28,644	39	29,515	83	186	13	326	24	40,734	57	88,956	94

Based on figures *World Military Expenditures and Arms Transfers 1998* (Washington, DC: US Department of State, Bureau of Verification and Compliance, 2000).

The United States has been deeply involved in the Persian Gulf region since the 1950s, both economically and militarily, *inter alia* in the form of direct military interventions, most recently in the war against Iraq for the liberation of Kuwait. This has been followed by the forging of ties with individual GCC countries and support for the GCC itself. Unfortunately for regional stability, however, it has also been followed by a practice of unilateral military interventions (1993, 1996 and 1998) and around twice-weekly air strikes against Iraq as well as open attempts at toppling the Iraqi regime (via the "Iraq Liberation Act" of 1998). While the United States might thus have played the stabilizing role as "external balancer", it has so far done the exact opposite, i.e. destabilized the region.

Even though the present and the immediate future thus look rather bleak, the Persian Gulf is surely not predestined to continuing instability and recurrent wars forever. The shared culture and common interests (e.g. with regard to oil prices) etc. might surely provide the foundations for much more collaborative relations, and might even point towards a future "security community" (Deutsch *et al.* 1957; Adler & Barnett 1998). The question is how to get from here to there.

The Roadmap: Cooperative Security

A relevant roadmap for this might be provided by the theory of "Common Security". It was developed in the early 1980s as a political strategy for dealing with a severe, systemic, ideological, and seemingly enduring conflict, namely that between East and West. As the conflict(s) in the Persian Gulf region bear an unmistakable resemblance to this it seems reasonable to assume that Common Security might (*mutatis mutandis*) also be relevant to the Gulf.

As formulated by the Palme Commission in its 1982 report on common security, what matters is for states to realize that lasting security cannot be obtained at the expense of one's adversaries (Independent Commission on Disarmament and Security Issues 1982). Because of the well-known "security dilemma" states often seek security by means which increase the insecurity of others, who then react with countervailing measures negating whatever security gains might have been achieved to begin with, thus making both sides increasingly insecure and the quest for security profoundly counterproductive (Collins 1997). An escape from this security dilemma must be sought in the form of means to security that represent no threats to other states, i.e. strictly defensive measures, be they military or political.

This general rule seems perfectly applicable to the Persian Gulf, where it is probably unwise and short-sighted of the smaller states to seek unilateral security at the expense of either Iraq or Iran (or both), if only because the potential of these two regional great powers may eventually manifest itself in military superiority. It is more likely to do so the more either state feels threatened by its neighbors or others. Should it do so, it will surely be to the smaller states' advantage to have a peaceful rather than a revengeful Iran or Iraq in their vicinity.

Common Security in its original formulation presupposed neither formal negotiations nor agreements, but was envisaged for implementation, if need be, in a unilateral, "tacit coordination, mode". However, it surely facilitates cooperation when parties can at least consult each other preferably even coordinate their policies—and even more so if an institutional framework is available for this, as was envisaged by the reinvigorated concept of Common Security that became fashionable in the nineties under the label "Cooperative Security" (Nolan 1994).

Seen from the point of view of the GCC, a cooperative security approach to the regional conflict(s) in the Persian Gulf would have to integrate, rather than contain, both Iran and Iraq. Expanded economic ties, pointing towards mutual interdependence, would be valuable, as this would give all states a stake in maintaining peace, but the lack of complementarity between regional economies may present an insurmountable obstacle to this. Hence, cooperative security may not be attainable by indirect means but would have to deal directly with military matters, rather than down-laying their saliency.

A relevant goal would be a situation where Iran, Iraq, and the GCC countries would be able to defend itself against each of the others—preferably even against both the others combined and ideally without external assistance. Such "mutual defensive superiority" may not be quite as unrealistic as it may sound (Møller 1992). It thus seems extremely unlikely that Iran and Iraq would gang up against the GCC, or that the latter (individually or jointly) would "bandwagon" with either of them as a putative aggressor against the respective other, however much they might disapprove of the victim. More likely is the, much less demanding, situation where an aggressor would risk having to fight the two others. Hence the actual worst-case scenario would be one in which either party would try to remain neutral in any war between the other two (as Iran did during the Gulf War). It further seems likely that the rest of the world would support whichever state would be attacked, albeit especially so with either of the two "rogues" cast in the role as aggressor. Not necessarily in the form of direct military assistance, but surely in the form of arms embargoes and economic sanctions, which would also help tilt the balance against an aggressor.

Presupposing that the military problems could thus be solved or their saliency reduced (more on which below) one could envision a process leading in the direction of a regional security community. Its nucleus would be the GCC, which would be well advised to emulate other regional organizations such as NATO, the European Union, and the Association of Southeast Asian Nations (ASEAN) by expanding in order to "embrace" its former enemies. By offering conditional security guarantees the United States could play an important role as a facilitator of this process, which would, in the fullness of time, allow the US to disengage completely. The four stages of such a process are outlined in Table 12.2.

Toolbox for Conflict Mitigation and Resolution

To launch a process such as the above requires, above everything else, political will, in the absence of which no progress will be made. Even in the presence of the requisite political will, however, it is important for the parties not to expect the conflict to disappear automatically, but to be mindful of the available panoply of mechanisms and instruments which might facilitate conflict mitigation and pave the way for conflict resolution (Burns 1993; Kurtz 1999). Even though instruments that have proven useful in one context (e.g. the East-West conflict) cannot be mechanically applied to a different regional setting such as that of the Persian Gulf, it makes perfect sense to at least make heuristic use of the available experience.

Table 12.2. Alternatives to Dual Containment

	IRAQ	**IRAN**	**GCC**
Present US strategy: "Dual Containment"	Roll Back (Militarily, economically)	Contain (Economically, militarily)	Support (Militarily)
Alternative strategy Phase 1	Contain (Militarily)	Normalize (Integrate)	Support (Militarily, defensively)
Phase 2	Normalize (Integrate)	Support (Security guarantee)	Support (Security guarantees)
Phase 3	Support (Security guarantee)	Support (Security guarantee)	Support (Security guarantees)
Phase 4		Disregard (Security community, collective security, general security guarantees)	

Political Tools

A good starting point for conflict mitigation is, for obvious reasons, **dialogue**, the purpose of which would simply be to acquaint the parties with each other's positions, which is a precondition for the empathy upon which any common security regime must be built. A good starting point, e.g. for the party wanting to initiate dialogue, is openness, as might be demonstrated by the publication of explicit security doctrines setting out threat perceptions, goals, and strategies—perhaps combined with invitations to other states to reciprocate. Bilateral consultations could be a useful second step, especially if the results are made public to other relevant actors, which could, in due course, lead to multilateral consultations that could become increasingly all encompassing. At each stage, and the more so the more sensitive the issues at stake, non-state actors could play important roles, as in the several initiatives for "Track-Two" or even "Track-Three" diplomacy.

It might be worth having a fresh look at **non-aggression treaties** as a possible instrument, even though such treaties have earned themselves a rather tarnished reputation in the past. One should, of course, realize that they, in and of themselves, afford no protection (viz. those signed, and subsequently broken, by Nazi Germany in the

1930s). One might, of course, object that they are superfluous and/or repetitious, as both the 1928 Kellogg-Briand Pact and the UN Charter (art. 2.4) already constitute explicit, and universally binding, prohibitions against aggression (Baratta 1993). First of all, however, there are already several regional treaties and agreements containing such repetition. Secondly, such "repetition" may actually provide some additional assurance of peaceful intent. Thirdly, and probably most importantly, unequivocal non-aggression commitments could provide a useful starting point for revisions of military doctrines, activities, and holdings. If a state has no aggressive intentions, it would seem to have no legitimate need for such weaponry as it has no defensive utility (long-range ballistic missiles might be a case in point), or for military exercises practicing large-scale offensives—and it would seem logical—to demand a revision of military doctrines with an offensive content.

The idea of **collective security**, likewise, suffers from past failures, especially associated with the League of Nations experience. Nevertheless, much of the recent criticism is logically flawed (Betts 1992; Mearsheimer 1994/95). For instance, such a system need neither be foolproof nor "automatic" for it to be useful. If prospective aggressors have to count with a probability above zero that the system would work as envisaged (as it did for Kuwait) then this would surely have *some* deterrent effect. The credibility of the commitment of the members to such an arrangement need therefore not be 100 percent (which is indeed unlikely), if only it is higher than zero. Nor does such an arrangement have to be completely egalitarian and/or universal for it to have some value. Even though the permanent members of the UN Security Council as well as, perhaps, their closest allies would be immune from reprisals, the system might still deter other states from wars of aggression that they might otherwise have felt tempted to launch. This is not an ideal safeguard, but surely better than none. Moreover, collective security commitments would also be a useful first step to preparations for actual mutual assistance, e.g. for the establishment of command structures, the holding of joint maneuvers, etc.

While both non-aggression treaties and regional collective security arrangements would have to rely mainly on indigenous efforts, external powers might play an important supportive role, simply by extending conditional security guarantees, i.e. guarantees that are not tied to any particular state and are valid in all eventualities, but guarantees to whatever state might be the victim of attack, but only for that eventuality.

Agreements on **non-interference in internal affairs** may be more controversial, even though they are also implicitly contained in, e.g. the UN Charter (arts 2.4 and 2.7), hence already constitute a binding norm for international relations. However, violations of this norm have been legion, and a re-confirmation thereof has proven an important component in peace processes, e.g. in Central America (Child 1992; Moreno 1994). For states to abstain from providing military support for guerilla movements abroad (as in the Algiers accord between Iran and Iraq committing both to discontinue support for the respective other's Kurds) may be a small, but still significant step in the direction of mutual recognition. It may thus be an indispensable ingredient in a "Westphalian" system that would surely be preferable to the present one. It would also help contain the spread of ethnic or ethno-religious conflict that might otherwise destabilize a region such as that of the Persian Gulf. As violators of human rights would, by implication, be protected against military intervention, there had better be other mechanisms in place to address such problems by non-military means.

Functional Arms Control Tools

Functional arms control pertains to military activities and are usually subdivided into confidence-building measures (CBMs) and confidence and security-building measures (CSBMs).

"Traditional" CBMs are mainly intended to mitigate the security dilemma by reducing misperceptions, i.e. by enhancing transparency of military affairs (Holst 1983). Not only does this relieve states of unwarranted concerns about their opponents; it also allows genuinely peaceful states to demonstrate their benign intentions to their adversaries. Relevant measures might include pre-notification of military maneuvers above a certain size (for instance in the form of an annual calendar) and invitation of observers to these maneuvers. Contrary to what has been the case in Europe, however, in the Persian Gulf region such measures would have to be extended to the maritime domain in order to really matter (Goldblat 1992). Also, in order to allay Iranian and Iraqi fears they should also involve US forces, at least in so far as these are collaborating with those of the GCC states. Most of these measures would also have the added advantage of acquainting military personnel with each other—which might also contribute to dismantling enemy images.

CSBMs would go a little further (hence may be more suitable for a later stage of a process), as they actually proscribe or regulate certain military activities. Relevant CSBMs would include a prohibition against exercises not listed in the annual calendar; a prohibition against military maneuvers above a certain size, either in general or merely in border areas; and limits on the annual number of exercises, *inter alia* in order to prevent circumvention of the size constraints by a substitution of many small for fewer large maneuvers. Such regulations should, among other things, rule out the (real or imagined) possibility that a state might conceal attack preparations as large-scale maneuvers, thus providing some insurance against surprise attacks.

In addition to these categories one might also mention other measures that would serve to promote confidence among parties that lack any basic trust in each other's intentions (in which case confidence building would be superfluous). An example might be the publication of **White Papers** on security and defense policies that would allow states to better interpret each other's military behavior. **Seminars on military doctrines and strategies** would be the ideal forum for exchanging information on military planning in general. The establishment of a **crisis management center** would be even more useful, as it could allow actual consultations about "suspicious" military activities.

Structural Arms Control

Structural arms control goes even further by regulating military holdings. In an intermediate position between the (mainly transparency-enhancing) CBMs and CSBMs and "genuine" structural arms control lies the promotion of transparency with regard to the configuration, deployment, and equipment of the armed forces. Full compliance with the **UN Register of Conventional Arms Transfers** would also be a significant first step in this direction (Anthony 1993). Ideally, it should be supplemented with a more detailed **regional arms register** that should also provide data on military holdings and indigenous arms production, and which could be extended to cover also small arms and weapons of mass destruction. While greater transparency in these matters would, in and of itself, do little to change the armed forces, it could be a useful first step in this direction, as certain deployments or arms purchases might be revealed as "illegitimate".

As far as "genuine" structural arms control the goal would be the aforementioned situation of "**mutual defensive superiority**", i.e. one where each state or alliance would be able to defend itself against any likely attack, but unable to launch a successful attack against any of the others. This is mainly a question of the size, configuration, deployment, and arming of the conventional armed forces, even though weapons of mass destruction (WMD) would also have an impact. However, it is emphatically *not* (as sometimes alleged by critics trying to ridicule the idea) a matter of singling out particular (categories of) weapons as "offensive" by their very nature, but of an assessment of total force postures for their offensive and defensive potential.

On the basis of such a holistic assessment the defensive criteria may be operationalized, e.g. in terms of re-deployment requirements or lists of weaponry to be reduced, as happened in Europe with the CFE Treaty on Conventional Armed Forces (Kelleher, Sharp, & Freedman 1996; Falkenrath 1994). While there was consensus between NATO and the Warsaw Pact on placing the emphasis on tanks, armored personnel carriers, artillery, combat aircraft, and helicopters, the relevant list of weapon systems may well be different in the Persian Gulf region (Arnett 1997). In any case, it stands to reason that it would have to include naval forces as well.

As far as WMD are concerned, the main problem is the danger of nuclear weapons proliferation. This would seem to speak in favor of making a **nuclear weapons-free zone** (NWFZ) a first priority. This would oblige regional states to abstain from developing or acquiring nuclear weapons, as well as to prevent other states from deploying such weapons on their territory. As a corollary (perhaps in an additional protocol to the main treaty) the nuclear powers could issue "negative security guarantees" to all parties to the treaty, i.e. commit themselves to neither threaten the use nor actually use nuclear weapons against any party—which would indeed be a small concession given that nuclear use has already been deemed illegal by the International Court of Justice (Boisson de Chazournes & Sands 1999). The nuclear powers could also make themselves useful by helping to monitor the treaty that would surely also correspond to their national interests, if only it would strengthen their nuclear monopoly.

What speaks against a "mere" NWFZ is the fact that the immediate neighbourhood of the Persian Gulf contains an undeclared nuclear power, namely Israel (Aronson 1992; Evron 1994; Shahak 1997; Cohen 1998), that would be difficult to ignore, but equally difficult to include. A solution to this dilemma might be to expand the scope of the treaty to include other weapons of mass destruction (i.e. chemical and biological weapons), hence to opt for a "**WMD-Free Zone**"(Prawitz & Leonard 1996)—an arrangement in which there would indeed be something for everybody.

Table 12.3. "Toolbox"

	Unilateral measures	**Bilateral/Multilateral measures**	**Third-party contributions**
Political: Goal: Common Security	Openness	Dialogue, e.g. on threat perceptions	Facilitation, moderation, mediation
	Non-aggression declarations	• Non-aggression treaties • Collective security	Conditional security guarantees
	Abstention from interference	Agreement on non-interference in internal affairs	Non-interference
Functional arms control: Goal: Mutual confidence through non-threatening military activities	Unilateral CBMs, e.g. • Calendar of exercises, invitation of observers • Publication of military doctrine	Multilateral CBMs, e.g. • Pre-notification of maneuvers • Invitation of observers • Seminars on military doctrines	Technical support: satellite data gathering and processing
	Unilateral CSBMs, e.g. • Maneuvers restraint • Defensive military doctrine and strategy	Multilateral CSBMs, e.g. • No exercises in border areas • No exercises above a certain size • No practising of offensive operations • Commitment to defensive military doctrines and strategies	Constraints on joint maneuvers
Structural arms control: Goal: Mutual confidence through non-threatening military postures	• NPT membership Chemical Weapons Convention accession • Defensive restructuring: (army, air force, navy)	• Nuclear-Weapons-Free Zone • Zone Free of Weapons of Mass Destruction • Limits on ballistic missiles • Limitations on capabilities for surprise attack and large-scale offensive action (armies air forces and navies)	• Negative security guarantees • Technical support for monitoring compliance • No export of weapons mainly useful for offensives purposes or to states with offensive doctrines

Conclusion

We have thus seen that there are many possible measures that might serve to stabilize the volatile Persian Gulf region. The "toolbox" for conflict mitigation is full of instruments and mechanisms that would appear applicable to the region. Whether or not they are relevant is, of course, up to the states of the region to determine; and whether they will be applied depends, above all, on the political will to escape from the present unstable and war-prone situation into one where military concerns have been allayed to the point where political solutions can be found to the mainly political problems of the region.

CHAPTER 13

Toward a Regional Security Regime for the Middle East

Peter Jones

The Stockholm International Peace Research Institute (SIPRI) inaugurated a Middle East Security and Arms Control Project in October 1995. As the first major initiative of the project a Middle East Expert Group, consisting of members from Europe, Japan, the Middle East, North America, and Russia, was formed to consider how a regional and comprehensive security regime might be developed in the Middle East. The Expert Group met four times over an 18-month period. The group did not intend to design a regional security regime for the Middle East. Rather, the aim was to identify and understand what issues would arise should regional governments try to establish such a regime.

From the beginning the group was keenly aware of the difficulties that face the Middle East in the coming decades. However, all of the members of the group expressed the view that an effort must be made to develop a new approach to security in the Middle East, leading to the evolution of a comprehensive regime for security of the region. They also believed that such a regime must adopt a more inclusive approach, both in terms of its agenda and membership, to security than has existed to date. Finally, they shared the view that any hope of addressing the long-term security issues that confront the region must rest on the foundation of a settlement to the Arab-Israeli dispute. Such a settlement will have to include security for Israel and self-determination with dignity for the Palestinian people.

Noting the rapid changes in the international scene following the Cold War, the members of the Expert Group based their work on the new and broader agenda for security that is developing throughout the world. They noted that principles of democracy, respect for human rights, and the peaceful resolution of conflicts are on the ascendant in the world and the Middle East cannot stand outside this process. But the Expert Group agreed that fundamental change in thinking about four important areas must underlie any future approach to regional security in the Middle East.

First, it was agreed that the Middle East region suffers from an almost total reliance on so-called "zero-sum" thinking regarding security matters. The group agreed that it is necessary slowly to develop a "sum-sum" approach, even if the gains are not equal on each security issue every time. Fundamental to the development of such an approach is the recognition that security is shared by all, rather than an object of competition and that such security is particularly important for the smaller states, although it is also important for larger ones.

Second, the members of the Expert Group expressed concern that the various organizing concepts or visions that are being discussed in many quarters for the future of the region's security are all based on the exclusion of certain states and peoples on national, ethnic or religious grounds. Some of these concepts even draw legitimacy by making certain excluded parties the villains against whom the others must band together. The group members agreed that this mentality must be challenged.

Third, it was recognized that the region is characterized by asymmetrical relations between its states in terms of wealth, resources, populations, and relationships with external actors. Although differences in the social, political, economic, and military power of the states exist in all regions, in the Middle East these discrepancies can mean the difference between a state living in fear of its survival and not. Indeed, many of the smaller and less powerful states live in genuine fear of their existence should the regional order be challenged.

Fourth, the Middle East is a region where the so-called "security dilemma" is acutely felt. Simply put, as each side tries to maximize its own security through unilateral steps, such as acquisition of more weapons, this causes others to feel increasingly insecure. They, in turn, take action designed to enhance their own security, and the cycle repeats itself with the result that no state's security is actually enhanced. The Middle East will not break out of this cycle overnight, but the group members feel that the security dilemma must be broken and the development of a new way of approaching security in the region is the only way to do so.

During the group's work the Middle East peace process was suffering a dangerous malaise. In such an atmosphere it was sometimes difficult for the participants in the Expert Group to devote their thinking to long-term issues. However, they were determined to do so and the following is the result of their efforts.

Basic Concepts

Comprehensive Security. The discussion of the Expert Group revealed that there are at least two basic and interrelated issues beyond military security which must be addressed in any discussion of comprehensive security in the Middle East: social cohesion within states and the region as a whole; and the growing demographic problem and its attendant impact on the resources and environment of the region. A useful distinction was made between actual *threats* to regional security (issues which have reached the point where conflict or unrest which will affect regional security is possible) and *risks* (issues which may develop into threats if left unattended). At a minimum, a regional security regime must provide mechanisms that will allow the states of the region to deal with threats and prevent them from becoming the cause of wider disorder. However, a more fully developed regional security regime would provide the countries of the region with ways to cooperatively address the risks as well.

The security of the region can be threatened by several risk factors. The most obvious of these is widespread suffering and need, which involves the second issue, demographic growth and resource scarcity. There are also other more intangible challenges such as a widespread sense in some states that the elite has become distant from its society's cultural and religious traditions. To be effective, a regional approach to security must be comprehensive to the extent that it recognizes these pressures and makes provisions for them. This does not mean that such a regime would necessarily call for intervention in the affairs of states but rather that the regime would strive to create an environment in which such internal tensions do not lead to a threat to basic national security.

Cooperative Security. There was consensus within the Expert Group that the only organizing principle that would be acceptable in the region was *cooperative* security. By cooperative security the group meant an approach to security that stresses largely informal cooperation and dialogue between the states of the region in the development and implementation of a set of agreed regional principles of conduct. Specific bilateral and subregional arrangements may be based on coordinated or even collective security, but they should not be in competition with the broader cooperative regional regime.

A Regional Security Regime. Drawing from the varied experiences of other security regimes, the Expert Group reached the following conclusions:

- There is no set pattern to the development of regional security regimes in the world (Europe has opted for a formal, institutionalized regime, Asia for an informal, dialogue-based regime, and Latin America for a regime that combines features of the other two);
- The key is the adoption of a set of agreed norms within a given region which best expresses the local traditions and desires;
- The creation of such regimes does not, in itself, guarantee an end to conflict, rather it signifies a desire to develop a regional way of dealing with differences by creating mechanisms which offer alternatives to conflict;
- Regional security regimes must be inclusive; they cannot automatically exclude any actor that wishes to join and abide by the agreed norms just because that actor has a point of view that is not subscribed by all;
- Membership in regional security regimes must be voluntary;
- In many respects, the evolutionary process of developing a regional security regime is most important because each actor's perceptions are shaped over time by this process; and
- This process is open-ended because any regional security regime must be able to adapt and develop in response to new concerns and issues.

In short, the Expert Group agreed that the essence of a regional security regime is not the creation of regional security by removing all differences among states. Rather it is a *way of trying to pursue regional security by developing an environment which recognizes the inevitability of the continuation of differences but seeks to prevent their getting out of hand.*

Elements of a Regional Security Regime for the Middle East

Political and Military Dimensions

Objectives and Elements of a Security Regime. In considering the potential objectives and elements of a security regime for the Middle East, the

Expert Group sought to avoid burdening such a regime with too many specific tasks and expectations. Indeed, in the initial stages of developing a regime, it was felt that it would be wise to avoid setting specific objectives if they would necessitate the creation of an overtly institutionalized approach. Instead, discussion focused on the more general objectives that included:

- Lessening of "zero-sum" mentality and its replacement by "positive sum-sum" mentality;
- Reducing incentives and prospects for escalation of disputes by allowing for discussion of problems before they become crises; and
- Providing a set of regional norms of conduct that can be useful in dealing with bilateral and subregional problems as well as regional concerns.

Based on these objectives, the Expert Group took the view that the elements of a future regional security regime should include a mechanism for regular and ongoing dialogue at the senior level over a wide range of issues of regional concerns. Between such meetings, groups should gather at less senior levels to review and discuss specific issues, as directed by the senior levels. Finally, group members identified the need for a Regional Security Center of a more standing nature. The tasks of such a center could vary but at the basic level it could provide for regular and continuing dialogue on regional security issues. In exceptional circumstances, and if parties agree, it could seek to provide a measure of "early warning" of possible disputes and to permit rapid exchanges of views on them.

The essential objective was perceived to be *substantive regular dialogue, within the framework of a set of guiding principles of regional conduct, as to how states in the region should conduct their relations and further the development of a cooperative security environment.* How best to develop this dialogue is a matter left for the governments of the region. But group members believed that it should be done in a voluntary, flexible, and pragmatic way and without overemphasis on institutions and formal mechanisms (with the possible exception of a model Regional Security Center), at least in the first stages of the process.

Guiding Principles. The elaboration of a set of guiding principles for a regional security regime has often proved to be one of the most vital aspects of its creation. Many regional forums have resorted to a mixture of ideas from the United Nations Charter and seemingly anodyne, if worthy, statements concerning non-use of force and the promotion of human rights and freedoms. This has sometimes led observers to criticize these documents as rather meaningless. However, the Helsinki Final Act, the Charter of the Organization of American States and the Association of South-East Asian Nations Zone of Peace, Friendship and Neutrality have had an impact far beyond what was expected when they were first promulgated.

The Expert Group considered what kinds of guiding principles should suffuse the creation of a security regime for the Middle East. Not surprisingly, they did not achieve consensus, nor did they try to. Such a list of principles will have to be worked out by negotiation over a period of time. Nevertheless, experience of other regional case studies point out that certain fundamental ideas are common. In no order of precedence they are:

- Respect for human rights and fundamental freedoms;
- Equal rights for all peoples and recognition of their right to self-determination;
- Non-interference in the internal affairs of others and respect for the sovereign equality of states;
- Settlement of disputes by peaceful means, including the renunciation of the use or threat of use of force to settle disputes;
- Recognition of the right to legitimate means of self-defense within an overall commitment to ensure that military establishments are kept to the lowest level consistent with purely self-defense needs; and
- Commitment to the principle that weapons of mass destruction should be abolished.

The Scope of a Future Middle East Security Regime. In considering this issue, the Expert Group recognized that it is impractical and impossible "scientifically" to define the term "Middle East". Hence it sought to develop practical ideas as to how the Middle East might be defined for the purposes of a security regime. Perhaps the most important idea to come out of the discussions was that any definition of the region should be both flexible and pragmatic, and that it should subscribe to a functional principle. This means that, within certain parameters, the definition should be a function of the issue being discussed. Furthermore, due consideration must be paid to how any extra-regional, but interested, states may interact with decisions, and the criteria for who these are should be based on the issue under consideration.

Generally, the members of the Expert Group believed that any definition of the region must include different layers, but the relationship between them would change depending on the issue being discussed. As a general rule, the first layer consists of the core states: the members of the League of Arab States, Iran, and Israel. The second layer consists of what can be called the "proximate" states, those which border the region and whose actions could affect its security (e.g. Turkey, Pakistan, India, Europe, some Central Asian states, and possible others). In this context, many group members indicated that the role of Turkey is especially critical in many different functional areas. The third layer consists of states and groups outside the region, which have a demonstrated role to play in its security, such as the Permanent Five members of the UN Security Council, Europe, Japan, and others.

Based on the essential qualities of flexibility, pragmatism, and functionalism delineated above, in some cases a region-wide arrangement would be the primary vehicle, backed up by the "proximate" states and other extra-regional actors. In others, subregional arrangements would take precedence, backed up by region-wide principles and the involvement of necessary extra-regional actors.

The Role of Extra-Regional States. Group Members believed that:

- Extra-regional states must respect and adhere to agreed regional norms and values in dealing with the region and its peoples;
- Such states can support and reinforce specific regional arrangements achieved within the framework of these norms;
- The provision of security guarantees from key extra-regional states will eventually be necessary but is unlikely to be possible at the initial stages of the creation of the regional security regime; and
- All extra-regional states can use good offices to assist in regional attempts to resolve differences, including NGOs and multilateral processes.

The Role of Subregions and the Relationship Between Bilateral, Subregional; and Global Security Arrangements. Broadly speaking the members of the Expert Group recognized the existence of three distinct subregions in the Middle East: The Persian Gulf, the states of the "central area" of the Middle East (Egypt, Israel, Jordan, Lebanon, Palestine, and Syria) and the Maghreb. Of course, these subregions overlap in terms of both membership and concerns. In an era of rapid communications, long-range missiles, and other developments, many of the distinctions between subregions are breaking down. The promotion of subregional independence and integration is a key stepping stone to greater regional integration throughout the Middle East.

Members of the group believed that the creation of a region-wide security regime should be undertaken in a manner that is synergistic with bilateral, multilateral or subregional approaches to security issues. This could best be accomplished by establishing a broad set of principles, as suggested in the above discussion on guiding principles, which would be relevant to all levels of discourse in the region. Then a functional approach as to which issues should be dealt with at which level and in what manner should be followed. Some issues, such as those related to weapons of mass destruction, will require a regional approach. Others may best be dealt with subregionally.

The relationship of a regional regime to global instruments should also be flexible and pragmatic. Widely recognized global arrangements, such as the UN Charter and various international agreements on security and other issues, provide a basis for the conduct of relations in the region. The Middle East, like any other region, has a particular history and reality and the application of many of these arrangements to the region will not itself ensure security. What seems to be required is an approach that provides for regional complements to these global arrangements, or even subregional ones where appropriate.

Institutionalization of the Regime. There was a strong sense that the initial phase of any Middle East security regime would feature minimal institutionalization and be based primarily on informal, political arrangements. In this sense, the Asia-Pacific model, with its emphasis on opportunities for quiet dialogue within the framework of a set of guiding norms, was seen as worthy of further consideration. The group members were also impressed with the way in which "Track-Two" dialogues (unofficial, academic workshops in which officials take part in their private capacities) have played a crucial role in the Asia-Pacific region.

It was accepted, however, that regional development on certain issues would be greatly assisted by the creation of institutions. The examples from the multilateral track of the peace process of various institutions such as a regional development bank and desalination program are instructive. However, it was agreed that any such institutions should be limited to clear and functional objectives (on an as-needed basis) and that participation could only be voluntary.

The idea that an informal, non-binding approach is best suited to the Middle East is relevant primarily to the initial stages of the creation of a regional security regime. Eventually, legally binding commitments and the creation of standing regional institutions will be necessary in such functional areas as a regional weapons of mass destruction-free zone.

Steps Towards a Regional Security Regime. The question of the sequence of the steps to be taken in the development of a regional security regime is complex and multifaceted. As an overriding concept, group members recognized that the issue will be conditioned by the need to accept a *geometry variable.* This concept recognizes that not all parties will be willing to proceed at the same rate on all the same issues, and it also provides the essential flexibility that group members identified as necessary to the initial steps of the creation of a regional security regime. Practically speaking, this recognition has two aspects. First, there is the question of *when* efforts can be made to begin the development of such a regime in relation to other political issues that are under consideration in the region. Second, there is the question of the *order in which* a regional security regime should attempt to deal with the issues on its agenda.

In terms of the first question, *when*, the Expert Group identified two critical issues which will affect the development of a regional security regime: the peace process, and the question of how many regional states will be prepared to join in the development of such a regime at its outset. In relation to the peace process, the group agreed that there is a need for further progress in the Middle East peace process in order to create a suitable political climate for the creation of a regional security regime. That being said, many argued that regional peoples should begin to explore ideas inherent in the creation of a regional security regime as soon as possible as these ideas may further the peace process. They may also prove helpful in dealing with many other regional security concerns of the region that exist outside of the Arab-Israeli dispute. In this context, many members of the Expert Group believed that the Regional Security Center should be created immediately as an investment in future regional stability.

As to the question related to countries willing to join, the Expert Group recognized that talks on the creation of such a security regime cannot take place until those countries prepared to take part believe that their number constitutes a meaningful quorum and this is primarily a political decision. The only rules that the group could determine were *start with the willing and leave a seat at the table for others to join when they are ready*. However, it was recognized that latecomers would have to accept that which had been agreed before they joined.

Views differed regarding the *order* in which the issues of future agenda should be addressed. Some advocated the establishment of an agenda that would set goals and develop a sequence for their realization. Others believed that discussion of specific goals and timetable (i.e. a road map) for their realization could create division until a new atmosphere of trust had been achieved in the region. Both these views have a high degree of conceptual and political validity. There is no right answer. Despite the objection of some to a road map, it is important to note that progress cannot be made towards more advanced stages without the previous stages having been accepted by all sides. However, it is important that a commitment be made to address the whole range of issues, which are important to all and recognize that progress will sometimes involve trade-offs between different issues.

Developmental, Economic and Social Issues

In considering what some refer to as the "soft security" aspects of the agenda the Expert Group members were strongly of the view that this is a profound misnomer. There was consensus that, of all the problems faced by the region over the long term, it was those that fall under this umbrella which are most likely to cause civil unrest, arms races and wars. In the Middle East, the issues of "soft" security have a very hard edge. They include questions related to refugees, development, debt, water, the "prosperity gap", and others. These problems are intertwined in both functional and political terms and usually involve questions traditionally associated with the internal affairs of the states of the region. Agreeing to a regional approach for dealing with them necessarily implies that all participants pool their sovereignty in the service of the greater good.

The Expert Group agreed that issues related to the management of rapid social, political, and economic change in the face of stagnant economic growth (if not decline) are among the most critical ones for the future of regional security. But members of the Expert Group were of two minds as to how a regional security regime might assist in dealing with them. On the one hand, they recognized that actively dealing with issues ranging from demographics to water to reallocation of economic power in traditional societies would require the establishment of many regional institutions. On the other hand, the Expert Group recognized such institutional development as not entirely consistent with the belief of the members that a future regional security regime for the Middle East should initially emphasize informality and caution in the creation of standing institutions. Group members were firm in their belief that an approach mirroring the European approach, which emphasizes the creation of many "baskets" and overlapping institutions to deal with different aspects of security in a broad sense, would not work in the Middle East for some time to come if it were made an integral part of a future regional security regime. This type of approach is simply not consistent with the political tradition of the region. On the other hand, a regional security regime based on dialogue and consultation may serve to create the necessary atmosphere of good will and trust to permit such institutions to be established on an as-needed and functional basis, even it they are formally outside the regime *per se*.

Confidence Building and Arms Control in the Middle East Security Regime

The control of the Middle East arms race will be one of the most significant challenges before any regional regime. For analytical ease the group members discussed this subject as different sub-topics. They recognized, however, that these issues are intrinsically interwoven. They also recognized the essential link between progress on the wider question of political rapprochement on several levels and the creation of successful arms control regime in the region. Moreover, group members recognized that there would be trade-offs among the issues on the regional arms control agenda.

Confidence- and Security-Building Measures. Confidence building is a psychological process. Confidence- and security-building measures (CSBMs) exist as part of a larger process to assist in transforming the views of former enemies throughout the region. Critical to the understanding of confidence building is the idea that it is a process. Over time the implementation in good faith of various specific measures has the potential to create a sum that is larger than its parts. A commitment to begin to work towards a set of guiding principles for regional conduct would be a critical CSBM in the Middle East at this stage and would lay a foundation for many others. The Expert Group was, in itself, a confidence-building exercise. Of course, there is already significant confidence building under way in the region.

Several Persian Gulf states are tentatively exploring the possibility of new relations with each other and are engaging in modest CSBMs. Several neighbors of Israel have also been prepared to enter into CSBMs with it, despite tense relations.

Confidence building has, at times, been regarded as the "poor sister" of arms control: a lesser form of activity in which states engage when they are not able to agree on arms control treaties. The group rejected this evaluation. Instead, they believed that CSBMs are both an essential aspect of the arms control process and worthy of pursuit in their own right. CSBMs are especially useful in that they are steps which countries can take without affecting their fundamental security decisions but which build trust over time. The cooperative aspect of the negotiation and implementation of CSBMs is critical in breaking down barriers of mistrust and misinformation. This makes them ideal for the beginning process of rapprochement between former adversaries, when trust is not yet developed.

At this time the most important single CSBM is the peace process. Another important CSBM would be for all sides in the region to tone down their rhetoric. Once established, CSBMs and other agreements must be rigorously observed, as tenuous progress towards reconciliation can be undone.

Weapons of Mass Destruction-Free Zone. The Expert Group noted that all of the regions' states have accepted the notion that the Middle East should be a weapons of mass destruction-free zone (WMDFZ). But the group members believed that a politically and legally binding WMDFZ agreement must be a central objective of a regional security regime for the Middle East. Such a regime must mandate the abolition of all weapons of mass destruction in all states of the region; there can be no exceptions. It must be recognized that weapons of mass destruction have been introduced into the region by many countries for many different reasons and any regional approach to them must address all of these cases within the context of a the larger security regime.

As a first step, all the states of the region should commit themselves to the creation of WDMFZ in the region and to entering into serious discussions regarding the nature and establishment of such a zone. The membership of such a zone must include at least all of the states of the Arab League, Iran and Israel, with associated protocols for "proximate" states whose observance and cooperation will be vital. Such a zone will also have to be backed by security guarantees from the P5 states.

A Middle East WMDFZ will have to include special verification provisions for intrusive and reciprocal inspections, including challenge inspections. Many members of the Expert Group also expressed the view that it will be necessary for all the states of the region ultimately to adhere to the international standards as regards to the non-proliferation of weapons of mass destruction within a WMDFZ.

Conventional Arms Control. Although weapons of mass destruction have commanded a considerable share of the public debate on Middle East security and arms control, it was recognized that conventional weapons have caused far more deaths in the regions and consumed a much greater proportion of its arms budgets than WMD. The group recognized that any proposal to eliminate conventional weapons from the region would be naïve, but they did believe that the countries of the Middle East spend a dangerously disproportionate share of their limited wealth on conventional weaponry and offered the following thoughts:

- A regional security regime must strive to create an environment that will make possible for the Middle East states to exercise restraint, while accepting the notion that all states have a right to acquire some arms for their legitimate self-defense requirements;
- Extra-regional suppliers of weapons must also accept this need and demonstrate a willingness to forgo excessive arms sales in the region;
- Unlike a regional WMDFZ, which must exist throughout the region, conventional arms control might best be dealt with subregionally, within the context of broad overall approach to the issue;
- As a first step towards a regional conventional arms control regime, states should begin to discuss with each other, on a subregional and non-committal basis, their threat perceptions, doctrines, and the reasons why they acquire various conventional weapons; and
- While formal, conventional arms control negotiations are unlikely to succeed in the region as a whole for some time, specific cases of bilateral and subregional concern may be amenable to such negotiations and such efforts must be encouraged.

Missile Control. The introduction of ballistic missiles into the Middle East is having a particularly destabilizing impact, regardless of whether they are armed with conventional warheads or used as delivery vehicles for WMD. The trend towards acquisition of anti-ballistic missile systems is also of concern. A regional security regime must seek to eliminate them from the region, although this will be a long-term goal.

Control of ballistic missiles is more likely to take the form of unilateral restraint by states than binding agreements, at least for the first few years, but binding agreements will ultimately be necessary. Steps that would be useful in this regard might be pre-notification of launches, range limitations and the capping of missile stocks. Ultimately the interplay between missiles and certain types of conventional weapons, such as long-range strike aircraft, must be recognized and understood.

A Way Ahead

In considering how to translate their ideas into concrete steps, the members of the Expert Group recognized that it may take time before the ideas of this report are broadly acceptable. However, that does not mean that some sort of dialogue on these ideas cannot take place. One possible avenue for such discussions might be Track-Two initiatives.

Track-Two permits experts from the region to put forward and consider ideas without necessarily having to adopt them as "policy" before they have had a chance to develop their thoughts and see how others will react. Track-Two is not a new idea. Such East-West dialogues were conducted throughout the Cold War. The Asia-Pacific approach to regional security has elevated Track-Two to a position of almost semi-official status. Even in the Middle East, the Track-Two approach has been a part of the regional dialogue for many years. There are presently several Track-Two initiatives under way on regional security of which this Expert Group is only one. Nevertheless, members of the group believed that there is a need to place Track-Two in the Middle East on a firmer footing. Governments must demonstrate greater commitment and meetings must begin to take on the character of a coherent *process* that is ongoing rather than a series of isolated meetings. This desire to create a continuing process was part of the reason why the SIPRI Middle East Expert Group was organized as it was.

However, nothing can replace official discussions on these issues. Track-Two can help prepare the ground but at some point governments must make the transition from talking about security in an academic setting to agreeing on it at the negotiating table. It is possible to construct many scenarios as to when and how that might happen, but the key is political leadership, courage, and vision. As in all of the great changes that have taken place in the world in recent years (e.g. Glasnost, the collapse of the Berlin Wall, and the end of Apartheid) and those that have taken place in the Middle East itself (the Camp David Accords and the Oslo Process), great leaders must recognize that they cannot continue as in the past and must accept the need for far-reaching change. The Middle East stands at such juncture today.

The Middle East stands poised at the edge of an era of rapid change from which there is no going back. Its citizens and their leaders have difficult choices to make. They can go on as before; this is the easy path in a political sense. Or they can summon the courage to attempt some difficult and even frightening changes; this will be much harder politically. However, all the members of the Expert Group were united in the view that change is coming to the region. The politically easy path, going on as before, will not prevent it. Instead, it will ultimately lead to change under conditions of great suffering and unpredictability. Nor will some states be able to shield themselves from the adverse effects of change by virtue of advanced technology or wealth. The kinds of crises that confront the Middle East in the near future will affect everyone in the region and many outside of it at a basic level. The only way to prevent them is to accept the notion that the security of the Middle East is an indivisible whole that its peoples must stop competing over and begin to shape together through cooperation.

CHAPTER 14

The Gulf, Iraq, and the Future

Saif A. Abdulla Dehrab

By December 31, 2000, Slobodan Milosevic, a tyrant who haunted Europe for thirteen years, was ejected by a furious Serbian revolution.[1] Saddam Hussein was in full power and authority in Baghdad. On January 20, president-elect George W. Bush was sworn in as president. President Bill Clinton followed George Bush into retirement. Both men fought Saddam Hussein who has outlasted them both in Office.

Just before the year's end, on December 31, the leaders of the six Gulf States met to ponder issues of security and how to deal with Saddam Hussein and his regime. The positions of the opposing states were softened towards Iraq and the UN embargo. At about the same time, the local press in the Gulf was carrying pictures of President Khatami and the Russian defense minister exchanging views on how to meet Iran's military shopping list.[2] Relations with Iran, which improved recently, are still tenuous. Recently, Iran has "rejected a GCC mediation bid to resolve a dispute with the UAE over three strategic Gulf islands, insisting on direct talks ... The islands of Abu Musa and the Greater and Lesser Tunbs are located near key shipping lanes in the Strait of Hormuz. They are claimed by both states and held by Iran."[3]

January 17, 2001, the day commemorating air war activities that started against Iraq during the liberation of Kuwait, was a good observation point on how the conflict between the Arab states can be protracted. On the one hand, the Kuwaitis celebrated the occasion as the start of their liberation while Iraq took the occasion to launch typical attacks on the traitors and their friends in Washington and London. Within a week, the rhetoric was scaled up to the point that Iraq called for a new map to be drawn for themselves that would include Kuwait. In the end Iraq threatened to withdraw its formal recognition of Kuwait if the latter would not stop plotting against Iraq.[4]

In all this, nothing, local, regional or international, brings peace of mind to the people of the Gulf. Iraq is defying the international embargo and relatively succeeding at the expense of its people. Many countries, big and small, are violating the UN sanctions. Several Arab and GCC countries are re-establishing diplomatic ties. Iran is rearming and Iraq is able to develop weapons of mass distruction.[5] It is no surprise, to say the least, that people in the region are confused and bewildered.

A local Kuwaiti daily, *Al-Rai Al-Aam*, on April 10, 1999 reported two statements that bore identical messages. The first statement was by the Crown Prince, the Prime Minister of Kuwait (CP&PM), and the second was by the American Ambassador to Kuwait. The CP&PM held that at this point in time, "the Iraqi regime suffers from isolation and that the system is abhorred even by those closest to it".[6] At the same time, the American Ambassador zeroed in on Saddam Hussein and emphatically stated that "when the American President says that Saddam will fall ... this will happen".[7] Granted that if Saddam Hussein falls no one is going to shed tears, yet, it is a mistake to form foreign policy based on the coming or the departure of one person. Only a few years ago it was Castro and Noriega, last year it was Saddam Hussein and Slobodan Milosevic and now it is Saddam Hussein alone.[8]

The Arabs have their own feuds and cold wars, but the United States that always, regrettably, has to have a "fixation" to form foreign policies around the world, as a superpower cannot continue like this. A sound policy should evolve systematically with or without Saddam Hussein. A sound foreign policy should realize that despised decisions and policies by opponents are results of institutions, psyche, history, and, some times, unbalanced and fanatic minds, whether in a democracy with full participation or in an autocracy with concentrated power (Al-Khouri 1993).

In India, among the countries of the East, there seems to be a realization of this fact, making it a pivot in their strategic thought and foreign policy. To India, it is not the realm of military planning and plan manipulation that counts when dealing with an opponent. In the words of one Indian planner:

> The assumption that principal application of strategic thought is in the realm of the military alone is a common error, a simplism, for the culture of strategy is not born in that crucible. It is an intermix of many influences: civilization, culture, evolution, and the functioning of a civil society all contribute. It is a by-product of the *political culture of a nation*, and its people; an extension of the

> functioning of a viable state, more particularly it's understanding of and subscription to the concept of power: the nature of that power, its application, and more importantly its limitations. For power is not merely military, it is diplomatic and economic, coercive, or persuasive; power of ideas and thought and example. And all in all these ways of power of a state can be used. But, of course, there has first to be an understanding of this "state power" [or limitations] in political-military leadership. And that is where history and racial memories influence strategic thought, its culture, as does a sense of geography, and this lasts much more significantly for this is born a sense of territoriality. (Singh 1999, 2) (Emphasis added)

This statement is generic in nature. However, in the case of the Gulf states this chapter will attempt to make this argument more justifiable. I will demonstrate that the thought, culture and geography of the people are one of the core problems of security and strategic thought. History and memories are central in creating *core problems* that education and socialization have neglected.

The Core Problem

In the early years of the 21st century, after so many active policy encounters such as the dual containment and isolation of Iraq, it is time to declare that the old policies did not bear their expected fruits. Also, as a result, it is time to search for new policies that are comprehensive and realistic.

To begin with, as facts become more available, and as we piece things together, it becomes evident that for Saddam Hussein and his political system the invasion of Kuwait was predetermined and was taken very seriously. Staying in Kuwait, a paramount national prize, was a goal that Iraq could not have given up easily. Furthermore, annexing Kuwait would have changed the balance of power in the area and would have opened a Pandora's box governing future inter-Arab relations. Indeed, to Iraq and her Arab supporters this would have been tantamount to changing the ill-fated and defunct Arab system.

More recently, a seminar held in Kuwait on the future relations of Kuwait and Iraq drew great attention, comments, and criticism from every sector in the Gulf.[9] All local papers carried in depth reports with comments on the seminar. The participants, Iraqis, Kuwaitis, Arabs from the Gulf and elsewhere, and the Europeans, for three days examined two major issues: the perspectives of Iraq and Kuwait on each other and the future of peace and security in the region. The scenarios that all participants considered entailed the examination of these issues in the case of the survival of Saddam Hussein's regime in Iraq or its demise.

In all scenarios, the consensus was that Kuwait could not live with this situation without international guarantees and/or *the rehabilitation of Iraq*. The core issue that was raised bluntly was that this results from the ideology of Arab nationalism, which is nurtured in Iraq by all regimes. Iraq as a society and system of government was well dissected. Conclusions were drawn to the effect that Iraq cannot live in harmony with its neighbors. The weakest link in the chain of neighbors around Iraq is Kuwait. At any moment in the future, under domestic pressure or political expedience, Kuwait will be the point of rupture.[10]

As we enter the new millennium, it becomes evident that the war, the economic embargo, applying the no-fly zones, supporting the opposition, and repeated punishing attacks on Iraq are not producing tangible or effective, let alone efficient, results as far as the dislodging of the regime in Iraq is concerned. On the contrary, the regime has been able to convert all these actions against it into anger among the masses, driving a wedge among the members of the Security Council, and making the status of the UNSCOM ambiguous. True, misery is not new to the Iraqi people since the Iran-Iraq War. However, resilience and perseverance seems to be becoming a pattern in Iraq.

On the other hand, to the rich and luxuriant life style of the Gulf States, things are not going as expected. Opposition groups are finding a niche to chisel at the systems foundations. Thanks to falling oil prices, and Asian collapsing economies and recession, budgets are cut and fragmented in order to distribute the ever-smaller social pie. This is not good news, neither for the Gulf States nor for the US, the lone global power in the area. The most unmanageable "risk facing American interest in the Persian Gulf is neither Saddam Hussein nor Iranian expansionism. Rather, it is the slow but sure decay of the economic and political structures of the United States' *key regional allies*" (Zanoyan 1995, 2) (Emphasis added). It is fair to assume that the United States can be better off defending allies exposed to foreign aggression rather than allies facing domestic upheavals.

For the Gulf States, the long holiday from economics of abundance which was characterized by, among other syndromes, "the lack of binding budgetary constraints, which reduced and sometimes even eliminated the need to set spending *priorities* and allocate *scarce* economic resource" (*Ibid.*) (Emphasis added), is something new. This requires swift, harsh, and hard adjustments. In the end this will prove fatal if the switch is not swift, *systemic, persistent, and fair*. In the past the financial pie was so large that even with the "highly skewed income distribution, all sectors of the society saw some measure of improvement in their standard of living. Unemployment was unimaginable and governments showed a seemingly infinite capacity to hire both citizens and foreigners in public jobs" (*ibid.*, 4).

At a point in time, employment will become a source of political control and appeasement that will open the door for nepotism and corruption leading to further grievances and preventing those sincere politicians from dealing with the most important function of the state, i.e. planning for the future. The day-to-day affairs of government, when proper channels of communications are not developed, will become a heavy burden and will pave the way for grapevines, rumors, and hearsay that will further weaken the credibility of the system.[11]

This economic hardship following the Gulf War and decline in oil prices is coupled with heightened anxiety about national security and defense, given the potential for "increased interstate conflicts. Saudi Arabia's ... multibillion-dollar commitment to new civilian and military hardware from the West, coming only a few months after its celebrated budget cut announcements, are good examples of both pressure and anxiety" (Zanoyan 1995). The established elite is willing to embrace neither these new facts nor a reduction in their traditional shares. But the money is not there any more and the political systems have to deal with the situation. In Kuwait, in April 1999,[12] Patriot missiles stand erect around important buildings at some residential areas facing east and north. At the same time, the government passed a law to gradually install Kuwaiti citizens in jobs held by expatriates, raising the financial burdens on the national budget.

Pressure and anxiety make Kuwaitis unable to believe totally in UNSCOM,[13] nor in Saddam Hussein's intentions. Their psyche makes them observe the old local adage: "That who was bitten by a snake will always remain scared of a rope."[14] Yet, neither fear nor hope seems to help a community divided about how to avert being invaded and made a people without a country. Reflecting on such an anxiety, a young Kuwaiti political scientist recently, after quoting contradictory captions from President Bush and others, wrote:

> President Bush's predictions were wrong. We have entered, after the Desert Storm and up to this day and for the last eight years, a dangerous arms race until we became arms warehouses ... We spent in the Gulf, the largest arm importer in the world, 100 billion dollars and we will spend another equal amount in the next five years. The Americans (our main suppliers), the French, the British, and a cartel of main arm suppliers will compete to sell us their arms. Due to our hunger and greed for weapons, arms sale went up by 12 percent in the world ... The GCC countries spend a fourth of their national income on armament and security at the same time when the leaders of these countries ask the people to tighten their belts and when they seek to prepare the people for a period of post welfare state ... and the failing dual containment policy continues. And the policy of dealing with Iraq falters. The contradictory statements continue, and we get confused and bewildered. We should blame ourselves as Gulf people because, and I say it with pain, we did not learn any lessons in security. We failed to develop our capacities, we did not coordinate and we did not meet the demand for a united Gulf army. (Al-Shayeji, 1999)

Figures on national incomes and spending on armament reveal a not-too pleasant picture.

Table 14.1. Military expenditures (millions of dollars)

Country	Rank	Amount
Iran	2	$5,787.0
Iraq*	–	NA
Saudi Arabia	1	$18,100.0
Kuwait	3	$2,703.5
UAE	4	$2,118.0
Oman	5	$1,672.0
Bahrain	7	$276.9
Qatar	6	$940.0

Data source: 1999 CIA World Factbook.
*For Iraq no accurate data is available. However, just before the second Gulf War commenced, Iraq was considered to have the fifth largest army in the world.

The fact that Saudi Arabia spends three times more than Iran should not be considered that Saudi Arabia is more capable to cause a threat to Iran. Saudi Arabia started to militarize quite late and the population dimension plays in favor of Iran. Nevertheless, the burden of military build up becomes obvious when observed in the light of GDP percentages for each country:

Table 14.2. Military expenditures as percent of GDP

Country	Rank per percentage	Percent
Iran	7	2.9%
Saudi Arabia	1	12.1%
Kuwait	4	7.9%
UAE	5	5.0%
Oman	2	11.1%
Bahrain	6	4.5%
Qatar	3	9.6%

Data source: 1999 CIA World Factbook.

The burden of military expenditures is heavier for a country like Iran with a large population that requires more social and educational services after a popular revolution. For a country like Oman the jeopardy is obvious. Oman does not rely on oil as a main source of national income. Hence, a Gulf integrated force is to her advantage, while a country such as Saudi Arabia may prefer a less integrated force.

It is obvious that different priorities come into play. Far from it, in the GCC region, it is not a question of guns or bread. It is more than that. It is a question of survival; a question of to be or not to be as in the case of Kuwait. Yet differentiation *vis-à-vis* some priorities do exist. For example, the World Health Organization's ranking of health systems of these countries is radically different from rankings in military expenditures:

Table 14.3. World Health Organization's ranking of health systems

Country	Rank (RM)*	VS.(RH)**
Iran	2	7
Saudi Arabia	1	2
Kuwait	3	6
UAE	4	3
Oman	5	1
Bahrain	7	4
Qatar	6	5

*RM= Rank in $ Military expenditures (CIA World Factbook).
**RH= Rank in world health system (World Health Organization, www.who.org).

Although the margin in health system between Iran and Kuwait is quite wide (Kuwait is ranked number 45 among 190 countries and Iran ranked number 93), it is amazing how badly the position of Kuwait has deteriorated since the second Gulf War. Oman, on the other hand, is ranked number eight after a list of countries headed by France and Italy. At the risk of being redundant, a comparison of education and other social services will reveal the abyss that the Gulf countries are heading toward.

Inconsistency in planning and budgetary allocations is widespread among the Gulf countries. In Saudi Arabia the petroleum sector accounts for roughly 75 percent of the national budget, 40 percent of the GDP, and 90 percent of export earnings. Roughly 4 million foreign workers play an important role in the Saudi economy.[15] Although oil prices were expected to remain relatively high in 2000, Riyadh expected "to have a $7.5 billion budget deficit in part because of increased spending for education and other social problems".[16]

The Not So Hidden Malaise: The Ember Under the Ashes

Through careful examination of the different political positions, it appears that during the invasion and occupation of Kuwait, but more clearly later on, that the two extremes, the Islamic right and extreme Arab nationalists, or the Arab left, both supported Saddam Hussein in various degrees, albeit some more openly than others (Piscatori 1991). This indicates that some unsympathetic ideologies are still simmering quietly under the ashes of the past and, should something of similar nature in the Arab world take place in the near future, a divisive reaction of similar characteristic and magnitude might eventuate.[17]

Not only this, but some members of the intelligentsia in the Gulf itself invite us to take a more antagonistic sentiment *vis-à-vis* the West to the point of embracing weapons of mass destruction, nuclear, chemical, and biological, to be introduced to the area. Without specifying Iraq as one country that deserves this privilege, and at the same time not excluding it, in the cry for Arab-Islamic power, glory, and solidarity, Abdulla al-Nifisi argues:

> We have mentioned that in our relations with the West the Arab and Islamic Nations have passed through five stages ... [the impact of weapons of mass destruction is tremendous] Pakistan has good achievements in this field ... It is the duty of the Arab and Islamic Nation to adopt this experiment and add it to

> the strategic resources of the Nation ... There has to be coordination between the Arab and Islamic Nation and Pakistan to realize some [military] balance in this area. (Al-Nifisi 1999, 3)

This needed "*balance in the area*" which is the gist of the article, is intended to achieve a balance of power against the West and Israel. The argument is of course neglectful of the fact that the Gulf countries and Iran faced and are still facing the by-products of only a fraction of these weapons that Iraq had in the past.

The core issue for such thinkers is not peace and security; rather, it is a question of "we" versus "them". It is a cultural suicide that professes that either we rule or Israel, and the West, shall rule. It is the essence and soul of annihilation thinking at large. This kind of reasoning illustrates vividly, that values, fanatic minds, and ethos, even in the Gulf, would permit acquiring these types of destructive weapons as long as they satisfy a psychological need under the banner of Islam or Arabism (Stowasser 1987, Part II).

One has to remember the suffering of the Arabs at the hand of militant regimes since independence in Iraq, Syria, Egypt, and Libya, just to mention a few. But this is the same reasoning that prevails in the belligerent countries in the Arab world. The irony with such writers from the Gulf is that they assume that once these weapons are achieved, their use will be limited only against the "enemies of Arabs and Islam". Saddam Hussein was willing to use these weapons against his Islamic neighbor and his own people. This indeed is not a monopoly for the recent Ba'thi regime to enjoy (Barnett 1992; Ajami 1981).[18]

Back in the early days of independence, when weapons of mass destruction were absent at the scene, the Iraqi army "had established its nationalist and patriotic credentials in the hearts of many members of the urban populations in the summer of 1933 by its campaign against the Assyrians, who were considered as an important adjunct of British presence" (Farouk-Sluglett & Sluglett 1990, 15). The massacre of the Assyrians was made possible by the orders of the Acting Commander in Chief Baker Sidqi, an instant national hero. Violence of this nature is not new in the area, but Iraq seems to be ahead (Makiya 1997). Quite often, nationalism and fascism coincide. This is a certitude that causes some leaders in the Gulf States to have sleepless nights (Batatu 1978). This is why Patriot batteries stand ready in Kuwait in so many residential areas. Their situation is unique and their dilemmas are complicated.

The Gulf states, rich, small, and relatively weak, are vulnerable to such acts of aggression by another stronger and bigger state. Notwithstanding this predicament, the Gulf states have gone through social and political transformations that in a way could have augmented their weakness and their historic vulnerability. It is in their social and political transformations that some find the malaise for this and other feebleness. That is to say that any social advancement, political change or integration might, and will, create new demands and problems that require new extractive and distributive capacities that these systems may not have at this stage of their development. It is to confirm the view that social change is risky. But social stagnation is seen to be worse.

Integration and Social Transformation

There is no credible disagreement that the Gulf States have realized decent achievement in the process of integration and social transformation.[19] However, there is a local debate about whether the achievement is enough qualitatively and quantitatively to meet the exigencies of the demands of a modern world. The demands of our modern world require that nations should be able to attain power and security domestically or seek other accommodations to guarantee their independence, sovereignty, and stability.[20]

The Arabian Peninsula United. In its quest for gaining power and security, in the 1920s, under King Abdul Aziz Al Saud, Saudi Arabia as a modern political entity came into existence, under the sword of the king and the Wahabi Islamic ideology. In the annals of Arabia, the integration of the Arabian Peninsula was one of the great achievements in our time.[21]

Democracy and Constitution Introduced. In 1961, albeit in a different fashion and style, when British forces were packing to leave East of the Suez, Kuwait gained its full independence and immediately adopted a modern constitutional political system with parliamentary, executive, and judicial separation of power. Since then, Kuwait cannot claim any other significant achievement of this magnitude.

On August 2, 1990, Kuwait was invaded and annexed by Iraq. On February 26, 1991, Kuwait was liberated by a coalition of international forces led by the United States. Since then, Kuwait has been physically rebuilt, but evidence of social stagnation and decay abound in the society and polity. Indeed, the country has taken several economic and political steps backward. The invasion, the threat of renewed aggression by Iraq, and the defense of Kuwait remain to be the critical issues that the political community has to grapple with daily. Democracy in the Arab world does not solve all the problems. As a result, along with Kuwait, Lebanon suffers more often than not. Other factors bear heavily on this situation.

It is the dilemma of small "golden" fish, in a big pond, that is being perpetually exposed to predators and cannot be safe, whether it sinks or floats. One experienced local Gulf writer, Hassan al-Ebraheem, calls this succinctly the predicament of small states. He warned, years before the Iraqi invasion, that the position of Kuwait and the Gulf countries was precarious, to say the least. The invasion revealed this naked fact, but the governments of the Gulf did not heed the warning nor accepted the depth and the essence of the problem (Al-Ebraheem 1984). The enigma is not Iraq versus Kuwait; it is rather an Arab Nation against itself. Jill Crystal, in the case of Kuwait and Qatar, detected this at times of creation, yet the real causes continued until the invasion and after (Crystal 1990).

James Piscatori, early after the Gulf War, was able to map the terrain and the trends that deserve serious attention. His focus was on the sympathies of the Islamic movements *vis-à-vis* Iraq and Kuwait during the crisis (Piscatori 1991). Mohammad al-Rumaihi focuses the Arab position on the invasion of Kuwait. He observes how the Arab mind has betrayed its masters (Al-Rumaihi 1994). Both works deserve thorough examination free of emotional and short-term considerations.

A United Polity Created. Further down in the Gulf, by 1971, Great Britain left behind several dependencies and small sheikdoms to their own fate. With the British blessing and individual vision, these seven principalities formed a loose union under the name of the United Arab Emirates (UAE). The union seems to be working and providing a reasonable framework for the better distribution of wealth among the sheikdoms themselves and among their publics. This has been an exemplary union in the Arab world, given the fact that so many attempts have failed bitterly in the past (Al-Anzi 1997; Peck 1986).

Regional Organization Established. By 1980, at the outbreak of the Iraq-Iran War, six members of the Gulf States formed a new regional organization dubbed the Gulf Cooperation Council (GCC). The GCC included Saudi Arabia, Kuwait, Bahrain, Qatar, the UAE, and Oman. It deliberately excluded Iraq and Yemen (Abdulkhaleq 1998). Since then, the GCC has played a vivid role in coordinating policies among its members. During the occupation and liberation of Kuwait, the GCC actions and voices were well coordinated and unanimous.

As time went by, except for Kuwait and Saudi Arabia, there was a softer attitude towards Iraq under the pretext that the people rather than the regime in Iraq are suffering from the UN embargo and repeated military punishment. Whether for public consumption or for the truth, the media is rich with such sympathy towards Iraq. But the basic principle of an abhorring invasion and aggression remains central to the claims heard daily in the media. Regrettably, as far as the suffering of the Iraqi people at the hands of the Iraqi regime is concerned, one hears very little, as human rights and democracy hold different rank in the priority lists of Arab governments in general.

In any case, the GCC still lags behind in implementing solid educational, cultural, and financial policies among its members. Exceptions to this are their coordinated efforts in the OPEC and in competitions held occasionally in the field of sports and other youth activities. Not surprisingly though, competition is fiercest in the area of television and the media in search of prestige and establishing added credibility in the new world order. However, these group activities, although encouraged by the GCC, are carried out through other arrangements.

The Sounds of the Past

A return to the glorification of the past, folklore, and heritage has been put to use recently. The hope of the intelligentsia in the Gulf states is that this return would concentrate on the more common, integrative, and general heritage of the Gulf States, rather than on the more parochial and individualistic single states. The creation of new national identities will be disadvantageous to the integrative efforts of the GCC, which should be, at the end, inspiring the creation of a "Gulfi" identity.[22] As local national wealth becomes pivotal in forming local allegiance, parochialism may grow while the institutions of GCC are to be developed. The paucity of the "peoples dimension" in the GCC makes the masses indifferent to the survival or growth of the organization. At times, the GCC has been under much strain by the conflict that surfaced among some of its members such as Qatar's conflict with Saudi Arabia and Bahrain. Other silent conflicts may brew any time in the future and it may wreck the unity of the GCC. It is feared that some members might pull out from the GCC for simply embarrassing another member. Recently, Qatar came very close to doing this, due to some not too serious conflicts with Saudi Arabia (Marhun 1996).

Danger on the Road?

It remains to be pointed out that due to the fact that there is huge disparity in size and power among the members of the GCC, some psychological by-products of big neighbor, small neighbor erupt from time to time. Saudi Arabia, because of some old historic claims and unsettled border issues, is looked upon as a big brother with a big stick. This leaves a huge burden upon the shoulders of the Saudi diplomacy, which has not learned, yet, to talk softly while carrying a big stick (Taylor 1982).[23] It would have been more advantageous to every one if the Saudi stick were absolutely inconspicuous. Saudi Arabia has a different perspective regarding this big brother complex, which during crisis Iran tried to exploit to her advantage. "Saudi Arabia will remain the big brother for the Gulf States not by imposition but rather by the choice of the people of the region."[24]

However, outside observers have a different view, albeit with some exaggeration. The Economist claims a set of rules placed by Riyadh for the GCC to follow:

> Don't be friendly to Iran, Iraq or Israel. Don't be nice to anyone who is causing a fellow-ruler trouble. Don't upset the local pattern of family rule with fanciful ideas like democracy. And, above all, don't question the importance of the [GCC] chairman, Saudi Arabia—especially when, as now, the Saudi royals are at each other's throat.[25] (Quoted in Khashan 1977)

Some Stubborn Facts of Life

1. During the Gulf crisis of 1990/1991, the hope of the allies rested on the removal of the government of Saddam Hussein as a favorable collateral result of the war. This hope became more intensified when the United States and its allies made it a declared policy that working with Saddam Hussein was impossible. His removal became a goal. Nine years later, while many of the contemporaneous leaders of the West have left office, Saddam Hussein alone is still there. The logic of "dual containment" however eloquently articulated, did not work (Indyk 1994; Gause 1994). The notion that there are rogue states has

no equivalent in the political vocabulary of so many countries and continues to be a source of puzzlement to some of US allies (Rouleau 1995, 61). Yet as Madeleine Albright pointed out, the US is determined to go along this path. She says, "we recognize this area [the Persian Gulf] as vital to US national interests, and we will behave with others multilaterally when we can and unilaterally when we must" (Quoted in *ibid.*, 67).

There is not much problem in this reasoning except that it is not working and that the wrong people in Iraq are punished as even the exiled archenemies of Saddam Hussein admit. Of course, the military and civilian leaders of Baghdad certainly must be fully "responsible for their savage destruction of Kuwait and the atrocities committed there" (*ibid.*), yet Kuwait is hardly accomplishing any of her demand for the return of her POW's or compensations for loss of life or property. As Eric Rouleau points out, the people in the region either "are not aware of or give little credence to analyses set forth in postwar books and mimeographs alleging that Bush was misinformed about the damage inflicted on the Republican Guard, the elite units serving as Saddam Hussein's Praetorian Guard, that Bush was worried about going beyond the UN mandate and so on" (*ibid.*, 68). Common sense here sounds more American than one would expect and goes like this: "when you do something do it right the first time".

2. Yet, even the changing of the regime in Iraq may not help peace and stability in the area. It is part of the Iraqi political culture to be idealist, castle-builder, utopian, and combative and this creates anxiety for her neighbors. Ambitions to obtain nuclear, biological, and chemical weapons, the initiation of a long war with Iran and the isolation of Egypt as a punishment for signing the Camp David Accord are testimony to this assertion.

Change of regime in Iraq may bring a representative regime that reflects Iraq's ethnic, regional, and religious diversity but this may not be a blessing for the other countries in the region. If basic changes and rehabilitation are not introduced and implemented, as we are suggesting here, no change might be better than change that would bring about a pandemonium.

3. The other Gulf countries are small states and lack the population base to have strong armies or a large local work force necessary for sustained economic development. Instead, they have to rely on the West for protection and end up investing heavily in arms and

armaments. For trained manpower, they have to rely on Arab and skilled and unskilled Asian expatriates. While doing this in the short run may provide a much needed factor of economic development and security cover, in the long run however, this policy remains to be an economic and social burden, opening the door wide to strife, opposition and unrest. Ten years after the Gulf War, nothing seems to be working right and the choices are becoming limited. An alternative survival path is becoming imperative.

Alternatives for Survival: A Bitter Medicine?

As it has been observed all over the Middle East, it is too early to arrive at more than a tentative understanding of the transformation and its positive and negative concomitants that lie beneath the surface. We have to admit that "not enough is known about the characteristics of the new social classes that have emerged or are in the process of emerging; too little is known about the decision-making process within the ruling elites in each state, their relationship to other social groups, and the nature and workings of the linkages between members of the ruling elite and private capital, both foreign and domestic" (Farouk-Sluglett & Sluglett 1990). Yet we can conclude safely that, in spite of the immense national wealth they enjoy, the Gulf states have limited choices and alternatives regarding long-running security and survival. Given the fixed costs and limited variables that they can juggle around with, three main courses of action avail themselves:

1. They may stay on course and continue the present pattern, containing Iraq and relying on the West along with their own limited capabilities. This one is a typical negative and fatalist approach to politics that is not foreign to the region. "Let things work themselves out", is a slogan well heard and well rehearsed by local policy makers. For example, appeasing Iraq in her war with Iran proved fatal at the end.
2. They may reactivate the GCC mechanism and move to coordinate their military buildup and strategic plans. This requires a set of psychological and mental adjustments that should reduce the occasional conflict that may arise due to border disputes and divergent political outlooks. This alternative has further unseen problems when spending on arms instead of other needed essentials and luxuries might cause their over-burdened national budgets to break down. However, the biggest danger here is the

creation of military societies, which are not known to tribal and traditional Arab communities. The activities of military societies in Third World countries created havoc for these societies and their neighbors.[26]

3. Ideally, and undeniably it might sound blasphemous now in the area, but it is advantageous to all, that Iraq should put an end to its belligerence and combative attitudes and look towards serious development. The Gulf states should be willing to help Iraq move into this direction. "To help move in this direction" goes beyond the typical diplomatic practices that exist in the Middle East. There will be domestic and international resistance to the idea. But gradual and step-by-step efforts should be employed with tough and arduous diplomatic toil based on goodwill and faith in the survival of the whole. These efforts would look too risky for some of the countries especially Kuwait and Saudi Arabia but the potential gains will outlast the inherited fear and suspicions. The Gulf states have to learn that the price of inaction could be far more costly than accepting a bitter medicine that in the end would be a healthy remedy. Admittedly there is no such precedence in the Arab world, but if the wars of past Europe were examined, there would be vivid testimony for such a hope. If Islam and Arabism have any bounding or gluing factors, it is time to test this at this historic moment. The gradual steps to be taken in this direction should proceed along these peaceful *diplomatic paths*:
   a. Improving relations with Iraq and Yemen and helping them disarm and finance many Iraqi and Yemeni projects that will create goodwill, and foment and generate development. Successful confidence-building techniques should be applied and tested in this region. It is an irony to believe that confidence-building measures could be effective in the Arab-Israeli case, but hesitate in trying and giving this concept a chance in the Gulf. We should give this a chance since everything else is failing big time any way.
   b. The Gulf states should reduce their arms gradually and seek international guarantees for their security.
   c. This plan should be a ten-year project supervised and guaranteed by the international community. The United States, Great Britain, France, and Russia should be the supervising big powers.
   d. The program should proceed gradually and result in creating a peaceful environment with the two protagonists, Iraq and Yemen, becoming members of the GCC.

e. Towards the end, the members of the GCC will be capable of forming deeper integration similar to the way it was done within the European Union.
f. The Gulf states should be able to define the maximum and minimum acceptable capitulation from Iraq. For Kuwait, it seems only four areas of grievances are negotiable:
    1. An official apology from Iraq and an unequivocal declaration of the sanctity of the borders is a reality that needs to be made part of the state-to-state coexistence.
    2. A serious effort should be put forth to determine the fate of the POWs and those missing in action.
    3. Compensation by Iraq for all the damages and losses incurred by Kuwait, private or public. GCC banks and financial institutions providing easement for Iraq and reparations for Kuwait and the Gulf States may finance compensations.
    4. As to the affront to the dignity and honor of Kuwait's ruling family one should say this in reality is not in existence anymore. The people that count most—the Kuwaiti people—have redeemed their dignity. Nowhere, that I know, was a regime exiled out of its home to return in triumph and respect. The one who lost dignity was the regime in Iraq. What needs to be done is to save the Iraqi people because of the indignity of their government. The longer we continue in this Iraqi people indignation, the deeper their hatred to Kuwait and the Gulf. We have to move in this direction, for our own sake and the sake of the Iraqi people.

Counter Arguments

The hope that one day the Gulf may become a sea of tranquility along the lines we suggested above has its opponents. Old habits do not die easily. Therefore, it is important to prognosticate some counter arguments down the road.

First is the assumption that Iran, both Islamic and imperial, represents a major source that seeks hegemony in the area. In the absence of strong military deterrence from the GCC, it is argued, Iran might seek to advance her influence. Notwithstanding the international security arrangements that the GCC countries enjoy, the GCC countries have a limited chance in warding against Iranian aggression. Iran as a peculiar democracy following a mass revolution and a country dominated by the aspirations of the youth, needs to provide plenty of social goods for its people. A good and secure atmosphere is conducive to a better society and better neighborly conduct. This so-called Iranian dialectic, could be applied to Germany *vis-à-vis* other smaller European countries. On the contrary, Germany today is a factor of stability and economic progress for many European countries.

Another counter argument is the perennial stigma and phobia created by Israel. Some argue that as Israel finds the Arabs disarmed, it will manipulate the situation to its advantage. This reasoning is hollow. Today the countries that signed peace treaties with Israel—Jordan and Egypt—have reduced their military spending without reducing their efficiency to defend their territories. These two countries were never as secure as they are today. Syria, which holds its military power on war alert, is by far less secure than Egypt or Jordan. If Israel attacks Jordan, for example, it would lose the sympathy and support of the American people and the US Congress. This is the worst calamity that might befall Israel. One can argue for the sake of argument what is it that the Gulf states can defend if Israel seriously decides to knock out. Only two minutes over Baghdad ended the Iraqi nuclear dream for a long time.

The other counter argument is that the New World Order makes coexistence with the present regime in Iraq impossible. The answer to this is that there are so many bad regimes in the world with which the United States has learned to coexist. The United States did not lose lives and material in Iraq as it did in Vietnam, nor can North Korea be considered a lesser menace than Iraq. Iran, and its revolution, caused more humiliation, by holding American diplomats as hostages. Evidence shows serious interest by the United States to deal with North Korea and Iran in the realm of economics and culture. The facts are that opening to China and lowering the status of Taiwan in US foreign policy started with a game of ping-pong. No one knows what would be the aftermath of the Orioles in Havana.

No one in the American administration has precluded the possibility of rehabilitating Iraq, with or without Saddam Hussein. The logical conclusion dictates that even if the US is seriously seeking the destabilization of the Iraqi regime, this is not going to happen by remote control. Controlled openness is the only way the people of Iraq may learn what they are missing. Had isolation been the policy of the allies after World War II, both Germany and Japan would have remained a burden of some sort.

The American Ambassador in his statement summoned the Kuwaiti business community to look forward and seek the fruits of the coming economic boom after the fall of the regime in Iraq. He is right in one postulation and wrong in the other.[27] Iraqi economic buildup is a boom for every one, especially Kuwait. He is wrong that everything has to wait for the fall of the regime. The world has learned that the economy of peace is genuine and more productive than the economy of war. The United States and President George Bush were not able to cash in as the result of the war economy. Eventually signs of recession showed up and President Bush, this American war hero, lost his office to a novice candidate, with no experience in foreign policy or military service.

Hence, it is fair to conclude that a peaceful environment with arms control and limitation is one that the area needs. A return to serious economic growth and economic gains will direct the attention of the regimes toward making peace and happiness for their people rather than war and oppression. I know of very few revolutions that erupted while things were going well. Only when anxiety grips the well to do middle class that the misery of the suffering masses becomes a contagious political slogan.

The logical justification of this "ideal" alternative is our principal focus in this chapter. To be able to further augment the validity of this assertion, we need to deal with a few basic and some secondary concepts, which are essential for the understanding of this situation. Needless to say, these concepts are not uniquely at work only in the Gulf area. Bahgat Korany finds in Keohane and Nye (In Hudson 1999, 35–59) a useful perspective that allows us to examine the new balance of power in the Middle East. From balance of power to balance of weakness and finally balance of benefits he visualizes a new Middle East. In my view the perspective does not apply adequately to the Gulf and some Arab states. The Arab-Arab relation among some states in the area is perceived as a domestic family business among the participants and, hence, concepts such as realism and complex interdependence are not at work (Khouri 1993).[28]

A quick examination of the concepts of realism and complex interdependence, as presented by Bahgat Korany (1999), makes it evident that the concepts that we present below is more akin to this Gulf situation. We assume that the Gulf region will take the central stage of events, especially as the peace process between Israel and the Palestinians shows glimpses of hope. It is imperative to develop helpful concepts in studying the area. Nonetheless, I shall present Keohane and Nye (1977) framework for comparison and contrast.

Table 14.4. Political process under conditions of realism and complex interdependence

	Realism	**Complex interdependence**
Goals of Actors	Military security will be the dominant goal.	Goals of states will vary by issue area. Trans-governmental politics will make goals difficult to define. Transitional actors will pursue their own goals.
Instruments of State Policy	Military force will be most effective, although economic and other instruments will also be used.	Power resources specific to issue areas will be most relevant. Manipulation of interdependence, international organizations, and transnational actors will be major instrument
Agenda Formation	Potential shifts in the balance of power and security threats will set the agenda in high politics and will strongly influence other agendas.	Agenda will be affected by changes in the distribution of power resources within issue areas; changes in the importance of transnational actors; linkages from other issues and politicization as a result of rising sensitivity interdependence.
Linkages of Issues	Linkages will reduce differences in outcomes among issue areas and reinforce international hierarchy.	Linkage by strong states will be more difficult to make since force will be ineffective. Linkages by weak states through international organizations will erode rather than reinforce hierarchy.
Roles of International Organizations	Roles are minor, limited by state power and the importance of military force.	Organizations will set agenda, induce coalition formation, and act as arenas for political action by weak states. Ability to choose the organizational forum for an issue and to mobilize votes will be an important political resource.

By a quick inspection, we may conclude that the major variables in this schema vary with the variables we choose for our study. While goals of actors, instruments of state policies, agenda formation, linkages of issues, and roles of international organizations are highly important variables in studying the political behavior of states, in a situation of conflict they are less outstanding as it will become obvious in our schema. Here quantification is very possible to attain by developing scales using indicators that can be measured comparatively.

We will present four sets of prepositions and attempt to demonstrate the validity of our assumptions. The interconnectedness of these concepts reveals the minefields that one should go through carefully when dealing with the area. The following study is a tentative road map for navigating safely.

Basic Concepts as Determinants of Political Behavior

1. Propensity for Violence (PV):

This is the real and/or the potential predilection for the use of physical violence for political purposes whether by state or the opposition. War, coercion, *coup d'état*, terrorism, political assassinations, and mass riots, especially those that use physical means in confronting the police forces, by definition, are acts of violence. Based on political myth and socio-psychological orientation, some cultures at some stages of social and economic development exhibit a readiness to get involved in violence more than others.

In the Arab world, some eschatological myths such as the destiny of the Arab Nation or the future of Arab unity are the driving forces behind so many acts of violence in the past and recent political actions. We have placed the countries of the GCC and Iraq in categories and assigned an ordinary scale and gave a value of high, medium or low to each entry. Our ranking pays keen observance to historic and recent events (Gurr 1980, 1964).

2. Propensity for Aggression (PA):

In using this concept we intend to arrange the countries of three GCC states and Iraq on an ordinary scale of their readiness to commit aggression against another state. Aggression is defined to denote any infliction of injury upon an opponent whether through the direct use of military means, sabotage or terrorism. Economic warfare is not a direct concern here, since the impact of economic boycott, embargoes, and other economic wars, are slow to show serious damage and quite often than not, before the impact of an economic warfare starts to bite, the combatants resolve their conflict under the slogan of Arab brotherhood (Khouri 1993).

This propensity as a potential is associated with social, political, and economic conditions of the conflicting parties. But as convergent evidence points, more than anything else, political belief and political myths are very instrumental in leading to conflict and the resort to use of aggression as a tool for settling disputes.[29] A review of the history of the area will speak for this assertion. Ideological orientation and personal feuds are causes for cold wars that last and shift partners as time goes by like quick moving sands (Taylor 1982).

3. Degree of Satiation (DS):
The degree of satiation is a function of the value one country represents as a prize for another country to occupy, annex, or defeat. Three factors are essential in determining the magnitude of such a value:

1. Location of the country sought, in relation to the country seeking to influence events. If country *A* seeks to influence *B* that is contiguous to *A*, then the value of such a prize is relatively higher. Kuwait represents such a case *vis-à-vis* Iraq. Iraq would gain more access to the Gulf and oil resources should Iraq be able to keep Kuwait annexed. In some other cases, the value of the sought after state is not in annexing the respective state but in keeping it ideologically a buffer state between two conflicting ideologies. The case of Saudi Arabia *vis-à-vis* Bahrain is a good example.
2. Natural and strategic resources are a key factor in determining the value of the sought after state. Although it is evident that Iraq has interests in Kuwait, with or without its oil, the fact remains that the strategic location of Kuwait was a key factor in invading and annexing Kuwait in August 1990.
3. The value added to the status of the aggressor locally or regionally is another factor that raises the value of the prize. Although we have no independent evidence to support or refute the official Iraqi claims, it is clear that the regime in Iraq tried to build support and credence for the invasion and occupation of Kuwait. In a democracy, examining public opinion or the free media can easily test this, but in autocratic society this is impossible. Yet it is possible that, at times, such actions of a regime might backfire and lead to a *coup d'état*.

4. Comparative Range[30] of Vulnerability (CRV):
This is a factor of proximity (see Table 14.5) to a source of danger, availability of outside help to the victim, and the presence or absence of a political alibi. If we examine the Iraqi invasion, the Gulf War of 1991 and its aftermath, we can be sure that Kuwait and Saudi Arabia fall in a high-risk area as far as Iraq is concerned. Other Gulf states can be ranked in lower risk areas, at least in the short run.[31] This factor may partially explain why other Gulf States developed a softer attitude toward Iraq in spite of the American hard position. Applying the comparative range of vulnerability to Iraq, Iraq itself falls in the high-risk area *vis-à-vis* Iran, Turkey, Syria, and Israel. More recently, Jordan represented a high-risk area for Iraq's comparative range of vulnerability. Other domestic factors, such as Arab domestic cold war syndrome, make Jordan a lesser threat than one expects. However, in this chapter we examine the case of Iraq in reference to her position relative to the Gulf States (see Table 14.5).

It is useful to view these basic concepts as "objective" factors in interstate relationship in the Gulf region. The other set of concepts that we labeled as secondary could be viewed as "subjective". Admittedly, the distinction between the two sets is not so neat. However, with scrutiny and some precision, it is possible to reach results that could explain political behavior in this area. Fortunately, previous observations regarding Arab cold wars and search for hegemony and influence do reveal the personal and objective factors in foreign policy among the Arabs (Taylor 1982).

Secondary Concepts as Catalyst in Political Behavior

Two dormant concepts at work that help activate the other variables are the concept of perceived hegemonic role and relative size of the opponent state.

1. Perceived Hegemonic Role (PHR):
It is established in the Islamic, Ba'thist, and other Arab Nationalist ideologies that it is the mission of the believers to dislodge the disbelievers from the position of leadership and responsibility. Examining the Iraqi media during the Gulf crisis makes this assertion self-evident. Not only in this case but also during the Arab Cold War at the high days of Nasser reveals the naïveté of some altruists who believe that they hold the truth and the whole truth. The two-camp syndromes, that of those who are believers and those who are infidels, have transpired from Islamic ideology to Arabism.

Table 14.5. Basic concepts as factors in inter-gulf politics: a hypothetical chart

Country	**PV**	**PA**	**CRV**	**DS**	**Results**
Iraq	Hi	Hi	Hi (Iran, Turkey)	NA. It is not expected that Iran or Turkey would take advantage of Iraq due to international and regional reactions	Vulnerable to aggression
Saudi Arabia	Lo	Lo	Med (Iraq or Yemen)	Hi. If Iraq changes border arrangement with Kuwait. Success here means Bismarkian approach	Vulnerable conditionally
Kuwait	Lo	Lo	Hi (Iraq)	Hi. Iraq values Kuwait as a prize	Aggression is always possible.
Bahrain	Lo	Lo	Med (Iran and Iraq)	Med. To Iran no desire of annexation. Influence and balance of power toward Saudi Arabia main goal.	Iran can cause trouble. No invasion possible. Invasion leads to total war: Arab vs. Persian. Iraq at Bismarkian stage will invade.
Qatar	Lo	Lo	Med (Iran) If sovereignty challenged	Med. Like Bahrain to Iraq and Iran.	Neither Iran nor Saudi Arabia will invade. Military pressure is possible.
UAE	Lo	Lo	Med/ Hi(Iran)	Med. (Iran).	Only local problem at economic austerity.
Oman	Med	Lo	Lo	Lo. No trouble. Sovereignty accepted.	Border troubles.

* Proximity is defined as relative to location of a country and whether a country shares borders with Iraq, Iran or Saudi Arabia as big neighbors.

Pluralism is not really accepted among Arab states even though the charter of the Arab League makes it imperative upon the members to respect the sovereignty and integrity of each other. As a result, those ideologically oriented countries are the hegemonists in orientation, and, deep in the heart of their leadership, the belief that some regimes do not deserve to rule is very obvious. *Our hypothesis tests this notion.*

Historically, some Arab states played the role of the hegemonists. However, recently, since the death of Nasser and the subsequent decline of Egypt's regional influence, there has been no "center" in the Arab political system around which smaller states might have opted to "bandwagon" in search for security away from the local hegemonists (Walt 1987). In the view of Michael Hudson, "even in Nasser's heyday, some small Arab states took advantage of the United States' influence to "balance" against the Egyptian leader" (Hudson 1999, 17). Nevertheless, in the 1970s, the security of individual states was enhanced by "the absence of a potential regional hegemon: unification or the Prussian model was no longer a plausible scenario" (*ibid.*). This was not the case by 1990. At this time, Iraq fully armed, financially broke, and psychologically prepared, was the perfect Prussian candidate.

2. Relative State Size: small/ big state (RS):
It is a fact that small states in the Arab system do not command the respect that sovereignty allows. Several small Arab countries are looked to as aberrations created by the colonial power. Anecdotes are abounding in this regard. Here my interest is how a state size might affect the behavior of a larger state to launch aggression against another one.

Table 14.6. Secondary concepts as factors for being exposed or cause for aggression: a hypothetical chart

Country	PHR	RS	Results
Iraq	Hi	NA	Ready to intervene
Saudi Arabia	Med	Big	Can stand firm, short of intervention
Kuwait	Lo	Small	Ready to use financial and media
Bahrain	Lo	Small	Play the victim role
Qatar	Lo	Small	No experience. Media effective
UAE	Lo	Small	Financial role
Oman	Med	Med	Expect respect

Propositions

Like fashion, ideas reach late to third world countries.[32] But, as fashion can be put to use, ideas take time to get used to (Tetreault 1997). The present day notions of security are still based on the pattern that Morgenthau laid many years ago (Morgenthau 1973; Buzan 1991; Gellman 1988). Morgenthau and followers saw that security was a derivative of power, hence the concept of power and peace. As such, acquiring power is a sure route to security. In the Arab world, this idea permeates all aspects of life, public and private. As a turn around, our conception here is radically different. Instead of power and pacification, I am suggesting that development[33] and peace be focal points for acquiring security. Many would place security as a final goal. Idealists tend to "see security as a correspondence of peace: a lasting peace would provide peace for all" (Buzan 1991, 2). I see the merit of this outlook, but I seek another concept that goes beyond security and power as motives for behavior and behavior modification. The taste of development, the joy of success, and the pleasure of happiness coupled with democracy and popular participation in decision making will make governments think twice before launching invasions or making wars.

A country such as Iraq, should feel, expect, or imagine an incentive for peace. From this point of view our propositions depart. Our propositions are some logical statements posed to stimulate further research and examination. As they stand now, they are subject to acceptance or rejection, no more or less. The statistical aid provided should add to the credence of each statement. Reference to the tables, back and forth, will make the propositions self-evident.

Proposition 1. Disarmament of Iraq will make available a reservoir of funds for development in Iraq while reducing the need for borrowing from neighbors.[34] The same result will accelerate economic development in other Gulf countries, which are facing a tremendous population growth. Soon, Iran alone needs to create near one million jobs a year.

In the literature on the cost of war one can find diverse outlooks that cannot but accept that wars are costly even when war is credited with major events such as capitalism and the emergence of representative institutions (Barnett 1992). Some find that armament from a different source might have a different result as far as war and peace are concerned (Kinsella & Tillema 1995).[35] Jochen Mayer and

Ralph Rotte (1999) see differently. They point out that the stabilizing effect of arms transfers clearly decreases with the total amount of armament supplied to the region. The economic burden to some of the Gulf States, to say the least, looks so wasteful.

Proposition 2. The GCC members (especially Kuwait) will provide a good base to spearhead economic development in Iraq. (Free Zone ports facilities, available capital, and communications). Iraq does not have many grievances against history. Yet it is in the subconscious of the Iraqi regime that geography is not fair to Iraq. All the conflicts Iraq has had with Kuwait or Iran have been geography-based. The free zone of Kuwait port facilities can provide all the services peaceful Iraq needs. The surplus capital in the area along with a first rate communication system will be heaven for Iraq.

Proposition 3. Disarmament of the GCC will provide a good population base for economic development. It is to the advantage of the Gulf States to benefit from the manpower capabilities of Iraq and Iran. Both countries have excess manpower that seeks employment in the Gulf countries. At present, the Gulf countries rely on manpower from Asia, Africa, and other places. Those who come to the Gulf carry a culture that can not always coexist peacefully with the local cultures. The taboo the Gulf states have against workers form Iraq and Iran is that they are highly political. Should politics become peaceful and pacific, labor movement will become uncongealed. Nevertheless, population distribution is lopsided relative to income. Although the GDP is not an accurate statistic due to the fact that it does not take into consideration the pattern of wealth distribution it can, nevertheless, give a good indication of the position of one country *vis-à-vis* another country on scale of national wealth. We should observe that the top three countries in terms of population (Iran, Iraq, and Saudi Arabia) have lower GDP *per capita* figures. These countries, however, are among the countries with high military spending. It is an irony that among the top five countries in military spending relative to their respective GDP, three are from the GCC. With the list topped by Eritrea, followed by Angola, and North Korea, Saudi Arabia, Oman, and Qatar spend 12.0 percent, 11.9 and 9.6 percent, respectively. Needless to say, the GDP difference between Qatar and Eritrea is tremendous (1999 CIA World Factbook). This is another travesty of this century.

Table 14.7. Population and GDP in the gulf region (*ibid.*)

Country	**Population**	**GDP *per capita***
Iran	65,179,752	5,000
Iraq	22,427,150	2,400
Saudi Arabia	21,504,613	9,000
Yemen	16,942,230	740
Oman	2,446,645	7,900
UAE	2,344,402	17,400
Kuwait	1,991,115	22,700
Qatar	723,542	17,100
Bahrain	629,090	18,100

Proposition 4. Economic development and peaceful environments will further augment cooperation for economic development and inter-Gulf integration. The example of the European Union is a good one. France and Germany fought for several hundred years. The results were disastrous for both. It is only under the banners of unity, democracy, and peace that both countries are facing the challenge of globalization, the demands of democracy, and the exigencies of social wellbeing. We find in the literature on democracy and peace, and non-military buildups and development a witness to the validity of this assumption. We believe that in a Guns versus Butter dialectic, different economies may have different cause/effect patterns on income. However, examining the economy of a non-industrial country with the view of economy being made up of four sectors, which are mutually exclusive and exhaustive with respect to output, is a useful abstraction that helps us understand the contribution of the military to the economy (Antonakis 1999, 504). Antonakis calls these sectors *M* for military, *G* for nonmilitary government, *E* for exports, and *R* for the rest of the economy (*ibid.*, 505). The sectors that create externalities on other sectors and impact the factors of productivity may vary from one economy to another, but it is safe to assume that in the non-industrialized rentier economies of the Gulf that mostly depend on the export of oil, the military does not create externalities and hence has no value added to the economy.[36]

Conclusions

This chapter was never intended to be a trip in fantasy or daydreaming. Iraq, Iran, and the Gulf states, sooner or later, have to face their own people demanding economic progress, dignity, and peace. The core problem is a burden of history. But the present day ideology that the leaders propagate cannot go very far. The "war against Israel" as a slogan has used all its steam and people are saying that if the Arab military cannot deliver war then the leaders should deliver peace and economic progress. This is a slogan heard in Egypt, Iran, Syria, and Iraq. The war of 1967 and the two Gulf wars have had sobering effects.

The Gulf states are at a crossroads and a quandary. They are not able to defend themselves in spite of the great wealth they have. Their neighbors are not so rich but overpopulated and relatively strong. Hence, the dilemma remains: who should defend the Gulf and at what price?

The Gulf states hope to see the day when Saddam Hussein is gone so that they may turn a new leaf. Nevertheless, paradoxically, it is no longer an ego or personality question. It is a question of survival. With or without Saddam Hussein, if the political culture is not refined, if the need for economic progress is not acknowledged, and the search for peace is not in earnest, the problem will stay with us for many generations to come. The Arab world lost half a century preoccupied with Israel. As the hope for peace with Israel becomes a viable possibility, Arab-Arab conflicts should not preoccupy the people for another half a century. As a result, Iraq has to join the caravan of peace now, if there should be any peace. It is a burden over the shoulders of those who want peace earnestly, to find the *incentives* for Iraq to do so. Otherwise, only Allah knows what is going to befall the Gulf area. This chapter is an attempt to point to the right direction.

Notes

1. See the full story in *Times* 156, No. 166. October 16, 2000.
2. Al-Qabas, No.9889. December 30, 2000: 17.
3. www.CNN.com. "Ties with Iran, Iraq dominates Gulf Arab summit." December 30, 2000.
4. For example see Al-Qabas starting January 17. On January 25, 2000 Al-Qabas, No. 9915, reported from Reuters the story that Iraq has threatened to withdraw her recognition of Kuwait.
5. *The Sunday Times* of London has reported, quoting an Iraqi source, that Saddam Hussein has ordered the Iraqi scientists to resume their nuclear research

activities since August 1998. This news item was reported in the local Gulf people with little comments. See Al-Qabas. No.9886. December 25, 2000:18.

6. Al-Rai Al-Aam. "Kuwait: Dar al-Jazeerah Press," *Printing and Publishing Co.* Vol.11615. April, 10, 1999: 1 & 27.
7. *Ibid.*, pp. 1 & 3. Now notice that President Clinton left office on January 20, 2001. Had something drastic happened to Saddam Husscin in thc interim period, wouldn't it have definitely added to the credibility of the ambassador?
8. I assume that Fidel Castro is a permanent enigma that the US foreign policy has learned to live with.
9. See Al-Qabas No. 9661. May 14, 2000: 1, 9 and 12.
10. This was the gist of the argument presented by some Iraqis in the conference.
11. Bernard Lewis warns us that in order "to approach some understanding of the politics of Islam, of movements and changes which are perceived and expressed in Islamic terms, we must first try to understand the language of political discourse among Muslims, the way in which words are used and understood, the framework of the metaphor and allusion which is a necessary part of all communication." (Lewis 1991, 5)
12. April 9, 1999 is a very significant day from the perspective of this writer. A child conceived by this date is expected to be delivered at the first day of the year 2000.
13. For a fine but not too recent evaluation of the UNSCOM experience see http://editors.sipri.se/pubs/Factssheet/unscom.html.
14. My own translation from Arabic.
15. http://www.cia;gov/cia/publications/factbook/geos/sa.html. p.5
16. *Ibid.*, p.6.
17. Notwithstanding the heroic resistance of the Kuwaiti people, given population size and the terrain, the total governmental and administrative system of Kuwait collapsed after less than six hours of Iraq's incursion and military operations.
18. The cost of war to Egypt and Israel is well documented by Barnett (1995) and in other places. What is interesting is how Barnett traces the development of state versus society in presumably two different settings. However, given the level of civic societies in the Arab world, the dominance of state over society because of military mobilization becomes more blatant in the Arab society than Israel. He argues, "The state's attempt to mobilize the instruments of coercion to defend its territorial integrity has been closely associated with the development of the state and changes in state-society relations." (p. 3) I do not think that Arab thinkers are not aware of the calamities that have inflicted on their societies at the hand of the military mobilizing regimes. Fouad Ajami (1981), for instance, discusses it.
19. The Gulf states, but especially Saudi Arabia, have not been very lucky in receiving objective studies about their conditions and policies. Both those who write to please the regimes and those debunkers, who seek to destroy any credibility that these regimes have, are not serving academia or the mass media. We presume that there are many achievements yet there is much waste as well. Our

opinion is that the Gulf states, with the great wealth they have, could have done much better.

20. It is obvious that the smaller European nations were able to preserve their identity and sovereignty through integration in a larger configuration, i.e. the European Union. It is interesting to observe that for smaller units when they become elements in larger units, they receive a larger status by virtue of becoming members of a larger whole. The smaller principalities of the UAE may have achieved some importance by joining the union. As such, today the UAE can demand better position for the claims of Sharjah and Abu Dhabi *vis-à-vis* Iran, than each one of them could have demanded separately.
21. Christine Moss Helms holds that it is superficial to present the unification of the present day Saudi Arabia to be the creation of one man. According to her the following statement is superficial:

    The Kingdom of Saudi Arabia as it is internationally recognized today is, historically speaking, of relatively recent origin. Within the first three decades of the twentieth century, the Al Saud recaptured al-Riyad, the city that had served as their political centre during the nineteenth century, and successfully expanded their authority over rival emirates and sheikhdoms in Central Arabia. During the same period both Arab leaders along the littoral regions of the Arabian Peninsula and European powers began to limit the expansion of Saudi authority with the result that its boundaries as an emerging nation-state began to crystallize and were formally established through a series of treaties. In 1932 Abd al-Aziz b. Abd al-Bahaman Al Fail Al Saud was proclaimed "king" of the nation-state, at which time both the Saudi kingship and the nation-state of Saudi Arabia were formally recognized by the international community. (Helms 1981, 17)
22. This term "Gulfi" was introduced anecdotally in several conferences that this writer attended in the US and Europe. The suffix "i" in Arabic is used to form an adjective or to attach something to something else such as in "Mr. X that belong to place Y, e.g. Khomeini." It has the same effect as "ski" in Polish, "de" in French or "of" in English. Hence when suffix "i" is added here to "Gulf" it Arabizes the English word to mean that that the person is from the Gulf.
23. Taylor does not deal with the Gulf and the GCC as newcomers to the scene, nevertheless his framework and analysis remain of great value in forming a good perspective on what moves and shakes the political behavior of Arab countries.
24. *Al-Yawm*. Riyadh. (December 11, 1995).
25. Quoted in Khashan (1977). Recently several high level official visits between Iran and Saudi Arabia took place. It has been announced that these visits will culminate in signing a security treaty between the two countries.
26. The last GCC summit in Bahrain, in December 2000, indicates that building a huge army is not in the minds of the leaders.
27. Al-Rai Al-Aam. op. cit. p. 3.
28. Indeed Khouri presents a good model on how behavior in an Arab family, tribe or community takes place. During the second Gulf crisis Saddam Hussein was

able to invoke many of these tactics, bewildering the Western observers. Within the framework of the one single Arab family and beyond the complexities of a nation state, one Arab country can inflict so much harm in a modern political environment.

29. I am not using the term "myth" in any pejorative sense whatsoever. The term myth as it is used here denotes a statement or and allegory for the purpose of "supporting or expressing political claim, principle or point of view" (Vernon Bogdanor in *The Blackwell Encyclopedia of Political Science*). For further details on the subject see H. Tudor (1972). To establish how language, reality, and myth may converge in the politics of the Middle East, I recommend Bernard Lewis (1991). Chapters 3, 4 and 5 are very much related, although indirectly, to the question of violence.
30. The term "range" is not used in its statistical meaning. In statistics the range equals the difference between the highest and lowest value in a data set. Here, by range it is meant to refer to the "extent" of some behavior occurring in an encounter.
31. By the short run I mean a situation where all variables in play remain the same. If a new variable is introduced, the situation will be defined as long run. For example, should a union between Syria and Iraq take place, the situation will bear a new factor that by definition makes it a long run situation. The interesting thing with this definition is that since the situation in the Middle East is ever changing, the difference between long run and short run becomes blurred.
32. I postulate that after the age of Arab-Islamic glory at the time of the "Abbasid, the area has been at the receiving end. Since Napoleon's invasion of Egypt, the age of European supremacy and the Pax Americana, the area has always consumed and regurgitated ideas, technology, and material. Security and nationalism, not excepted, are still the remnants of old time theories that have long been abandoned seriously in the West. The area has hardly awakened to the disintegration of the old Soviet Union. If it did, it has not adjusted nor calibrated its tools of foreign policy. Still, state, security, and power are examined in a classic fashion.
33. I am aware of the debate on the concept of development and the related literature. However, this concept is still useful for our study. For a recent examination of this topic see Colin Leys (1996).
34. We need to recall that the whole episode of the invasion of Kuwait started with an economic alibi. Iraq was deeply in debt to Saudi Arabia and Kuwait.
35. Kinsella and Tillema argue that American arms transfers to Israel exercised a restraining influence on both Israel and its Arab rivals, whereas Soviet transfers to Egypt and Syria tended to destabilize the region!
36. The literature on military spending and growth is full of examples supporting our assumption. Nicholas Antonakis (1999) provides a rich bibliography to which I recommend referring.

CHAPTER 15

Confidence-Building Measures in the Persian Gulf

Behzad Shahandeh

The Persian Gulf has gone through bitter experiences in the last two decades of the 20th century, including two wars that have inflicted enormous damage on its littoral states. The region has been so poisoned by these two wars that strategic attempts to alleviate the situation seem impossible and doomed to failure from the start. The lack of trust ingrained among many of the Persian Gulf states seems practically impossible to mend in the foreseeable future. When the possibility for a strategic union among the regional countries is closely scrutinized, wounds appear and bruises come to the surface. The situation deteriorates further when past animosities and differences are taken into account. Thus, it seems more logical to let the differences be as they are, since their discussion seems to lead to further loss of hope for reconciliation.

At the same time, fundamental changes, ushering a new geoeconomically-oriented multipolar system instead of the old ideologically oriented bipolar world, have provided unprecedented impetus for the formation of regional alliances or economic groupings. Naturally, a region as important as the Persian Gulf, given its economic and geopolitical significance, cannot afford to remain indifferent to the challenges generated by the geopolitical and geostrategic equations of the 21st century. In the following pages I will argue that the survival of the resource-rich Persian Gulf in the emerging geopolitical order depends on its ability to take advantage of the new dynamics as well as its ability to create an economic grouping of its own.

The geographic location of the Persian Gulf has always given the region significant strategic and economic positions. Oil and natural gas deposits, respectively 65 percent and 35 percent of the world's total reserves, give the region an unmatched capacity for hydrocarbon exports. The Persian Gulf has the potential of creating a regional alliance or regional economic grouping that can play a significant role in the emerging multipolar system of the 21st century; one that is comparable to the significant role played by the Organization of Petroleum-Exporting Countries (OPEC) in the 1970s.

Cooperation among the Persian Gulf littoral states is possible if national interests are put before the geopolitical considerations of big powers. In order to move towards an atmosphere of détente in the region, cooperation and confidence-building in non-political (i.e. non-sensitive) issues must be given precedence over political/strategic cooperation in the initial state, with an understanding that the former can be a prelude to the latter.

The Uses of Confidence-Building Measures

Confidence-building measures (CBMs), concepts born within the context of the East-West conflict in the Europe of the 1970s and 1980s, address themselves to the need to avoid outcomes that are unfavorable to conflicting parties (lose-lose situations). As such, they do not entail conflict resolution or peace process orientations. They assume that even in heated conflicts, there are many situations that parties in competition (or even in deep hostility) would wish to avoid. The measures taken can be preventive or confidence building or even include a combination of the two. Theoretically, preventive measures could be divorced from CBMs, but in reality this is very difficult since the two complement each other.

Communication plays an important role in CBMs. It can be said that bona fide transparency in actions will allow the other side to get better insight of (and even voice in) what the first party is doing. Letting the other (others) know about what you are planning to do has a soothing effect and actually precipitates reciprocity, starting a chain of goodwill gestures that would lead to negotiating and solving the outstanding problems.

As stated, CBMs do not foresee conflict resolution, but indirectly pave the way for the same. The *raison d'être* of CBMs is to avoid calamities and nothing more. It is rather a soft approach since hard approaches deepen the conflicts. This is due to lack of conviction that they will endure as grand programs since they are often thought of as empty gestures. For instance, unilateral disarmament programs are often perceived as not genuine, actually raising doubts and sensitivity about them being diversionary or even a conspiracy.

As mentioned, the more limited CBMs, on the other hand, can be used for communication. The other party for instance can be notified in advance of military maneuvers. This was practiced during the Cold War. The maneuver itself removes a great deal of secrecy from military buildups others always worry about. Such steps have also been taken by Iran to calm other Persian Gulf littoral states. Even if the entire military capability is not deployed (as some sceptics believe), announcing the action well ahead of time will boost trust since secrecy is a cause of doubt and removing it will be a successful CBM.

It must be reiterated that CBMs are to be embarked upon on the basis of enlightened self-interest. Each party must take the initiative for its own sake and in line with its own national interests. Of course, so much the better if the national interests of the two sides complement each other. It has been repeatedly said that there are no permanent enemies or friends, only permanent national interests. At this point in time the national interests of all parties in the Persian Gulf dictate that maneuvers be announced in advance. This has now become a norm to which all adhere; an initiative not many could have contemplated a few years ago.

Countries must take realities into consideration, grasp the changes and further the détente created in the Persian Gulf by taking small steps. Big steps are inappropriate now since the level of needed trust is not yet fully in place. As such big actions would appear empty and devoid of real content. But the measures that were initially designed as being merely preventive will in due time contribute to confidence-building. They will open up new opportunities to be explored, raising the initial relationship to new heights.

Currently in the Persian Gulf, Iran and Saudi Arabia have taken the initiative to establish trust among the existing states. This is having an effect on the region. For instance in the last meeting of the Persian Gulf Cooperation Council, the six member-states stressed the desire to befriend Iran. This is a confidence-building measure that has no strings attached. It is also a soft approach that will encourage even the difficult members of the council, that is the United Arab Emirates, not to antagonize the other members by dragging their feet in negotiating with Iran.

CBMs actually have two interlinked dimensions: creating self-trust and trust in others. Trust of oneself is a key factor in trusting others. If the party does not have confidence in itself, it will never be able to instill trust in others or trust others. All wars and hostilities arise from the very fact that a country feels cornered, isolated, and threatened, all boiling down to lack of self-trust.

Some argue that all politics is domestic politics, which is quite true since foreign policy is the continuation of domestic policy. If a county feels insecure internally, it will behave by not trusting others. Therefore for peace to ensue in a region as strategic as the Persian Gulf, the littoral countries must reach a level of feeling secure with themselves.

As a case in point, Iran has overcome its isolationist tendencies (some of which were intentional, some forced upon her) as the domestic scene has been transformed through a process of democratization. If a state can and does speak to its people, it can also speak to others, listen to neighbors, and have enough self-confidence to pursue negotiations with others. The changing situation in Iran has thus made Saudi Arabia change its approach as well. Genuine dialogue has been solidified to the point that Saudi Arabia has instructed its interior minister to explore the possibility of a security pact with Iran, something unimaginable just a few years ago.

For a genuine dialogue to be initiated some preconditions must first be met:

- Participants must be able to speak freely and without fear.
- Parties must be devoid of the will to dominate.
- A common logic for dialogue must exist. Participants must have a common interest to talk and listen (this can be called enlightened self-interest).
- Establishment of a win-win situation, based on a language of friendship and trust as a means to enhance the desire to conduct dialogue.
- Developing an appreciation of other cultures, civilizations, and politico-economic systems.

The emphasis on Iran is not to negate developments in other countries but to reiterate that the inauguration of détente in the region has risen out of the trust created within Iran itself. Developments in countries like Saudi Arabia, Oman, Kuwait, and Qatar are also worthy of note and allow these countries to represent themselves on the regional front with more confidence. Saudi Arabia, whose economic clout and influence in the Arab world has given it the confidence to be a pace-setter, at present is pioneering the effort to bring back Iran into the fold of the Persian Gulf littoral states. This is an enlightened endeavor since Saudi Arabia's present national interest calls for befriending and engaging with Iran (an approach very different from that of the 1980s and 1990s).

Unfortunately foreign presence has brought a third party—the US—that has vowed to stay in the region on the basis of its national interests. To be realistic, the Americans are hard to get rid of, since consensus among the Persian Gulf littoral states except Iran and Iraq favors their presence. In any case, it would probably undermine confidence-building if Iran, for instance, pushed hard to expel outsiders from the region. Iran for its part considers foreign presence in the Persian Gulf as an impediment to regional peace and cooperation. But its objections are subtle, since for outsiders to leave the insiders must trust themselves enough to be able to fill the vacuum created.

The Persian Gulf Arab states must bring themselves to a level where they can trust themselves and develop a consensus towards Iran. This is of course partially dependent on what Iran does. Once such a trust develops, foreign presence would become obsolete. This will be a subtle and long process, but one that will be long lasting and beneficial to all. What Iran offers as CBMs must make the Arabs realize their own interests in keeping the security of the Persian Gulf a regional affair. For Iran to achieve this, she must be transparent in her actions, not forcing her will on others, and in short creating the necessary ground for the gradual evolution from the present state of affairs. It will take time and perseverance on the part of all, with CBMs taken gradually and even indirectly. A good example of such an indirect approach is Iran's special care not to fortify its positions in the three islands in dispute with the United Arab Emirates. This is a soft approach, an indirect one, showing that the Iranians mean business in their efforts to pursue genuine trust with Arab neighbors.

It is also important that this soft and indirect approach entails both cognitive and affective dimensions. Undoubtedly confidence cannot be based on ignorance, which results in fear and misconceptions. The Persian Gulf littoral states are potential partners in the age of globalization and regionalism. Logic tells the players that friendship or partnership among neighbors will lead to a positive-sum game and security for all the Persian Gulf states. Not taking any relationship for granted and working to enhance relationships on the basis of more knowledge is an important requirement for confidence-building. Of course, knowledge by itself does not necessarily create a hostile or friendly relationship, but it does appear to be a necessary precondition for a stable relationship.

But the affective dimension must also be tended. The way countries feel about themselves and others has a strong impact on politics. When feelings about others have become so deeply ingrained by past deeds, it is difficult to change them overnight. To institutionalize détente between the Iranians and Arabs of the Persian Gulf (or Arabs in general), feelings must be changed. If feelings are not given attention, then deeds cannot be institutionalized. The question is how feelings can be changed. The only viable answer seems to come through the translation of goodwill into good deeds. This will gradually bring about changed feeling and it is again a soft approach. Certainly a heavy propaganda campaign will not do. People are slow to grasp the realities of the region, but will follow their leaders if actions speak louder than words. Accordingly, they will be moved to give support to their leaders gradually. The best way is to complement enlightened actions with the deepening of knowledge about each other. Dialogue must be pursued at the level of non-governmental organizations and universities.

How things are evaluated is also a very important dimension of confidence-building. Beyond knowledge and basic emotions about an adversary in conflict, an assessment of the intentions and capabilities of the other side is also necessary. The question of intentions is, of course, of prime importance. What does the potential partner want, what are the objectives in pushing beyond the given stage in conflict, how genuine is the commitment to conflict resolution or confidence-building? Evaluative answers will be given to these questions based on past experience but minds can be changed in response to strong stimuli such as perceived transformations in behavior.

To summarize, one may argue that confidence-building deals with attitudes about the self, the other, and the system based on a heritage derived from experience with the system. As such, confidence and confidence-building by definition have much to do with political culture. Unfortunately it is a fact that in some cultures political conflicts breed distrust in others, more so than in other cultures. Thus, to embark on CBMs in a region, cultures must be taken into account and special care must be taken not to arouse traits that breed on the distrust of outsiders. For the Persian Gulf littoral states to trust each other, the will and need to work together must be strong enough to dampen conflicting cultural traits and other differences. In the Persian Gulf, no external threat exists to make the littoral states gather around each other, so no urgency is felt. Thus the environment must be created. This will take time and patience and could be self-defeating if not properly approached. The conspiratorial mindset is strong among the Persian Gulf states, be it Iran to the north or the Arabs to the south. Past experience will be of no help; rather it will be an impediment.

Application of Confidence-Building Measures to the Persian Gulf

To instill trust among the Persian Gulf littoral states, the contemporary state of affairs must be taken into consideration. Confidence-building measures without attention to the realities of the time is simply not going to be productive. These realities and trends are as follows:

- Severe setback in Iraq's defeat of Pan-Arabist project.
- A new alignment of the Arab states system, with many things previously taken for granted coming under question.
- The trauma of Iraq's defeat for all Arab states, including those on the victorious side. The war's painful, embarrassing, humiliating effects has had tremendous repercussions for Arab solidarity.
- Persistent danger of Saddam's defiant and vindictive regime in Iraq, continuously issuing threats against Saudi Arabia, Kuwait, and Egypt.
- A democratization process in Iran, spelling positive results for its relations with the Arab world in general and the Persian Gulf Arab states in particular.
- Turkey's extensive cooperation with Israel, making the latter's entry into the Caucasus and Central Asia easier. The Persian Gulf states are also interested in expanding relations with the Caucasus and Central Asia but the project of connecting the Persian Gulf Cooperation Council with the Economic Cooperation Organization is not yet a priority.
- The emergence of the five new Central Asian states—the Muslim republics of the former USSR.
- The continuation of the arms race.
- The apparent paradox of stable and enduring regimes in deeply distressed societies, characterized by ongoing economic crisis compounded by exorbitant military budgets, high population growth and so on.

The question is how all these parameters affect the way CBMs in the Persian Gulf are to be formulated. To be sure there has been no "Iron Curtain" in the Persian Gulf and the region does not lack the instrumentalities and technical infrastructure necessary for confidence-building. But this conflict-ridden region lacks a compelling, overriding, legitimizing principle.

In short, it is deficient in mutual trust and confidence. The element that has increased the trust deficiency was the 1990 Iraqi invasion of Kuwait, which shattered many regional conventions and norms. This is why one could easily argue that the Persian Gulf security climate was in a suspended state between 1991 and 1997. On the one hand, the regional security system imposed by the US and its allies, failed to meet the region's power, security, and interaction requirements. On the other hand, conditions were not ripe for changes in the said model. All awaited a stimulus for change to instigate a more natural equation of power, security, and interaction on the basis of indigenous features and factors. The May 1997 events in Iran offered precisely such a stimulus.

At this point, regional countries are attempting their best to benefit from this new equation and convince supra-national elements to accept it as well. The emphasis now is on creating an indigenous model by the employment of soft power. In order for CBMs to be successful, an open-ended, flexible, soft approach is necessary that is not target-oriented in a way that would result in a closed system.

In the Persian Gulf, a situation has developed that has contributed to the littoral states being willing to listen and have dialogue with each other. The economic security of the regional states has become intertwined as never before. To explore why this is so will itself be a CBM since it will further highlight commonalities based on national interests. The countries on the southern shores of the Persian Gulf have embraced the idea of working with Iran as being in line with their national interests. This is because all the said countries are heavily in the red regarding their trade and economic situation in general. At the same time the perceived threat believed to come from Iran has dramatically declined. The two factors have combined to create an atmosphere conducive to CBMs never thought possible before.

To tap the present opening, the Persian Gulf states must not take steps that will be heavy or difficult to pursue. They must pursue a process of doing small things that do not arouse sensitivities or past ghosts.

A good place to focus is on the economic arena. The oil and gas industry needs to be tended. OPEC cooperation has paid off handsomely for the Persian Gulf states. The control of the price of oil is one way for cooperation. The other is for littoral states to benefit form each other's experiences and expertise to enhance their respective indigenous industry. As such, working in technical areas together will be a CBM whose success is guaranteed.

The problem of drug traffic is another common threat faced by all the littoral states that needs a coordinated approach to manage.

Recent agreements between Iran and Saudi Arabia, and Iran and Oman in this area are tantamount to CBMs.

Other CBMs, contributing to the creation of a family out of the regional states, are being established by the United Nations resolutions and the regional countries' vigilance in observing them. One area that comes to mind quickly is the special care taken not to allow territorial waters to be used for illegal transportation of oil. It is important to note that Iran has been particularly vigilant in showing commitment to the UN directives.

Another important issue is water. Close collaboration and investment in the water industry is very much needed. Iran, as a potential exporter of water, must be supported by investments from her southern neighbors. Huge amounts of water are currently being lost due to Iran's lack of water conservation technology.

A similar case could be made for a boost in food trade. Today a high percentage of the cost of the imported food (mostly fruits and vegetables) is related to transportation costs. Iran can become the vegetable garden of the region with minimal transportation costs. The variety of vegetables grown in Iran could be greatly increased by investments in Iran's food industry. Again creating a market for Iran's food resources will act as a double-edged strategy for the benefit of all concerned.

The environmental protection of the Persian Gulf is now a must and in need of an enlightened approach. Taking precautions to limit pollution of all kinds can amount to a CBM that will lead to other areas of cooperation not previously anticipated. The Persian Gulf is becoming more polluted as oil tankers and foreign naval ships increasingly dispose of their waste in the once blue waters of the Persian Gulf.

Soil erosion and prevention of desertification are two other possible avenues for cooperation among the littoral states. Iran's experience and expertise in the field of soil erosion prevention has been recognized by international agencies such as FAO, which has identified Iran as a model country in preventing desertification. Iran and the UAE have already worked together in controlling 3,000 hectares of sand deserts from expansion. The creation of a regional center for such activities is both necessary as well as filled with opportunities for cooperation.

Finally, it must be reiterated that these practical "soft" steps, which act as a base for ushering other measures enhancing cooperation, will not be completed without a people-to-people touch. For people to work together, they need to know each other as a means to overcome the prejudices of past generations. To be successful, elite contacts must set the pace for the populace to start or deepen dialogue. University scholars can cooperate on various topics. This must be done both at technical and theoretical levels. Exchange programs among the elite must be institutionalized. The elite will be pace-setters, pioneers, and image-makers. Exchanges will bring out the fact that differences are not so large as to justify animosity. This will allow elite links to trickle down after a period of time. Along the same lines, a joint committee can be set up to rid books in various countries of prejudices carried from the past. Of course, it must be stressed that differences must not be suppressed but valued since they give color to humanity. But commonalities must be allowed to come to the foreground.

This list of areas for cooperation is obviously not exhaustive. For dialogue to be endowed with purpose, it must acquire a demonstrable beneficial impact. So long as the setting is not imbued with trust, official exchanges and dialogues will be hollow exercises. Economic (non-sensitive) areas offer opportunities for giving dialogue concrete and beneficial contents, allowing trust to be developed gradually but firmly. This will set the stage for major undertakings in the direction of a comprehensive regional alliance at a later stage.

CHAPTER 16

Confidence-Building Through Regional Education

Leanne Piggott

Much of the work of the International Commission for Security and Cooperation in West Asia (SACWA) has thus far been dedicated to the articulation and analysis of systems which are aimed at limiting, managing, and ultimately resolving the present manifestations of inter-state conflict in the West Asia region. An effective peace strategy, however, must also be concerned with the prevention of conflict well into the future. This demands that not only the phenomena of conflict but also its causes be addressed. At previous meetings of this Commission, much of the discussion about causes barely went beyond pointing the finger of blame at one state or another, although, by the end of our time in Cyprus, a consensus had emerged that although history is important, it should not hold us prisoner. Other considerations are at least as worthy of our deliberations and they demand that we move beyond the verities and paradigms behind which we have hitherto taken refuge.

The purpose of this chapter, then, is to offer a practical suggestion both for conflict resolution strategies, generally, and for the intended Regional Center for Dialogue and Cooperation (RCDC) specifically. In short, I propose that the RCDC dedicate resources to facilitate the mutual development of cross-cultural and educational policies that will promote peace values throughout the schools and universities of participating states. Such an initiative would provide active and long-term confidence-building activities throughout the region. Hence the title of this chapter.

The point should be made at the outset that the mutual development of such policies could itself be considered to be a confidence-building measure in the context of inter-state relations and would have the advantage of bypassing unresolved historical grievances, at least in the short term. The focus of this chapter, however, is on the evolutionary, rather than revolutionary nature of such policies and the contribution they can make to the strengthening of civil society and to a pro-active rather than reactive approach to conflict resolution. In the longer term, seemingly prosaic issues such as the content of school curricula and the teaching of alternative dispute resolution procedures (both traditional and non-traditional), will be of paramount importance in delivering the kind of social consensus without which the permanency of even the most far-reaching inter-state agreements cannot be guaranteed.

The argument of this chapter, then, is that if we are successful in establishing the intended Regional Center for Dialogue and Cooperation, and if, as we have discussed, it is to be charged with the responsibility of developing policies and initiatives for the promotion of security and cooperation between member states, this must include a mandate for developing the necessary educational framework without which such policies cannot work effectively in the long-term. Therefore, whatever other policy development the RCDC might be called upon to undertake in the strategic, political, economic, environmental, and cultural areas, I propose that it also establishes a distinct section or department dedicated to the planning and development of a regional education policy that would incorporate such areas as a school curriculum in peace studies; university courses in conflict resolution; and similar courses in negotiation and mediation for policy makers and government officials.

Several Western governments have already embraced these ideas and have made studies in peace and non-violence a mandatory part of their school curricula.[1] The year 2000 also witnessed the launch of many interactive programs in peace education on the Internet, providing teachers with resources and lessons plans. UNESCO, for example, celebrated the International Year for the Culture of Peace, and the period 2001–10 has been designated as the International Decade for a Culture of Peace and Non-violence for the Children of the World. In support of these efforts, the UN Cyberschoolbus Peace Education Internet site promotes the global movement to build and sustain a culture of peace through education. The "Hague Agenda for Peace and Justice for the 21st Century" is another example of this work. One of the first principles of this document is the necessity of instituting systematic education for peace. According to the Agenda, their Global Campaign for Peace Education aims to "support the United Nations Decade for a Culture of Peace and Non-violence for the Children of the World and to introduce peace and human rights education into all educational institutions, including medical and law schools."[2]

"A culture of peace will be achieved when citizens of the world understand global problems, have the skills to resolve conflicts and struggle for justice non-violently, live by international standards of human rights and equity, appreciate cultural diversity, and respect the Earth and each other. Such learning can only be achieved with systematic education for peace." Hague Appeal for Peace Global Campaign for Peace Education

In the Middle East, successful peace education projects already in operation include the work of the Foundation for Human and Humanitarian Rights in Lebanon. The Foundation has developed a comprehensive course on the Theory and Practice of Human Rights, which has become mandatory for all students attending The Haigazian University College and The University of the Holy Spirit-Kaslik in Lebanon (The Foundation for Human and Humanitarian Rights 1996).

For convenience, I will refer to the section or department of the RCDC which would be responsible for the development and implementation of these proposals as "The Department of Education Policy" (See Figure 16.1 below). Its work would encompass curriculum development in conflict resolution and peace studies; academic

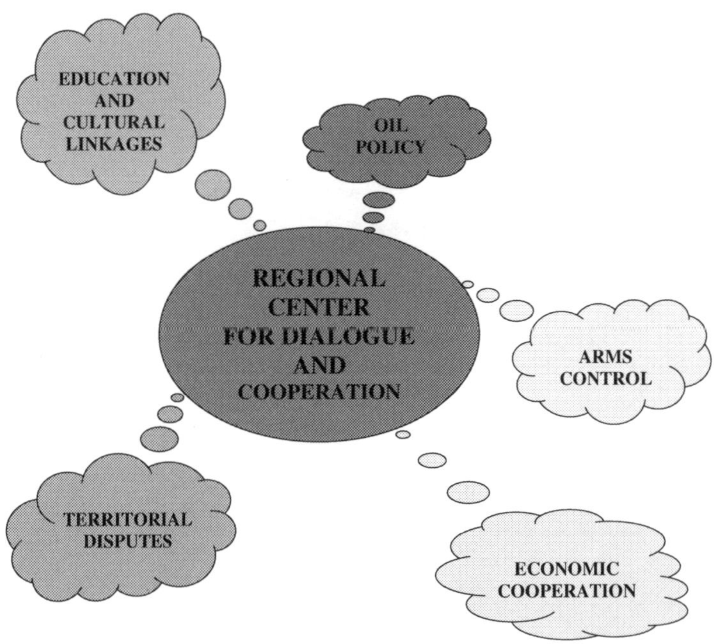

Figure 16.1. Regional center for dialogue and cooperation (RCDC)

and student exchanges; in-servicing for teachers; and any other area of education that could be positively affected (See Figure 16.2 below).

By way of illustration, I would like to highlight just one of these areas for detailed consideration, namely, peace education in schools and, in particular, the development of a regional peace studies curriculum. There is an abundance of research, which suggests that the influence of the family on children's psychology and social development is great. Education, too, plays a key role in shaping children's attitudes. The inculcation of peace values amongst students who will be both the citizens and the leaders of the future is essential for creating the habits and the expectations of peaceful resolution of conflict. Habitual behaviors are predominantly behaviors learned in childhood. Accordingly, in order to be effective, peace education must begin as early as elementary or primary school, to be reinforced throughout the remaining school years and as a part of higher education. If done effectively, a peace education program will

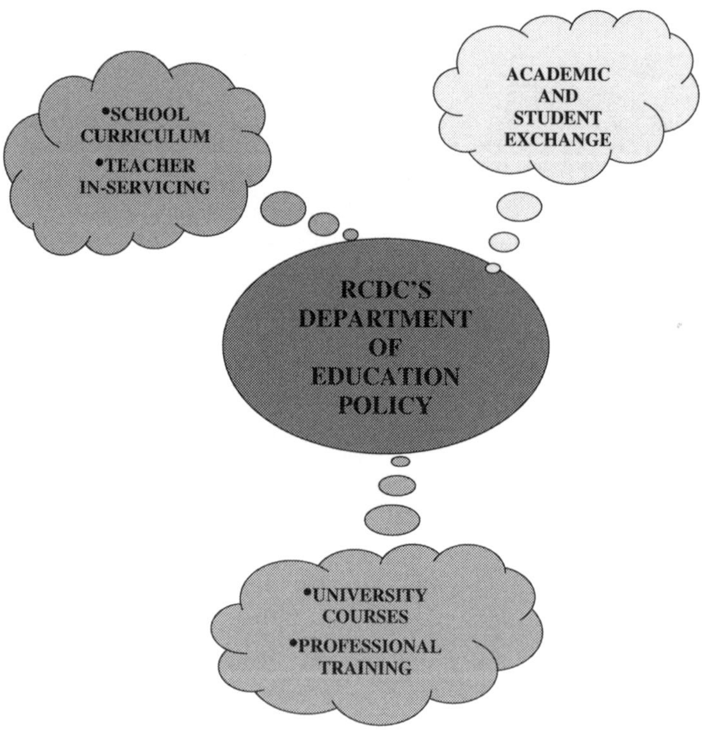

Figure 16.2. RCDC's department of education policy

obviate the necessity, which currently exists, of developing dispute resolution techniques that effectively require participants to *un*learn forms of behavior that are inimical to the peaceful resolution of conflict.

The classroom is a legitimate arena for engaging children in the process of peacemaking which fosters self-respect, respect for others, and effective communication. Once the classroom becomes a safe and nurturing learning environment, children are able to express their concerns and arrive at creative and spontaneous solutions. Through understanding, flexibility, and negotiation, children can learn to resolve problems assertively, without violence. As the children begin to understand and integrate peacemaking techniques in their classroom environment and, hopefully, outside their classroom among their peer group, the lessons can be extended to address issues within their wider community, the region, and in turn, global issues.[3]

As for the regional context, children are given the opportunity to explore the similarities and differences in customs, attitudes, and policies, and to believe in the possibility of a region at peace and not in perennial conflict. Through clarity about the goal for regional peace and perseverance in the commitment to effect peace, teachers are able to dispel the discouragement that comes from the belief that violence and war are inevitable. A wide range of opportunities exist for children to participate in global peace projects through the Internet. The World Peace Project for Children, for example, promotes peace concepts by "educating children about global matters that concern them and by giving them tools to build positive connections with children in other cultures".[4]

In practical terms, RCDC's work in the area of school education would need to focus on three areas. Its first task would be to devise peace education curricula in consultation with the various departments of education of participating states. Such consultation would be essential to ensure both the cultural sensitivity and overall acceptability of the curriculum content. Conflict resolution techniques, both traditional and modern, would be an important part of what would be taught. These would include mediation, negotiation and group problem solving (See Figures 16.3 & 16.4).

Frequent resort will need to be made to traditional religious and social values which continue to be of fundamental importance in West Asian societies. "*Reconciliation*", we learn, "*is a duty that every Muslim is ordered to perform*". There exists a long tradition of conflict resolution in the Middle East, known as *suhl* (settlement) and *musalaha* (reconciliation). The *Suhl* ritual, an institutionalized form of conflict

Figure 16.3. A regional school peace studies curriculum

management and control, originates in tribal and village paradigms. This particular element of Islamic society emphasizes the central link between psychological and political dimensions of communal life through recognition of the need to resolve local conflicts.[5]

Using the models made available by the plethora of peace education networks, textbooks, and Internet sites, these traditional models of conflict resolution can be incorporated into modern pedagogic models.[6] Translations of teaching materials into Arabic by organizations such as UNESCO already exist on the Internet that would be helpful in this process (Drew 1995; Bodine *et al.* 1994).[7]

Other elements of the curricula could also be drawn from the many recent developments in the area of peace education across the globe. For all of these topics, there is no shortage of material available in books, journals, newsletters, and of course, the Internet. RCDC's department of education policy would be required to adapt available materials (much of which has been developed for the Western school system) to the needs of participating states to make

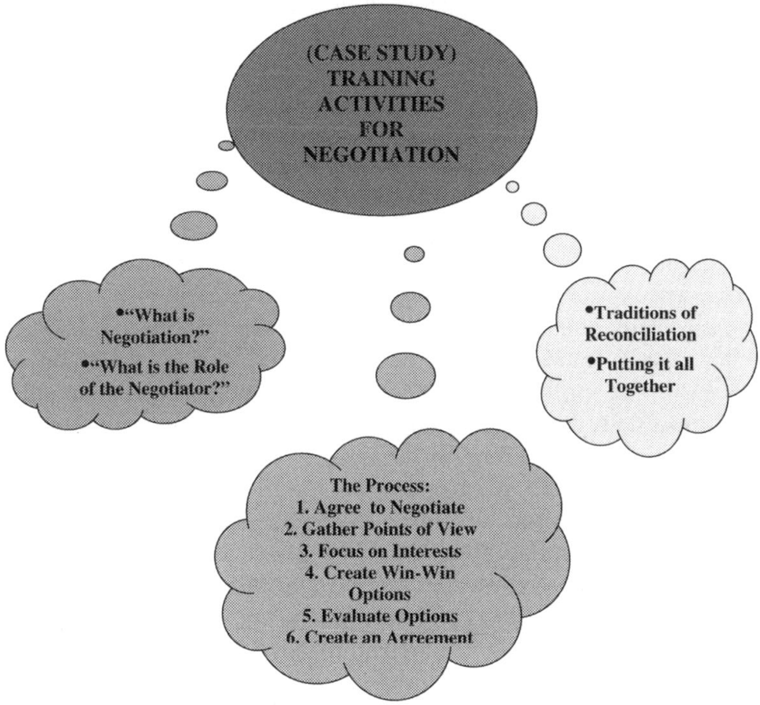

Figure 16.4. (Case study) training activities for negotiation

them culturally acceptable and relevant to their domestic needs (Irani 1999; Wolf 2000).[8]

The second task of the RCDC's department of education, in relation to school peace studies curriculum, would be for the training and professional development of peace educators. My experience as a professional educator confirms that the role of the teacher is critical to the success of any educational program. With peace education, as with any other form of education, the teachers themselves have to be educated. Only then can the principles of peace and non-violent responses to conflict emanate from adults and be instilled in children. RCDC would therefore need to devise training programs and make available regular in-servicing to hone and up-grade the skills of peace education teachers.[9] In time, the best teachers could be recruited from each of the participating states to form a curriculum development committee whose purpose would be to up-grade curricula on a regular basis and ensure that such curricula keep pace with international trends and improvements.

Third, the RCDC's department of education policy would need to develop a system for monitoring and inspecting the implementation of peace education curricula by participating states. The purpose of this would be to guarantee both the maintenance of high standards and quality in peace education and also the observance of mutuality between participating states. This will ensure that the RCDC's peace education program, apart from its intrinsic value in inculcating peaceful habits amongst the future citizens and leaders of the region, will also be a lasting confidence-building measure for the furtherance of security and cooperation in West Asia.

As already noted, the work of RCDC's department of education policy would not be confined to school education. Its resources should also be applied to many other areas. For example, the conflict resolution skills developed could also be taught to government officials and policy makers in especially convened seminars and workshops. RCDC's peace educators could teach techniques in mediation, negotiation, and group problem solving and this could also include the adaptation of the region's traditional forms of conflict resolution to contemporary circumstances and issues.

In time, the combined efforts of peace educators in the participating states in the area of curriculum development could provide the foundation for further confidence- building measures in the form of academic exchange programs and student exchange programs, which would not by any means need to be confined to peace education initiatives. By way of example, it is worth noting that the recent agreement between the Peoples' Republic of China and The Democratic Republic of Vietnam which resolved the long standing dispute between those two countries over their common border, also featured initiatives in the area of education, notably, the establishment of academic exchange programs between the two countries. The need for government involvement in the financing and administration of such programs could also provide a useful mechanism for maintaining regular government-to-government contacts in the field of education and perhaps in other areas as well, yet another benefit of RCDC's commitment to confidence-building through regional education.

Notes

1. For example, the "Citizen21" project in the United Kingdom.
2. *UN Document: Ref A/54/98*. For an interesting approach to peace education through mathematics, see http://www.xmaths.com.au/parentpage.html

3. It should also be noted that research has shown that in schools where conflict resolution techniques have been taught to students, academic achievement has increased.
4. www.sadako.org/foundingstatement.htm
5. According to *Shari'ia* (Islamic Law) "the purpose of *suhl* is to end conflict and hostility among believers so that they may conduct their relationships in peace and amity ... In Islamic law, *suhl* is a form of contract ('akd), legally binding on both the individual and community levels ... The purpose of [public] *suhl* is to suspend fighting between [two parties] and establish peace, called *muwada'a* (peace or gentle relationship), for a specific period of time." (Khadduri 1997, 845–6)
6. See, for one of many examples, the site for "The Consortium on Peace Research, Education and Development (COPRED). This organisation's mission statement reads as follows: "COPRED is a community of educators, activists and researchers working on alternatives to violence and war. COPRED spreads effective methods of non-violent social change among diverse racial and socio-economic populations. Founded in 1970 by a small group of teachers and scholars, COPRED has grown to almost 500 institutional and individual members, including K-12 educators, peace activists, conflict resolution practitioners, university professors and clergy. COPRED has become a central hub for over 300 university degree programs in the study of peace and non-violence around the world and works to strengthen public school programs and networks." The *International Peace Research Association*, founded with support from UNESCO, has a Peace Education Commission that brings together educators working to promote a culture of peace. The *Peace Education Network*, based in London, also works alongside the UN in promoting peace through education.
7. For material on the Internet, see www.oneday.net.arabic.htm; www.un.org/arabic/cybrschl/. The UNESCO site, "United Nations cyberschoolbus" (www.un.org/cyberschoolbus) provides an excellent educational tool for peace studies. The site holds peace education curricula, quizzes, games and other resources for the classroom. Also see http://erc.hrea.org/Library/index.html for an extensive resource list.
8. Case studies in regional and traditional approaches to conflict resolution can easily be incorporated as examples of dispute resolution techniques. For a recent work on traditional Middle Eastern conflict resolution techniques see Wolf (2000). Wolf draws on the parallels between modern approaches to alternative dispute resolution (ADR) and *suhl.* ADR refers to "a wide variety of consensual approaches with which parties in conflict voluntarily seek to reach a mutually acceptable settlement. It generally seeks to move parties away from zero-sum, or distributive, solutions, towards those in which all parties gain—positive-sum or integrative. The term ADR, and the methods generally described, are no more than twenty years old in western dispute resolution literature. In defining the methodologies for ADR, indigenous processes are rarely drawn upon. Both Berbers and Bedouin have apparently been practicing ADR for centuries." (http://terra.geo.orst.edu/users/tfdd/documents/indigenous/)

9. Again, there is a plethora of materials available in many formats. There are also many international organizations available for teachers to join. At the click of a button, the Internet provides an overwhelming number of sites that offer support groups, chat rooms and extensive teaching materials. The UN CyberSchoolBus, for example, is the on-line component of the United Nations Global Teaching and Learning Project, which promotes education about international issues by producing high quality teaching materials and activities designed for educational use (at primary, intermediate and secondary school levels). In the US, The Conflict Resolution Education Network (CREnet) provides curricula and teaching materials for the thousands of conflict resolution programs in American schools. See www.crenet.org

CHAPTER 17

Conclusion: Whither West Asia?

The worldwide trend toward regionalism can be better understood in the context of two other prevailing trends: globalization and democratization. Under the impact of globalization, a world order increasingly organized around the nation-state system has gradually lost its rationality. The national state is currently too small for the big problems (notably environmental) and too big for smaller problems (notably ethnic conflicts and migration). Under the impact of global market and communication, the national states have also lost much of their economic and cultural sovereignty while tenaciously hanging on to their territorial domains. Inaugurated by the Peace of Westphalia in 1648, the nation-state system was first undermined by the bipolar rivalries of the Cold War. It has been further eroded by the post-Cold War interlude of US hegemony in a unipolar world. The current drive toward a multipolar world order cannot succeed unless and until democratic regionalism can organize the various claimants to world power around competing interests. A greater system of checks and balances can then be obtained in the world system. That is the central meaning of the drives by the European Union, Russian-Chinese strategic alliance, and the East Asian efforts toward coordination of their long-term interests and policies.

But regionalism has had a variety of faces. What Hettne *et al.* (1999, 1–24) have called Old and New Regionalism corresponds to what Table 17.1 identifies as Hegemonic, Counter-Hegemonic, and Democratic Regionalism. Old Regionalism under the Cold War was primarily of the hegemonic and counter-hegemonic variety. To contain the Sino-Soviet bloc, the United States and its allies built a ring of military alliances from North Atlantic to Southeast Asia, including NATO, CENTO, and SEATO. In response, the Soviet Union organized the Warsaw Pact of Eastern European communist states. Caught between the bipolar rivalries of the capitalist and communist worlds, some Asian countries attempted to fend for themselves by organizing regional organizations for development such as the ASEAN, SAARC, and RCD.

The New or Democratic Regionalism has its roots in the European Coal and Steel Community, Treaty of Rome (1958), and the

Table 17.1. World regional formations

Regional formations	Military regionalism	Political regionalism	Economic regionalism	Comprehensive regionalism
Hegemonic Regionalism	NATO, SEATO, CENTO, Warsaw Pact		APEC, NAFTA	
Counter-Hegemonic Regionalism		Arab League, OSCE, GCC	MERCOSUR, ASEAN, SAARC, RCD, ECO	
Democratic Regionalism	EU	EU	EEC	EU

European Economic Community. Its aims are rooted not so much in military as in common security, social, political, and economic objectives. Motivated by the European anxieties concerning a recurrence of past tragic hostilities, the move toward European Union could take a leap forward only in the post-Cold War years. Relieved of the possibility of a Russian invasion, Europe could now aspire to striking an independent course from the United States. The European Union has consequently established its own common currency, armed forces, and foreign policy. It has also taken initiatives toward the Korean and West Asian security distinctly different from the United States.

Although the democratic conditions do not obtain in the Persian Gulf as they do in Europe, some of the same logic may apply in the case of West Asian regionalism. Relieved of a Russian threat, Iranian Revolution exports, and renewed Iraqi invasions, the region may be ready now for a regional grouping that could put it at a stronger bargaining position in world politics and economics. As in Europe, however, the movement for regional peace cannot succeed unless the West Asian civil societies are also mobilized to pressure their governments toward regional cooperation for security and development.

Drawing from the insights of the foregoing essays, this concluding chapter focuses on three fundamental questions. (1) Who are the main stakeholders in West Asian security and how their interests may converge or diverge? (2) What are the major arguments on behalf of regional cooperation for security and development? (3) How can the visions for regional peace, security, and cooperation presented in this volume turn into reality?

Who Are the Stakeholders?

Table 17.2 identifies the main domestic and international stakeholders. Governments, markets, and civil societies are the main domestic stakeholders, while Great Powers and transnational corporations, mainly in oil and arms industries, represent the international stakeholders. The table also points out the regime types, market systems, and degree of mobilization of civil societies from low to high. The Great Powers (notably US, Russia, Britain) have both staunch allies and adversaries in the region, while the transnational corporations generally pursue their commercial interests regardless of the regime type.

The table demonstrates an enormous diversity in the political, economic, and cultural orientations of the regimes in power. Common religion (Islam) and resource endowment (oil) sometimes act as disunifying rather than unifying factors. At first blush, therefore, the prospects for regional cooperation and integration seem extremely dim. However, further investigation provides some hopeful signs.

Table 17.2. West Asian region: stakeholders and orientations

Stake-holders	**Govern-ments**	**Markets**	**Civil societies**	**Western great powers**	**Trans-national corportions**
Big States: Turkey, Iran, Egypt	Divergent Ideologies	State Capitalism	Mobilized	Allies: Egypt, Turkey Adversary: Iran	Commercial partners
Middle States: Saudi Arabia, Iraq, Jordan, Israel, Lebanon, Syria, Yemen	Conflicting Nationalisms	Commercial and State Capitalism	Low to High Mobilized	Allies: Saudi Arabia, Jordan, Israel Adversaries: Iraq, Palestine, Syria, Yemen	Commercial partners
Small States: Kuwait, UAE, Qatar, Bahrain, Oman	Monarchical Sheikhdoms	Oil-generated rentier economies	Low Mobilized	US protectorates	Commercial partners

From Security Complex to Security Community

As this volume has demonstrated, most if not all of the major states in West Asia currently suffer from acute security complex. That may be the most compelling reason for them to take a serious look at regional approaches to common security and development. As Bjorn Hettne (Hettne *et al.* 1999, xxvi–xxvii) has suggested in a compelling study of globalism and regionalism, the arguments for developmental regionalism in West Asia may be summarized as follows:

- *The Sufficient Size Argument.* The smaller West Asian states do not have a sufficient size to enjoy economies of scale in any industry except oil. Whether they have oil resources or not, the micro states either have to cooperate to solve common problems or become client states of the Great Powers.
- *The Viable Economy Argument.* West Asian states can be divided into capital surplus, labor surplus, skill-importing, and skill-exporting countries (see Table 17.3). With the exception of Iraq, none of them can combine all of the necessary factors of production for balanced development. Iraq, however, has squandered its rich resource endowments in land, labor, water, capital, and skilled humanpower in military adventurism. Having learned the futility of that road, the regional states now can perhaps better see the complementarity among them for developmental regionalism. As capital surplus and labor deficient countries, the GCC can benefit from investment in Egypt, Iran, or Turkey while importing skilled humanpower from those countries. As labor surplus countries, Egypt, Jordan, and Iran already export a significant number of workers to the GCC states and have developed a stake in their political stability.
- *The Credibility Argument.* Coordination of economic policies among the West Asian states can lead to more viable industries as well as economies of scale and scope for the region as a whole. This will result in greater credibility and international competitiveness.
- *The Effective Articulation Argument.* Globalization is putting small and isolated states at a great disadvantage. Their bargaining power *vis-à-vis* bigger states, TNCs, and IGOs is seriously compromised. Collective bargaining at the level of the region can improve the economic position of the West Asian marginalized countries. It can also protect their export positions in their oil, petrochemicals, and other industries.

- *The Social and Political Stability Argument.* Most of the West Asian states face serious problems of social and political stability. Some of them have experienced revolutionary upheavals that have left their societies in a traumatic state. Nonetheless, it does not appear to be in the interest of the Great Powers or the regional states to see boundaries changed or a country dismembered. The example of Iraq clearly demonstrates this point. Despite Saddam Hussein's belligerence, neither the Great Powers nor Iran, Turkey, or the GCC has shown any interest in dismembering Iraq. The disintegration of any state in the region would bring about a more generalized regional instability. A regional security regime that guarantees existing borders would be thus in the interest of all stakeholders.
- *The Resource Management Argument.* Serious environmental problems in the Persian Gulf and the Caspian Sea as well as continuing conflicts over water resources among Iraq, Turkey, Syria, Iran, and Afghanistan call for a regional approach. That can be best approached as part of a sustainable development strategy for the entire region.
- *The Peace Dividend Argument.* In recent decades, the West Asian security complex has turned the region into a virtual arms bazaar. While this may be to the advantage of arms merchants, it is not in the interest of the states and peoples of the region. A security community resulting from regional cooperation would provide confidence-building, transparency, arms control, and collective action by all regional states against the aggressor. It would also eliminate arms races and distorted investment patterns.

Table 17.3. West Asian states: complementary of resource endowments

Capital Surplus	Manual Labor Surplus	Skilled Labor Surplus
GCC	Egypt, Iran, Turkey	Egypt, Jordan, Lebanon

The Imperative of Regionalism

Clearly, regionalism is not a panacea either for West Asia or elsewhere. However, in an age of globalization and regionalization, the choice facing the West Asian states is stark. Either they hang together or are hanged separately. The question is not whether to engage in regional formation but when, how, and with whom. West

Asian states have already experimented with regionalism in a variety of successful and not so successful ways. Due to premature Pan-Arabism, the formation of unions between Egypt, Syria, and Iraq collapsed in the 1960s. Due to regime changes in Iraq and Iran, the Baghdad Pact was first transformed into the Central Treaty Organization (CENTO) and then collapsed at the eve of the Iranian revolution of 1979. CENTO was part of the Western strategy of containing the Sino-Soviet bloc by a chain of military alliances extending from NATO to CENTO and SEATO (see Table 17.1).

Other regional formations, including some of the West Asian states, have survived at various levels of respectability. The Arab League continues its precarious life at a fluctuating level that depends on the degree of Arab unity at any moment in time. A more homogenous group, the GCC has survived and prospered because of the riches of its resources and its vulnerability to external threats. The latest addition to the regional alphabet soup, the Economic Cooperation Organization (ECO), is based on the old Regional Cooperation for Development (RCD) organization between Turkey, Iran, and Pakistan. It was established in 1985 but since 1992, it has expanded its membership to Afghanistan, Azerbaijan, Kazakhstan, Kyrgyztan, Tajikistan, Turkmenistan, and Uzbekistan. The ECO has primarily focused on trade and transportation among the member-states. But given the US opposition to Iran as a passage to sea for the land-locked countries of Central Asia, not much has been yet achieved.

Given this checkered history of regional formations in West Asia, what lessons can we draw for the future? To achieve better success, the region is well advised to consider the following recommendations for regional cooperation.

From Adversarial to Dialogic Communication. To build confidence, mutual understanding, and respect among the peoples and states of the region, the establishment of a regional center for dialogue as suggested by the Doha conference is highly recommended (see Chapter 1).

From Soft Security to Hard Security. The central function of the new institute should be to move carefully from soft to hard security issues by promoting regional dialogue among different sectors of the population, including youth, athletes, journalists, artists, educators, scientists, politicians, and military officers. For democratic regionalism to take root, active engagement of West Asian civil societies is necessary. Governments mainly preoccupy themselves with such hard security issues as military security, border disputes, and regime antagonisms. But to reach agreement on such issues, an atmosphere of trust and mutual respect much be first developed. Such a regional atmosphere can be created through the broadening and deepening of people-to-people exchanges.

From Limited to Comprehensive Cooperation. Cooperation should first focus on the most functional and practical aspects of regional life, including communications, transportation, environmental protection, and people-to-people exchanges. As greater mutual understanding and respect is built, cooperation can gradually extend to the more sensitive security, political, and economic arenas.

From Exclusive to Inclusive Regionalism. As the example of GCC demonstrates, it is normal that like-minded countries will achieve regional cooperation first. But closing their ranks to other states in the region, in this case Iran and Iraq, will be self-defeating in the long run. History has shown that the most successful regional organizations such as the European Union and ASEAN have gradually opened their doors to other less accepted countries. If this process takes place in a fashion in which group solidarity is built brick by brick, state by state, the resulting regional organization will have a more enduring and noteworthy life.

One last caveat! The Israeli-Palestinian conflict has been consciously left out of most of the discussions in this volume. This is not because the authors live in a dream world. Rather, it is because that this problem has taken a center-stage in the international discourse to the detriment of other equally pressing regional issues. A West Asian regional dialogue for security and cooperation must ultimately include the Israelis and Palestinians. Without a peace process between these two important West Asian nations, regional peace is inconceivable. Which comes first, the chicken or the egg? The answer is "both".

References

Abdel-Halim, A. 1996. *The Red Sea Security, Past, Present, and Future.* Strategic Papers Series No. 2. Cairo: The Arab Center for Strategic Studies. (In Arabic).

Abdulkhaleq, A. 1998. "Yemen-GCC relationship." *Journal of the Social Sciences.* (Kuwait) 26, No. 1.

Abu Dahab, F. 1999. "The Euro-Gulf dialogue: opportunities and challenges." *Shu'un Kalijiya.* (November): 10–14. (In Arabic).

Adler, E. and Barnett, M. 1998. (eds) *Security Communities.* Cambridge: Cambridge University Press.

Ahmad, A.A. 1992. "The resumption of diplomatic relations between the kingdom of Saudi Arabia and Iran." *Journal of Diplomatic Studies.* Ministry of Foreign Affairs, Riyadh: 159–163.

Ajami, F. 1981. *The Arab Predicament.* Cambridge: Cambridge University Press.

Al-Anzi, A.M. 1997. "Al-Nidham al-Ittihadi Lidawlat al-Emarat al-Mottaheda: Dirasah Moqarana." *Journal of the Social Sciences.* (Kuwait) 25. No. 3.

Al-Ebraheem, H.A. 1984. *Kuwait and the Gulf: Small States and the International System.* Washington, DC: Center for Contemporary Arab Studies.

Aliboni, R. 1985. *The Red Sea Region, Local Actors and Superpowers.* London: Croom Helm.

Al-Khouri, F.I. 1993. *Althehnia al-Arabia* (Arab Mentality). London: Dar al-Saqi.

Al-Nifisi, A. 1999. "The dialectic of relations between us and the West." *Al-Watan,* No. 8304 (March 31).

Al-Rumaihi, M. 1994. *Asda' Harb al-Kuwait* (Repercussions of the Kuwait War). Beirut: Al-Saqi.

Al-Saggaf, M. 2000. "Yemen and the European Union." *Al-Seyassa Al- Dawliya*, 36, No. 142 (Cairo): 115–127. (In Arabic).

Al-Shayeji, A. 1999. "The GCC ... To whom and why all this armament?" *Al-Watan.*

Al-Shayeji, A. 1997. "Dangerous perceptions: Gulf views of the U.S. role in the region." *Middle East Policy* 5, No. 3.

Al-Sultan, A. 1985. "The Red Sea and the Arab-Israeli conflict: rivalry between two strategies." Beirut: Center for Arab Unity Studies. (In Arabic).

Antonakis, N. 1999. "Guns versus butter." *Journal of Conflict Resolution* 43, No. 4.

Anthony, I. 1993. "Assessing the UN register of conventional arms." *Survival* 35, No. 4: 113–129.

Anthony, J.D. 1982. "The Gulf Cooperation Council." *Journal of South Asian and Middle Eastern Studies* 5, No. 4: 3–18.

Armstrong, A. 1981. "Saudis' AWACS just a beginning of a new strategy." *Washington Post.* (November 1).

Arnett, E. 1997. "Beyond threat perception: assessing military capability and reducing the risk of war in Southern Asia." In: *Military Capacity and the Risk of War. China, India, Pakistan and Iran* edited by Eric Arnett, 1–24. Oxford: Oxford University Press/ SIPRI.

Aronson, B. (with Brosh, O.). 1992. *The Politics and Strategy of Nuclear Weapons in the Middle East. Opacity, Theory, and Reality, 1960-1991. An Israeli Perspective.* Albany: State University of New York.

Baratta, J.P. 1993. "The Kellogg-Briand pact and the outlawry of War." In: *Encyclopedia of Arms Control and Disarmament* edited by Robert Dean Burns, 695–705. New York: Charles Scribner's.

Barnett, M.N. 1992. *Confronting the Costs of War: Military Power, State, and Society in Egypt and Israel.* Princeton: Princeton University Press.

Batatu, H. 1978. *The Social Classes and the Revolution Movements of Iraq: A Study of Iraq's Old Landed and Commercial Classes and of its Communists, Ba'thists and Free Officers.* Princeton: Princeton University Press.

Betts, R.K. 1992. "Systems for peace or causes of war? Collective security, arms control, and the new Europe." *International Security* 17, No. 1: 5–43.

Bodine, R. *et al.* 1994. *Creating the Peaceable School: A Comprehensive Program for Teaching Conflict Resolution.* Champaign: Research Press.

Boisson de Chazournes, L. and Sands, P. 1999. (eds) *International Law, the International Court of Justice and Nuclear Weapons*. Cambridge: Cambridge University Press.

Brown, M.E. 1996. (ed.) *The International Dimensions of Internal Conflict.* Cambridge, MA: MIT Press.

Bull, H. 1977. *The Anarchical Society. A Study of Order in World Politics.* London: Macmillan.

Burns, R.D. 1993. (ed.) *Encyclopedia of Arms Control and Disarmament, Vols. I-III.* New York: Charles Scribner's Sons.

Buzan, B. 1991. *People, States and Fear.* Boulder: Lynne Rienner Publishers.

Carroll, T.F. 1992. *Intermediary NGOs: The Supporting Link in Grassroots Development.* West Hartford: Kumarian Press.

Child, J. 1992. *The Central American Peace Process, 1983-1991. Sheathing Swords, Building Confidence.* Boulder: Lynne Rienner.

Cohen, A. 1998. *Israel and the Bomb.* New York: Columbia University Press.

Collins, A. 1997. *The Security Dilemma and the End of the Cold War.* Edinburgh: Keele University Press.

Cordesman, A. 1999. "The new balance of Gulf arms." *Middle East Policy* 7, No. 4.

Cordesman, A. 1998. "The changing military balance in the Gulf." *Middle East Policy* 6, No. 1.

Crampton, R. 2001. "Myths of the Balkans." *The New York Review of Books* (11 January): 14–18.

Crystal, J. 1990. *Oil and Politics in the Gulf: Rulers and Merchants in Kuwait and Qatar.* New York: Cambridge University Press.

Deutsch, K.W. *et al.* 1957. *Political Community and the North Atlantic Area. International Organization in the Light of Historical Experience.* Princeton: Princeton University Press.

Drew, N. 1995. *Learning the Skills of Peacemaking: A K-6 Activity Guide on Resolving Conflict, Communicating, Cooperating.* Torrance: Jalmar Press.

El-Misfer, M. 1998. "The European Union and the dimensions of its Mediterranean projects." *Al-Tawa'on* 47, No. 13 (Riyadh).

Evron, Y. 1994. *Israel's Nuclear Dilemma.* London: Routledge.

Fahmy, A. 1966. *Muslim Sea Power in the Eastern Mediterranean from the Seventh to the Tenth Century A. D.* Cairo: National Publications and Printing House. (In Arabic).

Falkenrath, R.A. 1994. *Shaping Europe's Military Order. The Origins and Consequences of the CFE Treaty.* Cambridge: The MIT Press.

Farouk-Sluglett, M. and Sluglett, P. 1990. *Iraq Since 1958.* London: I.B.Tauris.

Fisher, J. 1998. *Nongovernments: NGOs and the Political Development of the Third World*. West Hartford, CT: Kumarian Press.

Folger, J.P. and Jones, T.S. 1994. (eds) *New Directions in Mediation: Communication, Research, and Perspectives*. Thousand Oaks: Sage.

Foundation for Human and Humanitarian Rights. (ed.) 1996, *The Theory and Practice of Human Rights*, preliminary edition. Lebanon: Metn.

Gamlen, E. 1993. "United States strategic policy toward the Middle East: central command and the reflagging of Kuwaiti tankers." In: *The United States and the Middle East: A Search for New Perspectives* edited by Hooshang Amirahmadi, 213–25. New York: State University of New York Press.

Gause, G.F. 1994. "The illogic of Dual Containment." *Foreign Affairs* 73, No. 2: 22–44.

Gellman, P. 1988. " Hans J. Morgenthau and the legacy of political realism." *Review of International Studies* 14, No. 4.

Goldblat, J. 1992. (ed.) *Maritime Security: The Building of Confidence*. New York: United Nations/Geneva: UNIDIR.

Goodwin, J. 1998. *Lords of the Horizons: A History of the Ottoman Empire*. New York: Henry Holt and Co.

Gurr, T.R. 1980. (ed.) *Handbook of Political Conflict: Theory and Research*. New York: Free Press.

Gurr, T.R. 1964. *World Handbook of Political and Social Indicators*. New Heaven: Yale University Press.

Helms, C.M. 1981. *The Cohesion of Saudi Arabia*. Baltimore: The Johns Hopkins University Press.

Hettne, B., Inotai, A. and Sunkel, O. 1999. (eds) *Globalism and the New Regionalism*. New York: St. Martin's Press.

Holst, J.J. 1983. "Confidence-building measures: a conceptual framework." *Survival* 25, No. 1: 2–15.

Hudson, M.C. 1999. (ed.) *Middle East Dilemma*. New York: Columbia University Press: ????

Hume, C.R. 1994. *The United Nations, Iran, and Iraq: How Peacemaking Changed*. Bloomington: Indiana University Press.

Independent Commission on Disarmament and Security Issues. 1982. *Common Security. A Blueprint for Survival*. New York: Simon & Schuster.

Indyk, M. 1994. "Dual Containment." *Middle East Policy* 3: 1–26.

Irani, G. 1999. "Islamic mediation techniques for Middle East conflicts." *Middle East Review of International Affairs* 3, No. 2.

Jones, P. 1998. *Towards a Regional Security Regime for the Middle East: Issues and Options*. Stokholm, SIPRI.

Kechichian, J. 1993. *Political Dynamics and Security in the Arabian Peninsula Through the 1990s.* Santa Monica: Rand.

Kelleher, C.M., Sharp, J.M.O. and Freedman, L. 1996. (eds) *The Treaty on Conventional Armed Forces in Europe: The Politics of Post-Wall Arms Control.* Baden-Baden: Nomos Verlagsgesellschaft.

Kemp, G. 1997. *The Energy Superbowl: Strategic Politics and the Persian Gulf and Caspian Basin.* Nixon Center for Peace and Freedom, Washington DC: 14–16.

Keohane, R.O. and Nye, Jr., J.S. 1977. *Power and Interdependence.* Boston: Little Brown.

Khadduri, M. 1997. "Suhl." In: *The Encyclopedia of Islam*, Volume IX edited by C. E. Bosworth, E. van Donzel, W. P. Heinrichs, and G. Lecomte. Leiden, Holland: Brill.

Khashan, H. 1977. "The New Arab Cold War." *World Affairs* 59, No. 4.

Khedr, B. 1997. *Europe and the Arabian States of the Gulf: The Distant Partners.* Beirut: Center for Arab Unity Studies. (In Arabic).

Khouri, F. 1993. *Al-Thihnia al-Arabia: Al-Unf Said al-Ahkam* (The Arab mind: violence is the Master of the situation). London: Saqi Books.

Khrushchev, N. S. 1974. *Khrushchev Remembers: The Last Testament.* Translated into English and edited by Strobe Talbott. London.

Kinsella, D. and Tillema, H.K. 1995. "Arms and aggression in the Middle East: overt military interventions 1948–1991." *Journal of Conflict Resolution* 39: 306–29.

Klare, M.T. 1998. "The sole-superpower syndrome." *In These Times.* (March 22).

Klare, M.T. 1994. "Making enemies for the 90s: the new 'Rogue States' doctrine." *The Nation.*

Korany, B. 1999. "The Arab world and the new balance of power in the Middle East." In: *Middle East Dilemma* edited by Michael C. Hudson, 35–59. New York: Columbia University Press.

Krasner, S.D. 1999. *Sovereignty. Organized Hypocrisy.* Princeton: Princeton University Press.

Kriesberg, L. 1991. *Constructive Conflicts from Escalation to Resolution.* London: Rowman & Littlefield.

Kurtz, L. 1999. (ed.) *Encyclopedia of Violence, Peace and Conflict*, Vols. 1–3. San Diego: Academic Press.

Lake, D.A. and Rothchild, D. 1998. (eds) *The International Spread of Ethnic Conflict. Fear, Diffusion and Escalation.* Princeton: Princeton University Press.

Larrabee, S. *et al.* 1998. *NATO Mediterranean Initiative: Policy Issues and Dilemmas.* Santa Monica: Rand.

Lepgold, J. and Weiss, T.G. 1998. *Collective Conflict Management and Changing World Politics*. Albany: State University of New York Press.

Lewis, B. 1991. *The Political Language of Islam.* Chicago: The University of Chicago Press.

Lewis, B. 1984. *The Jews of Islam.* Princeton: Princeton University Press.

Lewis, B. 1968. *The Emergence of Modern Turkey*. London: Oxford University Press.

Lewis, B. 1958. *The Arabs in History*. London: Arrow Books.

Leys, C. 1996. *The Rise and Fall of Development Theory*. Bloomington: Indian University Press.

Mahan, A.T. 1894. The Influence of Sea Power Upon History, 1660–1783. Boston: Little, Brown.

Makiya, K. 1997. *Republic of Fear.* Los Angeles: University of California Press.

Marhun, A.A. 1996. "Hall Takhruj Qatar min Majlis al-Ta'awun al-Khaliji" (Would Qatar exit without the GCC?). *Shu'un al-Awsat* No. 48 (January): 131–34.

Mayer, J. and Rotte, R. 1999. "Arms and aggression in the Middle East, 1948–1991." *Journal of Conflict Resolution* 43, No. 1: 45–57.

Mayer, R.J. 1995. *Conflict Management: The Courage to Confront*, Columbus: (2nd edition) Battelle Press.

Mearsheimer, J.J. 1994/95. "The false promise of international institutions." *International Security* 19, No. 3: 5–49.

Mojtahed-Zadeh, P. 1999, *Security and Territoriality in the Persian Gulf.* London: Curzon Press.

Mojtahed-Zadeh, P. 1998a. "Regional alliance in the Persian Gulf: past trend and future prospects." *The Iranian Journal of International Affairs* 10, Nos. 1–2: 1–20.

Mojtahed-Zadeh, P. 1998b. "Iranian perspective on the Caspian Sea and Central Asia." In: *Central Eurasian Water Crisis* edited by Iwao Kobori and Michael H. Glantz, 105–124 Tokyo: UN Publications.

Mojtahed-Zadeh, P. 1994a. "A geopolitical triangle in the Persian Gulf." *The Iranian Journal of International Affairs* 6, Nos. 1 & 2: 47–59.

Mojtahed-Zadeh, P. 1994b. *The Islands of Tunb and Abu Musa.* London: CNMES/SOAS.

Mojtahed-Zadeh, P. 1990. *Political Geography of the Strait of Hormuz.* London: SOAS.

Møller, B. 2001. (ed.) (forthcoming). *Oil and Water. Towards Cooperative Security in the Persian Gulf.* London: I.B.Tauris.

Møller, B. 1992. *Common Security and Non-Offensive Defense. A Neorealist Perspective.* Boulder: Lynne Rienner.

Moreno, D. 1994. *The Struggle for Peace in Central America.* Gainesville: University Press of Florida.

Morgenthau. H.J. 1973. *Politics Among Nations.* New York: Knopf.

Nash'at, N. 2000. "The Euro-Gulf dialogue: an economic co-operation below the level of a strategic partnership." *Shu'un Khalijiya* (May): 24–30. (In Arabic).

Nolan, J. 1994. (ed.) *Global Engagement. Cooperation and Security in the 21st Century.* Washington, D.C.: The Brookings Institution.

Parrenas, J.C. 1998. *The GCC and the Development of ASEAN.* The Emirates Occasional Papers No. 26. Abu Dhabi: The Emirates Center for Strategic Studies.

Peck. M.C. 1986. *The United Arab Emirates: A Venture in Unity*. Boulder: Westview Press.

Piscatori, J. 1991. (ed.) *Islamic Fundamentalism and the Gulf Crisis.* Chicago: American Academy of Arts and Sciences.

Plano, J. and Olton, R. 1982. *The International Relations Dictionary.* Santa Barbara: ABC-CLO: 95–96.

Prawitz, J. and Leonard, J. 1996. *A Zone Free of Weapons of Mass Destruction in the Middle East.* Geneva: UNIDIR.

Richards, A. 1995. "Economic roots of instability in the Middle East." *Middle East Policy* 4, Nos. 1 & 2.

Rosenau, R. 1973. "Theorizing across systems: linkage politics revisited." In: *Conflict Behavior and Linkages Politics* edited by Jonathan Wilkenfeld, 25–58. New York: David McKay.

Rosenau, R. 1969. "Towards the study of National-International linkages." In: *Linkage Politics*, edited by James Rosenau. New York: Free Press.

Rouleau, E.R. 1995. "America's unyielding policy toward Iraq." *Foreign Affairs* 74, No. 1: 59–72.

Saeed, A. 1995-96. "An economic forum for the Indian Ocean region." *Regional Studies* (Islamabad) (Winter): 59–93.

Said, A.M. 1987. *The Arabs and the Geographically Contiguous Countries.* Beirut: Center for Arab Unity Studies. (In Arabic).

Selim, M. 2000. *Arab Perceptions of the Euro-Mediterranean Projects.* Abu Dhabi: The Emirates Center for Strategic Studies.

Selim, M. 1998. *Towards a Red Sea Forum for Security and Cooperation.* Strategic Papers Series No. 67. Cairo: Al-Ahram Center for Political and Strategic Studies (In Arabic).

Selim, M. 1995. *Mediterraneanism: A New Dimension in Egypt's Foreign Policy.* Strategic Papers No. 27. Cairo: Al-Ahram Center for Political and Strategic Studies.

Shahak, I. 1997. *Open Secrets. Israeli Foreign and Nuclear Policies.* London: Pluto Press.

Sick, G.G. and Potter, L.G. 1997. (ed.) *The Persian Gulf in the Millennium: Essays in Politics, Economy, Security, and Religion.* New York: St. Martin's Press.

Singh, S. 1999. *Defending India.* New York: St. Martin Press.

SIPRI, 1990. *Armament, Disarmament, and International Security, SIPRI Yearbook, 1998.* Oxford: Oxford University Press.

Soliman, S. 1999. "The European Union and the GCC: towards a Gulf strategy to deal with the European claims." *Shu'un Kalijiya* (January): 20–21. (In Arabic)

Stowasser, B.F. 1987. (ed.) *The Islamic Impulse.* London: Croom Helm.

Suez Canal Authority. 2000. *Yearly Report, 1999.* Ismailiya, Suez Canal Authority.

Taylor, A.R. 1982. *The Arab Balance of Power.* Syracuse: Syracuse University Press.

Tehranian, M. 1999. *Global Communication and World Politics: Domination, Development, and Discourse.* Boulder: Lynne Rienner.

Tetreault, M. A. 1997. "Designer democracy in Kuwait." *Current History* (January).

Tudor. H. 1972. *Political Myth.* London: Pall Mall.

Väyrynen, R. 1991. (ed.) *New Directions in Conflict Theory: Conflict Resolution and Conflict Transformation* (London: Sage, 1991).

Väyrynen, R. 1984. "Regional conflict formations: an intractable problem of international relations." *Journal of Peace Research* 21, No. 4: 337–59.

Wæver, O. 1995. "Securitization and desecuritization." In: *On Security* edited by Ronnie D. Lipschutz, 46–86. New York: Columbia University Press.

Walt, S.M. 1987. *The Origins of Alliances.* Ithaca: Cornell University Press.

Wolf, A. 2000. "Indigenous approaches to water conflict negotiations and implications for international waters." *International Negotiation: A Journal of Theory and Practice* (December).

Zanoyan, V. 1995. "After the oil boom: holidays end for the Gulf States." *Foreign Affairs* 74, No. 6.

Index